Children's Behavior

CHILDREN'S BEHAVIOR

Viewed by Adults and Children

BY

SOPHIE RITHOLZ, M.A.

*Registered and Certified Psychologist
and Psychoanalyst*

BOOKMAN ASSOCIATES

New York

MANUFACTURED IN THE UNITED STATES OF AMERICA BY
UNITED PRINTING SERVICES, INC.
NEW HAVEN, CONN.

Dedicated
to the memory of
my dearly beloved niece
HELEN JUNE BEDNO
Aged eight

Foreword

Present-day emphasis on juvenile delinquency in newspapers, magazines, radio, and television has given rise to parental concern about any behavior their children display that deviates from adult standards and has alerted them to try to correct these deviations as soon as they appear in the hope of averting potential cases of juvenile delinquency in their own families. Teachers of today, steeped in the knowledge of the seriousness of behavior disorders as portents of future personality maladjustments, are likewise behavior-conscious to the point where they, like parents, tend to focus too much attention on any childish behavior that deviates from the norm and to regard it as more serious than they otherwise would.

Furthermore, both parents and teachers, as is true of everyone else, view behavior from their own frame of reference. They judge the behavior of others in terms of how it affects them personally, how it helps or hinders what they have set out to do, and how it measures up to their expectations. Adult values, as many studies have revealed, are very different from those held by children or even by adolescents who are approaching the adult years. Consequently, when the child's behavior is seen through adult eyes, it is very differently interpreted than when seen through the eyes of children.

There have been many studies to date which report what parents, teachers, and mental hygienists find troublesome and antisocial in children's behavior at different age levels. In these studies, emphasis is placed on the fact that parents, and to a lesser extent teachers, report as problem behavior among children any behavior which is troublesome to them or interferes with what they have set out to do. A teacher, for example, who is trying to explain new subject matter to a class, will find whispering, note-passing, and other forms of inattention a hindrance to her goal and, therefore, she judges such behavior as problem behavior. Similarly, parents who want to create the impression of being good parents regard any childish behavior that militates against this impression as problem behavior. They are, thus, more concerned with having a good child than with what is good for the child.

The mental hygienist, these studies have revealed, judges childish behavior more from an objective than from a subjective frame of reference. To him, undesirable behavior is viewed more from future values, how such behavior will affect the child's adjustments to life, than from present values, how this behavior affects other people's interests and activities at the present time. In this long-term assessment of antisocial behavior, mental hygienists are emphasizing the child rather than the adult.

But, in doing so they are looking at the child and his behavior through adult eyes, ignoring the most important element in this complex pattern of human relationships, the child himself, his motives, his interests, and his values. Parents and teachers, far more than mental hygienists, are guilty of this error in their assessment of children's behavior. Their ego-centered judgments almost completely ignore the child's angle, nor do they trouble themselves to find out how he thinks and feels about the behavior they condemn. They fail to grant him the privilege of presenting his side of the story—a privilege he would be given if taken to a juvenile court. Instead, they condemn him on the grounds that he should "know better."

The seriousness of judging children's behavior from a personal frame of reference and according to adult standards does not end when one labels it as unfair to the child; it goes far deeper than that. Because every child sees himself through the eyes of the significant people in his life, and these significant people are his parents and teachers, his concept of himself as a person will be a reflection of what he *believes* they think of him. Constant criticism of his behavior and punishment for behavior which, as he sees it, is justified, will lead to an unfavorable self-concept. Furthermore, it is confusing to a child when these significant people in his life disagree as to what is right and wrong or the behavior they label as wrong. How is he to know what he should or should not do when they do not present a united front?

The author's study which constitutes this book is significant for two reasons. First, it fills the gap in our knowledge of how the different actors in this complex drama of interpersonal relationships—parents, teachers, mental hygienists, and children—view childish behavior. It shows us what other studies along the same line have not, to date, revealed, namely, the child's side of the story. In the second place, it has emphasized what other studies of children have hinted at but have failed to prove conclusively, the relative importance of parents' and teachers' roles in determining the child's self-concept after he reaches the school age.

This is of serious importance to our knowledge of personality development and which, until now, has received far too little attention in scientific investigations. It is equally important from a practical angle to fill in this gap so that parents and teachers will become aware of the serious consequences of dealing with childish behavior they consider troublesome in a manner that might leave a permanent scar on the child's personality.

It should highlight the warning that psychologists have given to parents, teachers, and all whose responsibility it is to guide the development of children, namely that one cannot assume that anything said or done to a child will have no more than temporary influence because a child's memory is short. He may not, it is true, remember specifically what was said or done to him but these will serve to reinforce impressions he has of himself, thus strengthening them so that, in time, they are no longer impressions but firmly rooted beliefs. If these beliefs are unfavorable, they can and often do have a lasting influence on the course of his development and the pattern of his entire life.

While written primarily for scientists as a report of a research study made by the author, this book offers much that can be of real value to both parents and teachers. Without reading between the lines, they can see the handwriting on the wall in the form of a warning to stop, look, and listen when dealing with childish behavior which, heretofore, they have automatically labelled as "problem behavior." If it serves the purpose of awakening them to the serious responsibility they have in dealing with such behavior, it will then have made an important contribution to our present knowledge.

ELIZABETH B. HURLOCK, PH.D.
University of Pennsylvania

Acknowledgments

Truism though it may be, it is nevertheless true that in attempting an evaluation or extension of work already done in any specialized field, or in projecting any new study, theoretical speculations are often totally without value unless such speculations can be proved or disproved by the touchstone of ascertained fact.

Expression of gratitude to Dr. Eugene A. Nifenecker, then Director of Reference, Research and Statistics, of the New York City Board of Education, and to Dr. May Lazar, Assistant Director, is therefore twofold in motivation: the confidence that they manifested in the worth-whileness of this contemplated investigation by giving their consent; and by this permitted access to the rich field of source material, the opportunity to translate theories into facts and figures.

This consent was predicated upon approval being granted by the principals of the respective schools which had been tentatively selected by the writer for the investigation. And it would take a great deal of appreciation, indeed, to be commensurate with the enthusiastic interest and cooperation which the heads of these schools have shown. Although the schools have been numbered symbolically throughout this study, as School I, II, and so on, instead of by their true designations, to this investigator they have also been symbolic of the highest of pedagogical aims and endeavors in the interest of the pupils in attendance.

The realization of these aims in the present instance was more than fully consummated by the faculty members in these schools where the ratings of teachers were obtained. And to these teachers there is a special feeling of gratitude due, for the gracious expenditure not only of their efforts but of their leisure time.

The approach to the liaison—and, in some ways, the most strategically important—group, the parents, was mediated through the kind offices of Mrs. Bess B. Lane, then Educational Director of the United Parents Associations of New York City. To Mrs. Lane and to these groups is expressed the hope that the thanks of the investigator will be expressed by this study; to whatever extent, however small, it adds to the welfare of children and to knowledge leading to fulfillment of that goal.

But, although chronologically the latest and last, yet shall they be first, for the warmest acknowledgments of all are due to the school children who participated in this investigation—whose furrowed brows and anguished erasures indicated that they gave us not only their best judgments but their best intentions as well.

May Life judge them kindly, always!

A separate statement of indebtedness is due the Commonwealth Fund for permission to quote from and otherwise utilize some of the material incorporated in E. K. Wickman's *Children's Behavior and Teachers' Attitudes.*

SOPHIE RITHOLZ

Contents

Chapter		Page
I.	Author's Introduction	19
II.	Some Preliminary and Elementary Considerations of Elementary Statistics	22
III.	Experimental Extension of Wickman's Investigations	29
	Résumé of a Major Phase of Wickman's Work	29
	Purpose of This Study	32
IV.	The Comparative Attitudes of Teachers in 1944-45 towards Children's Behavior	36
V.	Are the Comparisons Invidious?	47
VI.	How Do Teachers Compare with Mental Hygienists under Comparable Conditions?	51
VII.	What Do *Children* Think of Children's Behavior?	64
	The Purpose of Our Queries	64
	Questionnaire and Administration	65
	General Relationship between the Judgments of the Children, as against Those of the Teachers and Mental Hygienists	69
	To What Extent Were These Judgments *Acquired* by the Children?	84
	General Trends Shown by the Ratings of the Children	85
	Detailed Analysis of Ratings of the Items— Illustrating Uses and Usages of the Tables	86

Chapter   *Page*

The Extent to Which Children Agree in Their
Ratings Item by Item   106

Patterns Established when Our Data Are
Represented by Graphs   107

How Our Groups of Children Relate to Each Other   112

VIII.   How Parents View the Behavior of Children (With a
Side View towards a Successful Life)   116

IX.   Whose Influence, if Any, Is Strongest with the Child?   136

X.   The Anthropomorphism of Statistics   151

Define and Allot   151

Wherein Do We Disagree: How Ideal Is the
Mental Hygiene Ideal?   154

Wherein Do We Agree?   162

Shall Parents Abdicate a Primary Responsibility?   168

APPENDICES

A.   List of Schedules   175

B.   Figures   195

C.   Some Further, and More Advanced, Statistical
Considerations   223

Index   232

List of Tables

Table   *Page*

I Teachers' Ratings on the Seriousness of Behavior Problems of Children. Results from Schedule 1*a*   38

II Teachers' Ratings on the Seriousness of Behavior Problems of Children. (From E. K. Wickman, *Children's Behavior and Teachers' Attitudes.* Commonwealth Fund, 1928.)   40

III Clinicians' Ratings on the Seriousness of Behavior Problems of Children. (From E. K. Wickman, *Children's Behavior and Teachers' Attitudes.* Commonwealth Fund, 1928.)   42

IV Teachers' Ratings on the Seriousness of Behavior Problems of Children. Results from Schedule 1*b*   52

V Rank-difference Correlations   54

VI Rank-order of the 50 Items, Based on the Ratings Made by Six Groups   58

VII Critical Ratios for the Differences between the Mean Ratings of Teachers 1*a* and Teachers 1*b*   60

VIII Children's Ratings on the Seriousness of Behavior Problems of Children. (By Girls in Grade 5A)   70

IX Children's Ratings on the Seriousness of Behavior Problems of Children. (By Boys in Grade 5A)   72

X Children's Ratings on the Seriousness of Behavior Problems of Children. (By Girls in Grade 7A)   74

XI Children's Ratings on the Seriousness of Behavior Problems of Children. (By Boys in Grade 7A)   76

XII Children's Ratings on the Seriousness of Behavior Problems of Children. (By Girls in Grade 8B)   78

XIII Children's Ratings on the Seriousness of Behavior Problems of Children. (By Boys in Grade 8B)   80

XIV Rank-order of 46 Items, Based on the Ratings Made by All of Our Groups and the Mental Hygienists   88

XV   Critical Ratios for the Differences between the Mean
     Ratings of 5A Girls *versus* 7A Boys, 7A Girls, 8B Boys,
     8B Girls, Teachers 1*a*, and Teachers 1*b*   90

XVI Critical Ratios for the Differences between the Mean
     Ratings of 5A Boys *versus* 5A Girls, 7A Boys, 7A Girls,
     8B Boys, 8B Girls, Teachers 1*a*, and Teachers 1*b*   92

XVII Critical Ratios for the Differences between the Mean
     Ratings of 7A Girls *versus* 8B Boys, 8B Girls, Teachers
     1*a*, and Teachers 1*b*   94

XVIII Critical Ratios for the Differences between the Mean
      Ratings of 7A Boys *versus* 7A Girls, 8B Boys, 8B Girls,
      Teachers 1*a*, and Teachers 1*b*   96

XIX Critical Ratios for the Differences between the Mean
     Ratings of 8B Girls *versus* Teachers 1*a* and Teach-
     ers 1*b*   98

XX   Critical Ratios for the Differences between the Mean
     Ratings of 8B Boys *versus* 8B Girls, Teachers 1*a*, and
     Teachers 1*b*   100

XXI Critical Ratios for the Differences between the Mean
     Ratings of Mental Hygienists *versus* Each of Our Ten
     Groups   102

XXII Mothers' Ratings on the Seriousness of Behavior Prob-
     lems of Children   122

XXIII Fathers' Ratings on the Seriousness of Behavior Prob-
      lems of Children   124

XXIV Critical Ratios for the Differences between the Mean
     Ratings of the Fathers *versus* Each of Our Other Nine
     Groups   126

XXV Critical Ratios for the Differences between the Mean
     Ratings of the Mothers *versus* 5A Boys, 5A Girls, 7A
     Boys, 7A Girls, 8B Boys, 8B Girls, Teachers 1*a*, and
     Teachers 1*b*   128

XXVI Relative Ratings Given to Salient Mental Hygiene Items
     by the Fathers, Mothers, and Teachers   166

List of Figures

Figure		*Page*
1.	Tardiness	197
2.	Truancy	197
3.	Destroying School Materials	198
4.	Untruthfulness (Lying)	198
5.	Imaginative Lying	199
6.	Cheating	199
7.	Stealing	200
8.	Profanity	200
9.	Smoking	201
10.	Disorderliness	201
11.	Whispering and Note-writing	202
12.	Interrupting	202
13.	Restlessness	203
14.	Inattention	203
15.	Lack of Interest in Work	204
16.	Carelessness in Work	204
17.	Laziness	205
18.	Unreliableness	205
19.	Disobedience	206
20.	Impertinence	206
21.	Cruelty, Bullying	207
22.	Quarrelsomeness	207
23.	Tattling	208
24.	Stubbornness, Contrariness	208
25.	Sullenness	209
26.	Temper Tantrums	209

Figure		Page
27.	Impudence	210
28.	Selfishness	210
29.	Domineering, Overbearing	211
30.	Shyness	211
31.	Sensitiveness	212
32.	Unsocial, Withdrawing	212
33.	Overcritical of Others	213
34.	Thoughtlessness	213
35.	Inquisitiveness	214
36.	Silliness	214
37.	Unhappy, Depressed	215
38.	Resentfulness	215
39.	Nervousness	216
40.	Fearfulness	216
41.	Dreaminess	217
42.	Slovenly in Personal Appearance	217
43.	Suspiciousness	218
44.	Physical Coward	218
45.	Easily Discouraged	219
46.	Suggestible	219
47.	Is It a Sin to Talk in School? (After McGrath)	220
48.	Would It Be Wrong to Take a Nickel out of Your Mother's Pocketbook without Asking Her? (After McGrath)	221
49.	Is It a Sin to Cheat? (After McGrath)	222

Author's Introduction

The very words "conscience," "morality," have latterly taken on the connotations of a concept that is taboo except in certain settings (ecclesiastical), and under certain temporal conditions; as though conscience, like the appendix, were a certain vestigium which one does not politely mention unless it becomes troublesome.

But now, in this age of nuclear fissions and cosmic upheavals, in which Man against himself has now mastered the forces of Nature, too, against himself, wherein the new Atlantis bodes fair to be no new fable, conscience is no longer a spiritual luxury, a nosegay to counteract the noisomeness of an ethical morass. Nor is it a static idea, a bound code of conduct, which can be solved by Neo-Statism, the cult of the State which, despite its arrogant seizing of the question merely begs the question, pauperizing as it does man's individual responsibility to a commonage of no responsibility.

Rather, Man must now look to his conscience, his own morality, if he is to survive. It is no longer a case of spiritualism versus materialism, but of literal and actual survival; a return to primitive survival in this age of civilization.

In this connection, the study of prehistoric and protohistoric man[1] offers not only one of the most fascinating subjects in the science of social psychology but also one of the most salutary object lessons in the art of not taking too much for granted. Being born in a civilized community, we are somewhat apt to assume our civilized status as our natural-born right, as much a part of us as our integumentary inheritance, without realizing the mighty nature of this slow, upward climb.

As we go back perhaps one hundred thousand years, we find the remains of Neanderthal man, one of the ancestors of the human race today, with his Mousterian culture. Dying out some twenty-five to thirty-five thousand years ago, this type disappeared and was supplanted by men who fell within the range of Homo sapiens, their era in turn constituting the Late or Upper Paleolithic age of Europe. Then, some ten thousand years ago the Neolithic men came upon the scene, and from them the line leads straight to the modern races of Europe.

Throughout this vast space of years, of ascension up the scale of human evolution, there ran consistently the threads of an increasing fraternity among men, of an increasing utilization of the tools and usages of civilization.

Neanderthal man had learned to make fire and to fashion stone implements. Although the social unit was the family, he had learned the advantages of meeting with his fellows in order to hunt the wooly mammoth and other primeval beasts. With the careful laying out of their dead, a faint glimmer of religious sense seemed to be shedding its first nascent glow.

And ever more, as modern man evolved, did his social structures reach outward and his usages and customs become more intricate: wherein even Neolithic man showed a *developed* civilization, with his social unit now the village, his cultivation of wheat and the domestication and breeding of animals, his use of the sewing needle, and his pottery which was no longer purely utilitarian but bore the impress of a civilized aestheticism in its zigzag incisions. Here, too, elaborate inhumation procedures and burial of equipment to provide for a future existence showed the rudimentary stirrings of standards and morality, even of spirituality, of belief in a life beyond death.

The very names of their periods—and of those which followed—Lower and Upper Paleolithic, Neolithic, Copper Age, Bronze Age, Iron Age—all bear out Tylor's exposition that there exists no known record of any people who did not have the knowledge of fire, cooking, and tools.[2]

Concomitantly, a study of their burial habits would indicate to this present writer that there exists no known record of any people, during that tremendous epoch that bridged the period from prehistory through protohistory, that did not observe careful burial rites, most or all of which made provision for a future life; that there exists no known record of any people that did not harbor and foster this ancient spark, distinguishing primitive man from his brute fellow dwellers that prowled the earth, a spark which enlarged and expanded with evolutionary process, so that finally out of the seething chaos, like a new celestial body, the sun of morality emerged.

And all this leads straight down to the modern inheritor and transmitter of this heritage, both testator and legatee, the bearer of this Promethean flame—the child.

In this study, then, our attention will be occupied with children, their conscience and morality. Or, better said—and more in keeping with the age of our subjects—with the more prosaic, and it might be termed, diminutive counterparts of conscience and morality, the every-day behavior disorders of everyday children.

More concretely: What do adults—parents, teachers, mental hygienists—think about these characteristics as they manifest them-selves in the child? What do these answers mean to us from a peda-gogical and psychological point of view?

Should we judge from a moral standpoint? Or from the standpoint of what is good for him? Is there a necessary difference, or are the two intertwined? Does that depend on what we consider "good" for him, such as our idea of success? Does good necessarily have to mean good, behaviorally?

Furthermore, what does the child himself think of these charac-teristics? How does the adult affect these judgments of the child and how does he, in his turn, affect and effect theirs? Who has the greatest influence over him, the home or the teacher, and how does each affect the child's evaluations of his own conduct?

These evaluations of right and wrong—are they learned, are they inherent?

These are some of the questions this investigation attempts to deal with and partially answer, although it does not purport to lay down any dicta about applications. And since facts are the foundation stones upon which to construct any edifice of theory, tenet, and ther-apy—if any of our facts shall succeed in replacing any existing arti-facts, to that extent shall we have succeeded in the full attainment of our purpose.

REFERENCES

1. Scholarly development and rich presentation of the facts briefly alluded to here may be found in the following references:

McGregor, James H. "Human Origins and Early Man." *General Anthropology.* Edited by Franz Boas. Boston: D.C. Heath & Co., 1938. Pp. 24-94.

Homo, Léon. *Primitive Italy and the Beginnings of Roman Imperialism.* Book I, *Origins and Invasions.* New York: Alfred A. Knopf, 1927. Pp. 23-36.

Whatmough, Joshua. *The Foundations of Roman Italy.* London: Methuen & Co. Ltd., 1937. Chapter 3.

Coon, Carleton Stevens. *The Races of Europe.* New York: Macmillan Co., 1939. Pp. 12-15; Chapters 2, 4, and 5.

2. Tylor, Edward B. *Researches into the Early History of Man-kind and the Development of Civilization.* New York: Henry Holt & Co., 1878. Chapters 8 and 9.

CHAPTER II

Some Preliminary and Elementary Considerations of Elementary Statistics

There are few experiences more frustrating than the attempt to digest the contents of an article or book, only to find concentration rudely broken by the intrusion of esoteric terms and cryptic symbols. For this reason, a very simplified explanation will be made in this chapter of certain elementary concepts of statistics as they have been utilized and applied in this report, for the benefit of those who have not been initiated into the devices of that field.

Inasmuch as references to footnotes and appendices in the body of a text have an equally distracting effect, at least so it seems to this present investigator, these statistical explanations are thus being put boldly into a small section of their own—convenient both for those who wish to consult it and for those who wish to skip it!

And, for those who find statistics and other mathematical studies agencies of confusion rather than otherwise, and who are willing to repose a certain amount of confidence in the present writer's judgment, assurance is given that reference to the more descriptive tables and figures will suffice; although desirable, studying of this chapter, and other statistical data, is not mandatory for an adequate understanding and descriptive knowledge of the material presented in this study.

The first term that appears is *correlation*. Webster's abridged dictionary defines its verb: "To connect by disclosure of a mutual relation." Unfortunately, this definition is too patently abridged, so perhaps our own data will offer supplementary information, remembering that the key word is *relationship*.

Positive relationship, then, would mean a positive correlation, the coefficients falling anywhere from .00 up to 1.00.

Negative relationship would mean negative correlation, the coefficients now falling anywhere from −1.00 up to .00.

Where there is no consistent relationship, the correlation is zero or approximately zero, showing small coefficients of positive or negative numerical value.

To illustrate, let us use this present study, comparing the list of ratings made by Teachers 1a as against mothers, say.

If teachers rated:

Cruelty as first in seriousness and mothers did the same

Stealing as second in seriousness and mothers did the same

Truancy as third in seriousness and mothers did the same

and this were done all the way down the list for the fifty items, then we would say that the correlation between the ratings made by Teachers 1a and those made by mothers was 1.00. The pattern of such ratings presents itself graphically in horizontal lines as shown below:

Teachers' ratings   *Mothers' ratings*

Cruelty ———————— Cruelty
Stealing ———————— Stealing
Truancy ———————— Truancy

Etc.

If, however, both groups had reversed these ratings so that

Teachers rated:

Cruelty as *first* and mothers as *last* in seriousness

Stealing as second from the *top* and mothers as second from the *bottom*

Truancy as third from the *top* and mothers as third from the *bottom* ,

and so on for the fifty items, we would then have a completely negative or inverse relationship, which would have the correlation coefficient of —1.00. This type of correlation would look like this, graphically:

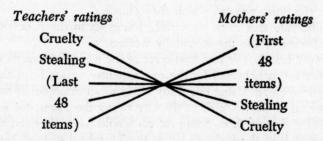

In the first case, of positive correlation, we could say that high ratings of various traits by teachers tend to go with high ratings of the same traits by the mothers, et cetera; and when the correlation coefficient is as high as 1.00, as here given, to the point of one-to-one correspondence.

In the second case, of negative correlation, we would say that high ratings of various traits by teachers tend to go with low ratings of the same traits by mothers; and when the correlation coefficient is as high as −1.00, to the point of one-to-one correspondence, but in a reverse (inverse) direction.

If there were no consistent relationship at all, so that for some items both groups of raters might agree on a high rating, for others they might be diametrically opposed, for still others they might show no systematic trend, *so that in general no definite tendencies could be postulated,* then we would expect a correlation of zero or near zero, either plus or minus in sign.

Symbolically, this correlation coefficient may be represented by r or ρ, depending on the method of computation. In this study, because the rank-difference correlation coefficient is being utilized, ρ would be more correct technically, but r will be used for purposes of convenience.

It may be pointed out that the examples used above were merely examples, and do not necessarily represent the results of actual relationships found between the judgments made by the teachers and those made by the mothers.

Another term which is used often, in the tables among others, is the term *standard deviation,* often abbreviated as SD, for which the symbol is σ, the Greek letter sigma. The standard deviation is a measure of variability, and in our case informs us how the ratings range around the arithmetical mean (average) of all ratings obtained from a given group for any given item. A large standard deviation means that the ratings are widely distributed; a small one means that the ratings tend to stay within a narrow range so that the arithmetical mean is the point around which they cluster.

To illustrate this more concretely brings us to the concept of the *standard error of the mean,* usually written: σ_m

Put very briefly, the standard error of the mean informs us to what extent the mean obtained by the experimenter varies from the theoretically true mean. Using our study again as an example: If we could have had all of the 7A girls in the city rating the items, for instance, instead of eighty of them doing so, we would have obtained the true mean for each of the items so far as the 7A school girls of New York City were concerned. But experimentally we had to depend on a "sample" of children. In all such cases, no matter how properly it is carried out, fluctuations are a *normal* component of such sampling procedure.

Hence it will be seen that the term standard error may be misleading, for it does not carry within itself actually the connotation of mistakes in methodology, as its name might imply, but rather the meaning of deviation.

And to find out thus to what extent our obtained mean for each item varies (deviates) from the theoretically true mean, the statistical device of the standard deviation is therefore invoked in the formula

$$\sigma_m = \frac{\sigma}{\sqrt{N}}$$

in which σ_m is the standard error of the mean; σ is the standard deviation; and $\sqrt{N}$ is the square root of the number of individuals rating the item in question.

To put it more concretely, and applying it to our data: Table X will show us that the 7A girls had rated sullenness with an average of 13.16, the standard deviation (σ) being 5.01. N, the number of girls, was 80. Applying our formula we find that the standard error of this mean of 13.16 would then be:

$$\sigma_m = \frac{\sigma}{\sqrt{N}} = \frac{5.01}{\sqrt{80}} = \frac{5.01}{8.944} = .560$$

This would mean that the chances are approximately 68 in 100 that the true mean would be somewhere between 13.16 minus .560 and 13.16 plus .560, or between 12.60 and 13.72. In other words, if *all* the 7A girls in New York City had rated this item of sullenness, the chances are 68 in 100 that the average obtained from them, the true mean, would have been between 12.60 and 13.72. Similarly, the chances are 9,973 in 10,000 or 99.73 in 100 that the true mean would lie between $13.16 \pm 3 \times .560$; that is, between 14.84 and 11.48.

Another concept closely allied to that of standard error of the mean, is the one that deals with the *reliability* of the difference between two means. We have just noted, for instance, that our 7A girls had rated sullenness with an average of 13.16, while our Table XI reveals that our 7A boys had rated it with an average of 10.34, producing a difference of 2.82. But how can we be certain that this is a true difference, that other groups of 7A girls and 7A boys would also judge it in the same *relative* way; that is, with the girls rating it less seriously than the boys would? Conceivably, other groups of 7A girls and 7A boys might judge sullenness equally for seriousness, or the girls might even give a higher value to sullenness than would be true of the boys.

Fearful and wondrous are the ways of statistics! In order to ascertain this information, one calculates what is called the *critical ratio*, based on the standard error of the difference between the two means, and according to the following methods and formulae:

The standard error of the difference between the two means, expressed also as σ_d, is computed according to the formula,

$$\sigma_d \;=\; \sigma_{m_1 - m_2} \;=\; \sqrt{\sigma^2_{m_1} + \sigma^2_{m_2}}$$

Then the actual, obtained difference between the means (D) is divided by this standard error, giving us the critical ratio,

$$\mathrm{CR} \;=\; \frac{D}{\sigma_d} \;=\; \frac{M_1 - M_2}{\sqrt{\sigma^2_{m_1} + \sigma^2_{m_2}}}$$

$M_1 - M_2$ — is the actual, obtained difference between the means, also expressed as D

σ_d — stands for the standard error of the difference

σ_{m_1} — stands for the standard error of the first mean (in this instance, the average for sullenness as rated by the 7A girls)

σ_{m_2} — stands for the standard error of the second mean (the average for sullenness as rated by the 7A boys)

Reference to appropriate statistical tables shows that the critical ratios ($\frac{D}{\sigma_d}$) range from .00 to 3.00 (and may go much higher). When the critical ratio is as high as 3, it is generally spoken of as a significant one—that is, the chances are 99.9 in 100 that there is a real difference between the means, and a virtual guarantee that the ratings would be in the same relative position if they were repeated. If the critical ratio is only 1.00, for instance, we know that it is only 1/3 as large as it should be to guarantee virtual certainty, the chances now being 84 in 100 that there is such guarantee of the same direction of rating (that is, that 7A girls would again regard sullenness as being less serious than 7A boys would).

To use our example again as an illustration of what this means in concrete application, we present our data and computations as follows:

13.16 is the average of the ratings for sullenness, obtained from 7A girls

10.34 is the average of the ratings for sullenness, obtained from 7A boys

Therefore, M_1-M_2 (D) is 2.82, the actual difference obtained

Sigma (σ) for sullenness as rated by girls 7A is 5.01

Sigma (σ) for sullenness as rated by boys 7A is 6.04

N of girls is 80

N of boys is 81

Hence, $$\sigma_{m_1} = \frac{5.01}{\sqrt{80}} = .560$$

And $$\sigma_{m_2} = \frac{6.04}{\sqrt{81}} = .671$$

Substituting in our formula, we thus obtain

$$\sigma_d = \sqrt{.560^2 + .671^2} = \sqrt{.763841} = .874$$

Hence, our critical ratio $= \dfrac{2.82}{.874} \dfrac{(D)}{(\sigma_d)} = 3.23$

Which means that there is a statistically significant difference between the average ratings made by our 7A girls and by our 7A boys for the item of sullenness, with a margin of extra safety. In other words, this quotient of 3.23 is more than enough to give us virtual certainty that other groups of 7A girls as compared to 7A boys would always rate sullenness in the same relative direction; that is, the 7A girls, on the average, would continue to evaluate sullenness as being less serious than the 7A boys would.

And, finally, may be briefly mentioned the term of *reliability*, as used in its more technical and restricted sense, in which case it takes on the meaning of *consistency* of ratings. In other words, if our 7A girls, or any of our groups, were to rate the entire list of items again, to what extent would their second set of listed items agree with their own first set, so far as the relative position of each item was concerned?

However, it may be stated that the ratings for all of our groups do show the necessary consistency, or reliability, and hence this more difficult phase, what may perhaps be termed applied statistics, need not confront the statistical neophyte beyond this point. Further discussion of reliability in this narrow sense will be found in the appendix (Appendix C), entitled, "Some Further, and More Advanced, Statistical Considerations."

This brief, almost schematically sketched, survey of some basic statistical principles may serve the purpose of clarifying the statistical references made in this study for those who desire such clarification. If amplification should be necessary, any one of several standard textbooks on the subject will be found to be readily helpful in supplying this need.

CHAPTER III

Experimental Extension of Wickman's Investigations

Résumé of a Major Phase of Wickman's Work

During the years 1924 to 1928, E. K. Wickman carried on a series of investigations on the subject of behavior problems of children in elementary schools, in the course of which was evolved an ingenious list of fifty behavior characteristics, designed to ascertain the comparative reactions of individuals to the behavior and personality traits of children.[1] A copy of this list is to be found in the appendix (Appendix A).

This schedule, with minor changes, set up in the form of a rating scale, was submitted by Wickman to teachers in public schools who, under certain specified conditions, were to rate the respective seriousness of the fifty traits specified in this list. The schedules and the schools were as follows:

1. Schedule B-1; administered in October, 1925, to all teachers in a Cleveland school, twenty-eight persons in all. This was followed by Schedule B-2, similar to Schedule B-1, but which had had certain amplifications made, and which was administered to the same teachers a week later. This group of raters was considered to be the experimental group by Wickman.

2. Schedule B-3, was administered to:

  a) Thirty teachers at Senior Teachers College, Cleveland—December, 1925-26.

  b) Forty-one teachers enrolled in a class at Teachers College, Columbia University—1927.

  c) Ten men teachers, comprising the entire faculty of a progressive private school for boys—1927.

3. Schedule B-4, was administered in 1927 to 511 teachers, constituting the entire teaching staff of thirteen elementary public schools, ten of which were located in Newark, New Jersey, New York City,

and Cleveland, Ohio, with the balance situated in three villages in New York State and Minnesota. These teachers represented the second control group, for the purposes of this study.

Then, in order to obtain the comparative judgments of mental hygienists towards these selfsame items, in 1926-27 Schedule B-5 was given to the entire professional staffs of the demonstration Child Guidance Clinics in Cleveland and in Philadelphia, and to the Department of Child Guidance in the public schools of Newark—thirty clinicians in all. The results obtained from these rating scales were compared with the judgments made by the teachers, as evidenced by the ratings made on the schedules administered to them.

The instructions to the mental hygienists and the conditions of rating were definitely, and designedly, different from those given to the teachers, the most notable differences being: Whereas the intent was to obtain from the teachers their innate and emotional reactions to these problems, Wickman so planned the experiment that the responses of the mental hygienists were to represent their professional and intellectual judgments.[2] Also, the teachers were required to view the problem from the standpoint of its immediate, *present* effect on the child,[3] the mental hygienists were urged to view it from the perspective of its importance and effect on the *future* of the child.[4] Finally, a time limit was imposed upon the teachers for completion of these ratings, while the mental hygienists were urged to allow sufficient and unlimited time in order to insure that their judgments were carefully considered ones.[5] Hence, presumably intellectually controlled ones.

To give an exceedingly brief summary of this important phase of a rather elaborate investigation, the following points may be related:

It was found that there was a "fairly close" relationship between the ratings made by the various groups of teachers, respectively: when completely permutative intergroup comparisons between the Cleveland school and the first three control groups were made, the intercorrelations between the rank-order arrangements for the fifty items were found to range from .670 to .897.[6] However, Wickman was of the opinion that these first three control groups were not very representative teacher groups,[7] and put more weight on the findings elicited from the second control group, the group of 511 teachers. Here the correlation between the fifty items arranged in rank-order was .895 when the two groups, the Cleveland experimental group and the group of 511 teachers, were compared.[8] On the whole, Wickman concludes that "the four methods of investigation yielded consistent results with respect to the differential reactions which teachers make to selected types of behavior disorders of children."[9]

But when comparisons were made between each of these teacher groups and the mental hygienists, it was found that there were important differences shown between the judgments rendered by the teachers as against those made by the mental hygienists: so that a negative correlation of −.22 was obtained between the ratings made by the mental hygienists and those made by the Cleveland (experimental) group of twenty-eight teachers; while the correlation between the ratings made by the mental hygienists and those made by the 511 teachers in the second control group was −.11.[10]

Basing his final analyses upon the data obtained from the 511 teachers who constituted the second control group and the clinicians, Wickman's final conclusions may be summarized as follows:

Teachers stressed "the importance of problems relating to sex, dishonesty, disobedience, disorderliness and failure to learn. For them, the problems that indicate withdrawing, recessive characteristics in children are of comparatively little significance."[11] More concretely, teachers estimated that problems such as stealing, heterosexual activity, untruthfulness, cheating, disobedience, impertinence, disorderliness in class, inattentiveness, lack of interest in work, laziness, and the like, were of the utmost seriousness, according to their ratings; whereas characteristics such as shyness, unsocialness, sensitiveness, fearfulness, suspiciousness, imaginative lying, and dreaminess were of the least importance.[12]

"Mental hygienists, on the other hand, consider these unsocial forms of behavior most serious and discount the stress which teachers lay on anti-social conduct."[13] In other words, in the case of the withdrawing and recessive personality and behavior traits, the judgments of the mental hygienists showed a "complete reversal" as compared with those of the teachers; for the former regarded these characteristics of shyness, sensitiveness, unsocialness, fearfulness, dreaminess, and the like, as being among the most serious of all fifty traits listed.[14]

However, as expressed by the smallness of the negative correlation between the rank-order placements of the ratings secured from the two groups, the problems considered most serious by the teachers did not meet with a completely opposing viewpoint on the part of the clinicians.

Perusal of some concrete items bears out this statistical expectation: Items such as untruthfulness, unreliableness, stealing, and lack of interest in work, to which the teachers' ratings had ascribed great importance, were viewed with considerable concern by mental hygienists also, although to a considerably attenuated extent. Others, however, also deemed to be very serious by the teachers, such as impertinence and disobedience, were regarded as being among the least important characteristics by the mental hygienists, along with laziness, profanity, destroying school materials, and smoking. While truancy, dishonesties, heterosexual activity, and obscene notes, pictures, etc., which were also among the problems receiving the highest ratings by teachers, were reduced to an approximately intermediate zone of significance by the mental hygienists.

Other traits, regarded with less concern by the teachers, such as those pertaining to poor adjustment in school—carelessness and inattention—were also discounted in importance by the mental hygienists; while the item of disorderliness in class was also depreciated by the clinicians to a position very far down the list of graduated significance.

In similar fashion, but contrariwise, items such as unhappiness, easily discouraged, resentfulness, physical coward, and suggestible were ranked as among the highest in importance by the mental hygienists; while the ratings of the teachers showed a marked reduction of these evaluations, placing them in a category of comparatively high but more moderated seriousness. Hence, here, too, there was no complete evaluatory reversal shown.[15]

Purpose of This Study

This present study was undertaken with a series of tasks in view: To repeat one phase of Wickman's procedures and to go further, launching into both vertical and horizontal comparisons, and extending its scope into additional sources of information. To find out in absolute terms how the teacher of 1944-45 would judge these same behavior characteristics of children concerning which Wickman interrogated his teachers, and also, how her views compare with the views thus expressed almost twenty years previously, as educed from schedules identical with those devised and utilized at that time by Wickman. In addition, techniques were herein utilized to ascertain how teachers would react if a series of schedules, the same in all respects as those given to mental hygienists, were administered to them: would their ratings on this second type of schedule be similar to the judgments they make on the first type of schedule, ordered to produce distinctive differences between teachers and clinicians, or would their evaluations be in conformity with those made by mental hygienists?

This information by itself, however, does not give a well-rounded answer to questions that arise, confining itself too rigorously to restricted groupings of interested persons. Questionnaires were therefore utilized and submitted to another very important group of adults

In all, the number of forms distributed were:

Schedule 1*a* was distributed to 130 school teachers of New York
_y.

Schedule 1*b* was given to the same school teachers a week later
r rating.

Schedule 2 was submitted to 460 parents, the majority being
_others.

Schedule 3 was administered to more than 400 boys and girls in
_rades 5A, 7A, and 8B.

However, some of the responses had to be discarded, so that the
_otal number of schedules that were utilized for each participating
_roup was then as follows:

School teachers 1*a*	110
School teachers 1*b*	110
Fathers	40
Mothers	102

School children of Grades 5A, 7A, and 8B:

Girls	206
Boys	200
Total	768

Here, too, the scale of measurement was taken to be 20.5 units
and the ratings were scored by a rule calibrated according to inches
and their subdivisions. Although this procedure was rather tedious
and seemed to be an overrefinement, perhaps, of what were essentially judgmental approximations, exact precedence had to be followed
in this instance also in order to insure legitimacy of comparisons with
Wickman's findings.

—the parents. But, and perhaps most important
of those most clearly concerned, the children th
solicited in this present study.

Inasmuch as the views of the mental hygienist
thermost, "ideal" point at the time of Wickman'
considered an experimental redundance, for the pu
ent survey, to obtain any new data from mental h
Wickman did, but with no commitment to any inter
regarding their merits, these views of the mental l
be used as a convenient point of reference: by wl
not necessarily to judge, a standard of measureme
matically one of opinion.

In order to make for strict comparability, the bulle
ent study were necessarily based upon those devise
in some cases, schedules and instructions were iden
models, in others there were variations as dictated b

These bulletins, used in the present research projec
duced in the appendix and are, briefly, as follows:

Schedule 1a was distributed to the full teaching st
mentary schools in New York City. In order to reprodu
conditions, this bulletin was kept identical in all respects
B-4, which had been devised and employed by Wickma
the ratings of the largest and last groups of teachers q
his investigation.

Schedule 1b is an exact reproduction of Schedule B-5
been designed for the consideration of the mental hygienis
man. In this present case, it was given to the same scho
for rating a week after the first questionnaire, Schedule 1a
completed by them.

Schedule 2 was issued to 460 parents. The instructions v
different presentation by the present investigator, whereas
behavior items are the same as those used by Wickman.

Schedule 3 was administered to groups of children atten
mentary schools of New York City, pupils in Grades 5A, 7A,
respectively. Unlike the other three schedules, this consists o
six items instead of fifty. Four traits were deleted as being un
for the scrutiny of children under these specific circumstanc
traits being: obscene notes, pictures, talk; masturbation; heter
activity; and enuresis.

REFERENCES

1. WICKMAN, E. K. *Children's Behavior and Teachers' Attitudes.* New York: The Commonwealth Fund, 1928.
2. *Ibid.,* pp. 117-18.
3. *Ibid.,* p. 119.
4. *Ibid.,* p. 120.
5. *Ibid.,* pp. 120-21.
6. *Ibid.,* p. 105.
7. *Ibid.,* p. 110.
8. *Ibid.,* p. 112 n.
9. *Ibid.,* p. 117.
10. *Ibid.,* p. 122.
11. *Ibid.,* p. 129.
12. *Ibid.,* p. 115.
13. *Ibid.,* p. 129.
14. *Ibid.,* pp. 126, 130.
15. *Ibid., passim.*
16. *Ibid.,* p. 118.

CHAPTER IV

The Comparative Attitudes of Teachers
in 1944-45 towards Children's Behavior

One of the first objectives of this present study, then, was to elicit the attitudes of contemporary teachers towards the identical behavior characteristics which had formed the basis of Wickman's inquiries; and also, to compare these secured judgments with those expressed by teachers almost two decades earlier. Theoretical expectation would lead to the supposition that the gap between teachers' ratings and those of the mental hygienists had narrowed during this period of time, while that between current teachers and those antecedent by twenty years had widened in the direction of closer approximation towards attitudes evinced by the mental hygienists.

Accordingly, to test these assumptions, schedules identical with those devised and administered during the course of Wickman's investigations were submitted to 130 school teachers, representing the total faculties of five elementary schools in the City of New York, during the academic year of 1944-45. For various reasons, 20 schedules of this series had to be discarded; so that 110 schedules were finally utilized, which distributed themselves as follows: School I—14 schedules; School II—20 schedules; School III—28 schedules; School IV—25 schedules; and School V—23 schedules.*

This schedule was now called Schedule 1a in the present investigation, and is to be found in Appendix A. In order to keep identification clear, we shall refer to these participating teachers as *Teachers 1a*. The instructions† and contents reproduced faithfully those devised by Wickman, except for one noteworthy exception: in Wickman's study,

---

* Terms such as "School I," "School II," and the like, do not represent the actual designations of any of the schools. They are, rather, symbolic denotations which take the place of the real numerical descriptions of the respective schools; and are invoked because some form of identification is necessary for coherence and clarity.

† In this study a note was attached to the instruction sheet proper for the guidance of those who could not finish in the time allotted (see Appendix A). But since no such cases developed, this problem remained a purely academic one.

the teachers of New York City had made no ratings for the behavior characteristics relating to sex. The data thus obtained from the present-day New York school teachers, as educed from Schedule 1a, statistically treated and tabulated in rank-order of decreasing seriousness, are presented in Table I, pages 38 and 39. Tables II and III, following Table I, are reproductions of Wickman's tables and are inserted here for the convenience of the reader.

Contrary to reasonable expectation, even a cursory inspection of two of the tables, Table I as against Table II, will show a marked correspondence between the evaluations of the teachers of 1944-45 as compared to those made approximately twenty years previously— a correspondence which is verified by statistical treatment. Using the method of rank-differences, and computing rho by the formula,

$$\rho = 1 - \frac{6\Sigma D^2}{N(N^2-1)}$$

we find that the correlation between the two series of ratings is .922.

Comparison of the standing of the items in these tables reveals that both sets of teachers consider heterosexual activity to be the most serious offense, topping the list in each case; stealing claims 2d place in each; while impertinence has moved up 2 steps in our latest rank-order arrangement. In short, except for two discrepant items in each list, both sets of teachers' ratings assign to the same disorders of behavior—namely, heterosexual activity, stealing, truancy, cruelty, impertinence, disobedience, masturbation, obscene notes, untruthfulness, destroying school materials, temper tantrums, unreliability, impudence, and cheating—the topmost placements of seriousness. Adoption of Wickman's phraseology would categorize these traits variously as representing immoralities; overt, attacking, extravagant behavior; violation of application to school work, and the like.[1]

However, despite this close conformity between the teachers of 1944-45 and those of 1927, there are some interesting exceptions; not many, but perhaps prophetic. In four items the teachers of 1945 in contrast to those of 1927 moved strongly in the direction of the mental hygienists' ratings: unsocial, domineering, suggestible, all of which rank among the first eleven in the clinicians' ratings of serious problems, have each moved up 10 steps in the contemporary teachers' estimates; while stubbornness, ranked 20th in seriousness by the clinicians, has also been raised 10 steps in our teachers' evaluations of undesirability. Similarly, in respect of two items, our present-day teachers parallel the mental hygienists' greater *leniency* of rating: so that whereas the teacher of 1927 ascribed a placement of 19 to

TABLE I

TEACHERS' RATINGS ON THE SERIOUSNESS OF BEHAVIOR PROBLEMS OF CHILDREN

(Results from Schedule 1a, as Filled Out by 110 Teachers in Five Public Schools of New York City)*

Behavior Problems	Averages	Standard Deviations
Heterosexual Activity	14.09	7.04
Stealing	14.08	6.71
Truancy	13.67	6.33
Cruelty, Bullying	13.22	6.45
Impertinence, Defiance	13.10	5.99
Disobedience	13.03	5.73
Masturbation	12.76	6.90
Obscene Notes, Pictures, etc	12.70	6.98
Untruthfulness	12.34	5.97
Destroying School Materials	12.12	5.59
Temper Tantrums	11.51	6.42
Unreliable, Irresponsible	11.28	4.99
Impudence, Rudeness	10.85	5.14
Disorderliness	10.78	4.60
Cheating	10.71	5.97
Quarrelsomeness	10.61	5.31
Lack of Interest in Work	10.31	5.19
Suggestible	10.18	6.05
Unhappy, Depressed	9.88	6.13
Laziness	9.59	4.94

* This schedule was given to 130 teachers, and, after an interval of one week, Schedule 1b was given to the same teachers.

For reasons already stated, 20 schedules of this series had to be discarded. The 110 schedules that were utilized distribute themselves as follows: School I—14; School II—20; School III—28; School IV—25; School V—23.

TABLE I—*Continued*

Behavior Problems	Averages	Standard Deviations
Profanity	9.15	6.06
Stubbornness, Contrariness	9.04	4.93
Domineering, Overbearing	9.01	5.60
Inattention	8.98	4.64
Carelessness in Work	8.97	4.31
Resentfulness	8.95	5.54
Nervousness	8.94	5.28
Selfishness, Unsportsmanship	8.82	4.75
Enuresis	8.78	6.36
Unsocial, Withdrawing	8.48	5.75
Physical Coward	8.09	5.22
Easily Discouraged	8.06	5.17
Smoking	8.04	6.78
Slovenly in Appearance	7.96	4.68
Interrupting, Talkativeness	7.91	4.83
Fearfulness	7.74	5.52
Silliness	7.73	5.26
Sullenness, Sulkiness	7.67	4.61
Tardiness	7.65	3.88
Restlessness	7.49	5.33
Suspiciousness	7.20	4.98
Dreaminess	7.06	4.76
Overcritical of Others	6.98	4.64
Thoughtlessness	6.80	4.54
Inquisitiveness	6.65	4.60
Whispering	6.41	4.11
Sensitiveness	6.40	4.29
Shyness	6.02	4.86
Imaginative Lying	5.92	4.61
Tattling	5.66	4.50

TABLE II

TEACHERS' RATINGS ON THE SERIOUSNESS OF BEHAVIOR PROBLEMS OF CHILDREN

(Results from Schedule B-4 Administered to Teachers in 13 Public Schools)*

AVERAGES OF COMPOSITE RATINGS

BEHAVIOR PROBLEMS	Newark, N. J.		New York City				Cleveland, Ohio				Three Villages	Total	
	Sch'l A	Sch'l B	Sch'l C	Sch'l D	Sch'l E	Sch'l F	Sch'l G	Sch'l H	Sch'l I	Sch'l J	Sch'ls K-L-M	Aver.	S.D.
(Number of Teachers Rating)	53	38	44	63	82	57	21	35	19	64	35	511	
Heterosexual Activity	17.9	17.3					17.3	16.9	17.1	18.3	15.2	17.3	4.6
Stealing	18.2	17.1	17.7	17.8	18.2	13.9	17.1	15.7	17.2	18.4	13.9	17.0	3.1
Masturbation	17.1	16.8					17.3	16.3	15.7	17.7	15.1	16.7	4.2
Obscene Notes, Pictures, etc.	16.1	16.4					15.3	15.7	16.8	17.2	15.3	16.6	4.6
Untruthfulness, Lying	16.1	16.4	13.3	15.8	15.1	16.0	17.0	14.4	17.4	17.8	14.8	15.8	4.6
Truancy	16.1	16.8	15.6	14.5	16.1	15.5	13.6	14.3	16.0	17.5	13.7	15.6	3.0
Impertinence, Defiance	15.5	15.4	16.3	15.6	15.3	13.8	14.5	13.8	14.7	15.5	13.0	15.0	4.7
Cruelty, Bullying	14.7	14.7	14.0	14.8	14.5	14.9	15.4	14.7	14.0	16.9	13.0	14.8	4.7
Cheating	15.4	15.8	14.0	14.7	14.6	13.9	16.3	13.9	14.7	16.8	13.7	14.7	4.8
Destroying School Materials	14.1	14.5	14.6	14.7	13.0	12.8	14.6	14.2	13.0	16.9	14.1	14.3	4.8
Disobedience	13.8	14.8	15.0	13.0	14.1	13.1	14.7	12.8	14.0	16.3	13.4	14.1	4.6
Unreliableness, Irresponsible	13.7	12.4	13.5	13.9	12.5	14.4	15.6	13.5	15.0	16.7	12.4	13.9	5.8
Temper Tantrums	12.0	13.3	11.6	17.1	12.2	10.5	13.2	12.7	12.8	13.8	12.7	13.0	5.8
Lack of Interest in Work	12.5	13.2	12.1	10.6	17.9	14.1	12.2	12.8	14.0	13.9	12.8	12.8	4.8
Profanity	12.8	13.0	10.5	13.1	11.6	10.7	12.7	11.4	14.0	14.1	13.6	12.3	5.6
Impudence, Rudeness	13.2	12.1	12.1	11.9	12.1	11.9	11.1	10.8	11.9	13.4	12.9	12.2	4.7
Laziness	12.3	12.5	10.3	11.9	10.7	12.4	13.8	12.1	12.9	14.6	11.3	12.2	4.6
Smoking	11.3	10.9	9.8	11.5	12.0	13.1	12.0	12.2	12.7	13.3	13.3	12.0	6.5
Enuresis	11.6	11.4					11.3	12.0	10.9	13.0	10.7	11.8	5.7
Nervousness	12.0	11.7	12.0	9.8	10.8	13.7	12.9	9.4	9.6	12.3	11.3	11.7	6.2

	A	B	C	D	E	F	G	H	I	J	K-L-M	Total	
Disorderliness in Class	11.4	11.4	11.9	11.2	11.4	10.4	12.2	12.1	11.8	12.9	12.5	11.7	4.1
Unhappy, Depressed	11.6	11.3	10.7	10.1	12.0	10.1	14.3	7.1	11.5	14.6	10.4	11.5	5.3
Easily Discouraged	11.9	12.0	9.9	10.5	10.4	12.4	13.2	12.1	12.2	12.6	10.8	11.5	5.1
Selfishness, Unsportsmanly	11.5	10.2	10.2	11.3	11.4	11.1	12.1	10.8	10.8	13.1	13.2	11.3	4.5
Carelessness in Work	11.4	11.5	9.6	10.9	10.6	10.6	12.6	11.5	10.6	13.2	11.9	11.3	2.6
Inattention	10.5	11.9	9.8	10.2	10.5	11.2	11.4	10.9	12.1	13.5	12.1	11.2	3.9
Quarrelsomeness	11.9	10.7	11.0	10.5	11.5	10.1	11.5	11.5	9.3	12.3	10.9	11.1	4.3
Suggestible	11.9	12.4	10.3	12.0	10.5	10.9	12.4	10.6	12.5	14.8	11.3	11.0	5.8
Resentfulness	11.5	12.1	9.9	10.2	9.8	10.0	10.6	11.1	11.9	12.4	11.0	10.8	4.7
Tardiness	10.4	11.1	9.5	9.6	10.1	9.4	9.2	10.6	9.7	14.7	9.3	10.5	4.2
Physical Coward	10.8	11.2	10.1	10.4	8.4	10.2	10.2	11.1	11.3	12.7	10.0	10.4	5.8
Stubbornness, Contrariness	9.9	11.2	10.2	9.5	9.9	9.4	11.5	10.2	9.8	11.1	12.3	10.3	4.2
Domineering, Overbearing	10.9	10.3	8.7	10.2	9.7	7.6	11.1	10.2	11.5	12.8	11.2	10.3	4.8
Slovenly in Appearance	11.0	10.5	7.7	9.7	8.9	10.0	10.4	11.1	8.5	12.8	9.7	10.1	4.9
Sullenness, Sulkiness	10.4	10.9	8.8	8.4	9.3	8.3	11.0	9.4	10.5	11.4	12.7	9.9	4.4
Fearfulness	10.3	8.3	8.7	8.7	8.5	10.6	12.3	9.6	9.1	11.8	9.7	9.7	5.0
Suspiciousness	9.5	8.5	8.7	8.8	7.4	8.9	9.0	10.0	8.2	11.5	9.2	9.1	4.9
Thoughtlessness	8.4	9.2	7.0	7.3	7.5	8.2	9.9	9.5	8.6	11.5	9.8	8.7	4.7
Silliness	8.9	10.2	8.7	6.6	7.9	7.0	7.7	9.6	10.1	10.1	9.7	8.5	4.8
Unsocial, Withdrawing	8.4	8.1	7.3	7.4	6.4	7.3	12.4	9.2	9.3	10.4	9.7	8.3	5.2
Dreaminess	9.0	8.8	6.4	5.5	5.9	6.3	9.3	8.9	9.0	14.2	10.1	8.3	5.1
Imaginative Lying	8.2	7.8	8.5	6.9	8.2	7.6	8.1	7.5	8.7	9.4	8.2	8.1	5.7
Interrupting, Talkativeness	8.0	7.6	7.2	6.5	6.8	7.4	8.5	7.7	7.0	9.8	13.2	8.0	4.2
Inquisitiveness	8.1	8.5	7.5	6.9	7.2	6.7	7.7	9.0	8.6	9.8	9.3	8.0	4.4
Overcritical of Others	8.0	7.9	6.7	8.1	6.0	7.2	8.9	8.3	8.6	9.9	8.6	7.9	3.1
Tattling	7.9	8.9	5.6	8.3	6.3	6.9	9.0	7.1	5.8	8.8	8.4	7.5	6.1
Whispering	8.2	7.2	6.7	5.9	7.2	6.1	6.4	7.9	6.5	9.8	9.9	7.5	4.1
Sensitiveness	7.7	7.2	6.8	6.1	5.7	5.4	9.1	8.0	5.9	8.9	8.6	7.0	4.6
Restlessness	7.8	7.1	6.2	6.6	5.7	7.2	7.1	7.0	6.6	8.5	9.3	6.9	4.6
Shyness	5.7	6.3	4.3	4.4	4.4	3.3	6.9	6.6	3.4	8.0	6.8	5.4	4.4

* From E. K. Wickman, *Children's Behavior and Teachers' Attitudes.* Commonwealth Fund, 1928, pp. 246-47.

TABLE III

CLINICIANS' RATINGS ON THE SERIOUSNESS OF BEHAVIOR PROBLEMS OF CHILDREN

(Results from Schedule B-5 Administered to 30 Mental Hygienists) *

Behavior Problems	Averages	Standard Deviations
Unsocial, Withdrawing	17.3	3.4
Suspiciousness	16.4	3.8
Unhappy, Depressed	16.2	3.5
Resentfulness	14.1	3.9
Fearfulness	14.0	4.8
Cruelty, Bullying	13.5	3.8
Easily Discouraged	13.4	3.4
Suggestible	13.3	3.5
Overcritical of Others	13.2	4.0
Sensitiveness	13.1	4.5
Domineering, Overbearing	13.0	4.5
Sullenness, Sulkiness	12.6	3.3
Stealing	12.5	3.2
Shyness	12.5	4.6
Physical Coward	12.0	3.9
Selfishness, Unsportsmanly	11.8	3.7
Temper Tantrums	11.7	4.4
Dreaminess	11.3	4.4
Nervousness	11.3	5.8
Stubbornness, Contrariness	10.9	3.9
Unreliable, Irresponsible	10.4	3.9

* From E. K. Wickman, *Children's Behavior and Teachers' Attitudes.* Commonwealth Fund, 1928, p. 243.

TABLE III—*Continued*

Behavior Problems	Averages	Standard Deviations
Truancy	10.3	3.9
Untruthfulness	10.3	2.9
Cheating	10.3	4.5
Lack of Interest in Work	9.6	5.0
Heterosexual Activity	9.9	4.6
Enuresis	9.2	4.0
Obscene Notes, Pictures, etc.	8.8	4.9
Tattling	8.8	5.6
Silliness	8.5	4.9
Quarrelsomeness	8.3	3.7
Impudence, Rudeness	7.6	4.1
Imaginative Lying	7.5	6.2
Inattention	7.3	3.6
Slovenly in Appearance	7.2	5.3
Laziness	7.2	4.1
Impertinence, Defiance	7.1	3.3
Carelessness in Work	7.1	3.1
Thoughtlessness	6.8	3.7
Restlessness	6.4	4.5
Masturbation	6.4	3.8
Disobedience	6.4	2.9
Tardiness	5.6	2.6
Inquisitiveness	5.3	4.1
Destroying School Materials	5.1	3.4
Disorderliness	3.4	2.9
Profanity	2.9	2.7
Interrupting, Talkativeness	2.8	2.4
Smoking	2.3	2.1
Whispering	0.8	1.1

enuresis and 18 to smoking, the teachers of 1944-45 lowered them to a standing of 29th and 33d in importance.

Contrariwise, however, easily discouraged and nervousness, both of which rank among the nineteen most serious behavior problems among the clinicians' ratings, were viewed less seriously by Teachers 1a, 9 and 7 steps respectively, than by their counterparts of 1927.

Many interpretations can undoubtedly be read into the reading of these two tables or, rather, as to why the tables read as they do. Sherif in his "The Psychology of Social Norms" presents an extensive account of the development, incorporation, ubiquitousness, diversity, influence, and persistence of norms—moral and social;[2] which would furnish partial explanation as to why our teachers, as individuals, hold fast to their views. However, there are special factors at work in this judgmental task which would precipitate out specific attitudes, operative during the original judging and regenerative after a span of practically two decades. Whether these attitudes are unique and extrusive to the general context of the times and what these special considerations are, will be developed later in our discussion.

But suffice it for the moment to point out that, among all other explanations, the one of basic attitude, "Einstellung," must not be forgotten. For, essentially, the teacher was asked to rate as a teacher, not as an individual. This was inherent in the instructions given to the teachers and in the intentions of the original Wickman bulletins, as Wickman carefully explains.

Accordingly, the teacher's basic *attitude* gave rise to a series of differential basic *attitudes* to each of these items insofar as her criterion for each judgment was the reaching of her goals as a teacher. Included in the scope of this problem there were, then, two compelling factors: the children about whom these estimates were given and the person giving the judgments. They did not, nor were they asked to, divest themselves of their roles as teachers while making their ratings. As an individual, the teacher may believe that fearfulness is the most serious problem for a *child*, for example, but not for the *pupil* in her charge.

To put it more succinctly, no matter how objective the teacher may try to be, the fact remains, nevertheless, that the way she will view the child is bound to be a function of her function (as a teacher). Nor would it have been desirable that the teacher conceive of the child purely in the abstract or of herself as an abstract rater; had she done so, the results we thereby obtained would undoubtedly have been too much of an abstraction!

In essence, there are really two sets of questions in each bulletin:

one which deals with the rating of objective characteristics, such as destroying property, disorderliness in class, etc., and the other which deals with more personal, subjective characteristics, such as shyness, nervousness, and the like. Further, when the bulletin confronts the rater with the query, "How serious is this trait?", the automatic response may well be: "Serious for *what*?" The teacher will see one aspect, the mental hygienist another, each conditioned by his own professional goals. In a sense, a biserial list is presented for their scrutiny.

However, for an understanding of the forces that actively concern the child, this questionnaire has an invaluable importance in that it does furnish a common meeting place despite the seeming diversity of its components. For each item is weighed against a common standard of reference—what is good for the child?—and thus these items are indirectly comparable, each with the other, judgment being expressed by the numerical values yielded. In this fashion, based on relative weighting of each, these items thus form a continuum, instead of a discrete series of disparate traits or a double list of opposing ranks based on subjectivity or objectivity of their component parts. This continuum, which thus gives a generic homogeneity to the items, is revealed and realized when the listings of the various items are set up in tabulated, sequential form, according to the judgments made by the individual rater and by the groups, respectively.

Similarly, and as a by-product, we obtain the judgment of the various groups of raters as to the relative importance of subjectiveness versus objectiveness, inherent in each of the characteristics, along with the ratings of the characteristics themselves.

Let us take as an example, truancy as against nervousness. By evaluating truancy as 3d in seriousness and nervousness as 27th, Teachers 1a show that, as a group, they deem an objective factor to be more serious than a subjective one in this case. Although the two items were not compared directly, nor were the teachers directly concerned about whether the individual items of truancy and nervousness were objective or subjective in character—nevertheless, and indirectly, they revealed their view as to the comparative importance of an objective trait as against a subjective one; thereby adding an accrual value to their basic task of establishing numerical values for the traits themselves.

An alternative procedure, of having two separate lists, would not produce results as ultimately satisfying; there would not be the same opportunity for immediacy of comparison and there would be even more emphasis on the differences existing. Two separate lists of traits, bringing out in relief outward conduct of the child as a *pupil* as against inward feelings of the child as a *child*, would emphasize various facets of the child's personality and character to an undesirable degree; whereas Wickman's method of listing tends to keep before the rater's eyes the view of the child as a totality, in whose conduct the appraiser picks out the points of emphasis as he sees them. In other words, instead of beforehandedly ascribing any degree of importance to traits in prejudgment, the viewer looks at the child in the process of behaving, gives his selective attention to the traits thus manifested, and then evaluates them according to his beliefs.

REFERENCES

1. WICKMAN, E. K. *Children's Behavior and Teachers' Attitudes.* New York: The Commonwealth Fund, 1928. Pp. 114-15, 130, *et passim*.

2. SHERIF, MUZAFER. *The Psychology of Social Norms.* New York: Harper, 1936.

CHAPTER V

Are the Comparisons Invidious?

This leading question led to the second phase of this present investigation: the attempt to find out to what extent the end is a reciprocal of the means. Wickman explains that "unfortunately . . . the results may appear to the disadvantage of the teaching profession. . . . It is not our intention to draw invidious comparisons between the two professional groups";[1] etc.

However, our succeeding discussion addresses itself to the query: In comparing the answers given by the mental hygienists and the teachers, is the comparison necessarily invidious to the latter when taken in full context, and in view of the results secured experimentally by Schedule 1a of this present study and possibly to be obtained by further and subsequent investigations projected herein?

As has already been noted, Wickman conscientiously points out that his investigation was so ordered as to evoke responses from teachers which would be most representative of their duties as teachers. But his subsequent interpretations of the bases underlying their ratings, and his analysis of what motivates teachers in making such judgments, would appear to show significant deviation from this initial premise. In his section on "The Psychology of Teachers' Attitudes," Wickman presents the thesis that the teachers respond as they do because their teaching purposes are frustrated: "To the extent that any kind of behavior signifies attack upon the teachers and upon their professional endeavors does such behavior rise in their estimation as a serious problem."[2] And that these reactions, by interpretation, are "personal, emotional responses to children who exhibit problems in behavior."[3] By extension of these assumptions there is further postulated a whole psychology of teachers' attitudes, finally evolving into the theory that any seeming intellectual convictions on the part of the teachers are really rationalizations which merely justify the underlying emotional reactions of the teachers.[4]

With the basic tenets put forth there can be no dissent: the behavior items do lend themselves to such terms as "attacking" and "withdrawing," and one can set the experiment in such fashion as to favor

emotional responses. But further interpretations would seem to be
purely speculative unless the experiment had yielded evidence to
bear them out or refute them. For the classifications of attacking and
withdrawing, schematically correct and convenient though they may
be, are not necessarily conceived as such in the minds of the teachers,
nor are the types of conduct upon which they are based necessarily
evocative of emotional reactions upon the part of teachers, and less
likely so to any determining extent when engaged in a task so relatively
objective as filling out questionnaires away from provocative stimuli.
And without any introspective or other subjective data being available,
it would seem that there is an insufficiency of evidence upon which
to predicate such constructions.

Consistently applied, this method of interpretation would lead to
the deduction that, in rating the behavior characteristic of "unsocial"
as highest on their list, the mental hygienists were also reacting to the
psychology of frustration. For, inasmuch as unsociability is a difficult
trait to alter and the purpose of the mental hygienist is to heal, his
purposes are thereby frustrated; and hence, the characteristic designated as "unsocial" is rated uppermost on the list of seriousness. But
this reasoning along syllogistic lines reveals its own fallacy when
examined in the light of the actual situation.

The problem resolves itself, then, into the following parallel: Is
it necessary that the teacher undergo a complete reorientation so that
she will more closely approach the views of the mental hygienists, as
Wickman suggests? In other words, shall we ask that there be a
re-education of the educator, or shall we merely ask that she redefine
her goals? If the teachers are responding primarily and upon intellectual bases to types of behavior which are regarded as interference with
professional or pedagogical objectives, with the emotional components
being purely concomitant or corollary in nature, the answer would
seem to point to the latter direction. But if the teachers are evidencing, fundamentally, emotionally conditioned types of response, alternative to the first, then the answer would point in affirmation of the
views set forth in Wickman's doctrine.

All this has its functional importance in the practical applicability
of the doctrine later to be enunciated in this present study, of *define*
and *allot.* For, if the first conjecture is correct, if teachers respond
intellectually for the most part, their attitudes can be approached intellectually, and a relatively simple solution of the problem is possible.
But if their reactions are emotionally prompted, basically, then the
undertaking would, of necessity, be much more difficult and more

specifically along the rather laborious lines that Wickman has suggested.

These foregoing speculations have, so far, taken no affirmative stand, but there are two lines of evidence that may be positive in nature:

1. The first one consists of a possibility of interpretation that has not been made and yet, logically, could have been invoked. In one of the studies made by Wickman in his investigation, preceding the issuance of Bulletin B-4, the teachers in a Cleveland school reported that only 6 per cent of the children were free from any type of disturbances of conduct, while 53 per cent were said to have exhibited disturbances of behavior ranging, in their opinion, from "considerable" to "very serious difficulty." But, two days later, when asked to report on the total behavior of the pupils in their school, the teachers reported that 51 per cent were "exceptionally well-adjusted," only 7 per cent being considered important behavior-problem cases.[5] Wickman's explanation bases itself on the argument that the teachers fail to "recognize the significance of many of the problems which they encounter frequently in their children," etc.[6] From all the foregoing, the assumption has to be made that by "problems," Wickman's reference includes behavior traits which the mental hygienists consider serious.

But this deals with only one side of the coin. The obverse, which has not been pointed out anywhere would, to this present writer, also seem to follow: namely, even though teachers consider classroom offenses, etc., to be serious, regarding the *child* as a *pupil*, they are by implication also stating, most definitely, that so far as the *child* as a *child* is concerned, these problems are not of comparable import. In other words, *they are* discounting their own high ratings for misconduct, and the like, when viewing the child in the context of his changed status. And thus, even if the reverse conclusion to this does not necessarily in and of itself follow, namely, that teachers agree with the mental hygienists about the seriousness of behavior disorders such as shyness, unsociability, etc., there seems little doubt that they do, even if indirectly, show this considerable insight into the child's needs and development.

2. However, to test the possibility of this reverse conclusion developing, under comparable conditions, this study undertook the submitting of a second questionnaire to the *same teachers* who had participated in filling out the first one issued in this present investigation. This schedule was called Schedule 1*b* (to be found in Appen-

dix A), and was the duplicate, deliberatedly so, of the schedule that Wickman had given to the mental hygienists in 1926-27.

As may be noted, and in consonance with the differences which have already been pointed out in Chapter III, the rating scales and instructions pertaining to Schedule 1b differed in important ways from those appearing in Schedule 1a:

a) The teacher was given an unlimited amount of time in which to make her ratings, thus affording the opportunity of supplying the requested *intellectual* evaluations rather than the more hurried, *emotional* judgments.

b) Instead of evoking her reaction to the *present* importance of each problem, the view of the teacher was sought so far as the later effects on the *future* happiness and adjustment of the child as an adult were concerned.

c) Whereas the rating scale in Schedule 1a was captioned: *Of no consequence, Of only slight consequence, Makes for considerable difficulty, An extremely grave problem,* Schedule 1b referred to various degrees of *importance* of the individual items. Similarly, in the instructions, the concept of importance now coshared the previous stress that had been laid upon *seriousness* of the various traits exhibited.

REFERENCES

1. WICKMAN, E. K. *Children's Behavior and Teachers' Attitudes.* New York: The Commonwealth Fund, 1928. P. 118.
2. *Ibid.,* pp. 159-60.
3. *Ibid.,* p. 160.
4. *Ibid.,* p. 165.
5. *Ibid.,* pp. 54-55.
6. *Ibid.,* p. 59.

CHAPTER VI

How Do Teachers Compare with
Mental Hygienists under
Comparable Conditions?

And so, a week later we distributed Schedule 1b to the same teachers who had filled out Schedule 1a, to ascertain what the ratings would be when the judgments were elicited under conditions identical with those which had been set up for the mental hygienists. For identification purposes, these teachers will be called Teachers 1b when the discussion deals with the ratings they marked on Schedule 1b. This is analogous to our terming the same teachers, Teachers 1a, when reference is made to their ratings on Schedule 1a. Some rather interesting results were thereby obtained, as may be seen from the information available in Table III, and in Tables IV and V following.

For one thing, as evidenced by their valuations which appeared on Schedule 1b, these same teachers no longer expressed so close an agreement with the Wickman teachers as they had done a week earlier. Table V shows that the first rank-order correlation between the ratings made by "Teachers (Wickman's data)" and Teachers 1a was .922; whereas now the correlation between "Teachers (Wickman's data)" and Teachers 1b is .854. This is still a high correlation but does, nevertheless, portray a definite lowering in correspondence of ratings.

But of more importance are the data referring to Teachers 1a in comparison with Teachers 1b: in other words, a comparison of two lists of ratings representing the one and same group of individuals under two sets of experimental conditions. The correlation between Teachers 1a and Teachers 1b is, according to expectation, manifestly high, .921; and in and of itself, therefore, would indicate no great change in attitude on the part of the teachers.

Again, scrutiny of Table V informs us of the correlation that was now obtained between Teachers 1b and the mental hygienists. It will be remembered that the correlation between Teachers 1a and the mental hygienists was negative, being −.016. Although small and by

TABLE IV

TEACHERS' RATINGS ON THE SERIOUSNESS OF BEHAVIOR PROBLEMS OF CHILDREN

(Results from Schedule 1b, as Filled Out by 110 Teachers in Five Public Schools of New York City)*

Behavior Problems	Averages	Standard Deviations
Stealing	15.70	5.81
Heterosexual Activity	14.73	6.15
Cruelty, Bullying	14.24	6.15
Untruthfulness	13.98	5.41
Impertinence, Defiance	13.93	5.82
Unreliable, Irresponsible	13.89	5.19
Truancy	13.54	6.06
Disobedience	13.53	5.16
Masturbation	13.26	6.89
Obscene Notes, Pictures, etc.	12.87	6.58
Cheating	12.70	5.70
Temper Tantrums	12.39	5.92
Suggestible	12.08	6.07
Destroying School Materials	11.60	5.52
Domineering, Overbearing	11.51	5.76
Lack of Interest in Work	11.47	5.03
Impudence, Rudeness	11.42	4.90
Unhappy, Depressed	11.05	5.86
Disorderliness	11.00	5.19
Selfishness, Unsportsmanship	10.99	4.86

* Schedule 1a was given to 130 teachers and, after an interval of one week, this schedule was given to the same teachers.

For reasons already stated, 20 schedules of this series had to be discarded. The 110 schedules that were utilized distribute themselves as follows: School I—14; School II—20; School III—28; School IV—25; School V—23.

TABLE IV—*Continued*

Behavior Problems	Averages	Standard Deviations
Quarrelsomeness	10.92	5.20
Carelessness in Work	10.88	5.28
Laziness	10.88	5.00
Resentfulness	10.72	5.29
Slovenly in Appearance	10.61	5.11
Easily Discouraged	10.61	5.74
Physical Coward	10.48	5.74
Unsocial, Withdrawing	10.24	5.63
Nervousness	9.82	4.92
Inattention	9.75	4.65
Suspiciousness	9.53	5.06
Profanity	9.43	5.97
Enuresis	9.11	6.39
Fearfulness	9.02	5.05
Overcritical of Others	8.94	5.09
Tardiness	8.75	4.97
Sullenness, Sulkiness	8.71	4.64
Stubbornness, Contrariness	8.67	4.59
Sensitiveness	8.49	4.46
Thoughtlessness	8.27	4.88
Dreaminess	7.94	4.94
Silliness	7.89	5.14
Shyness	7.85	4.49
Inquisitiveness	7.45	4.32
Restlessness	7.17	4.79
Interrupting, Talkativeness	6.79	4.59
Tattling	6.48	4.72
Imaginative Lying	6.39	5.11
Smoking	6.39	5.69
Whispering	5.22	4.03

TABLE V

RANK-DIFFERENCE CORRELATIONS

	Mothers	5A Boys	5A Girls	7A Boys	7A Girls	8B Boys	8B Girls	Teachers 1a	Teachers 1b	Mental Hygienists (Wickman's data)
Fathers .... .945	.945	.625	.542	.630	.711	.752	.632	.789	.880	.330
Mothers		.583	.542	.613	.671	.689	.584	.801	.885	.357
5A Boys			.837	.866	.866	.796	.839	.760	.661	−.231
5A Girls				.880	.893	.818	.880	.655	.589	−.220
7A Boys					.845	.859	.895	.728	.653	−.161
7A Girls						.860	.893	.750	.707	−.130
8B Boys							.883	.719	.762	.047
8B Girls								.705	.693	−.112
Teachers 1a ..									.921	−.016
Teachers 1b ..										.229
Teachers (Wickman's data)								.922	.854	

no means indicating reversal, nevertheless it was negative. But now, under the new, comparable sets of instructions, the correlation is .229, which indicates a small but *positive* degree of affinity. In other words, the teachers and mental hygienists are now .245 points of unity closer to agreement than they had been when our sampling of teachers filled out Schedule 1a.

However, analysis of the individual items furnishes some important insights not easily derived from general correlation figures and reveals that there were important shifts in rated seriousness of a considerable number of items. And, to make this analysis more meaningful, it would be best to make a double presentation from this point on; namely, to make a concurrent multiple comparison between the three groups:

Teachers 1a .... Teachers 1b .... Mental Hygienists

Study of Tables I, III, and IV reveals that at least twelve items were moved upward in point of undesirability by Teachers 1b in comparison with their first ratings, and that these twelve items were all among the group categorized by the ratings of the mental hygienists as comprising the top sixteen rankings of seriousness. Arrangement One illustrates this somewhat graphically.

ARRANGEMENT ONE

UPWARD RATINGS BY TEACHERS, IN THE DIRECTION OF THE MOST SERIOUS EVALUATIONS MADE BY MENTAL HYGIENISTS

	From Schedule 1a	To Schedule 1b	Ratings Made by Mental Hygienists	Critical Ratios Means of 1a and Means of 1b
	Rank-order	Rank-order	Rank-order	
Suggestible	18 →	13	8	2.29
Domineering	23 →	15	11	3.25
Resentful	26 →	24	4	2.42
Selfishness	28 →	20	16	3.34
Unsocial, etc.	30 →	28	1	2.29
Physical coward	31 →	27	15	3.19
Easily discouraged	32 →	26	7	3.45
Fearfulness	36 →	34	5	1.78
Suspiciousness	41 →	31	2	3.43
Overcritical of others	43 →	35	9	2.97
Sensitiveness	47 →	39	10	3.54
Shyness	48 →	43	14	2.90

Correspondingly, the teachers now depreciated the importance of twelve traits, as compared to their first evaluations. Most of these items had been characterized (by Wickman) as attacking, extravagant, aggressive characteristics and violations of classroom discipline and school work, and all of them were items which the mental hygienists had rated as among the least serious. More specifically, when filling out Schedule 1b, the ratings of the teachers reduced the rank-order of destroying school materials, by 4 steps, to 14th place; disorderliness went down from rank 14 to 19; and quarrelsomeness was also lowered from 16th to 21st place. Not a great distance in any case, to be sure, but nevertheless some distance downwards. Smoking, profanity, interrupting, inattention, restlessness, impudence, whispering, laziness, and disobedience follow a similar pattern in a diminishing order of 16, 11, 11, 6, 5, 4, 4, 3, and 2 steps, respectively. These are presented in Arrangement Two.

ARRANGEMENT TWO

DOWNWARD RATINGS BY TEACHERS, IN THE DIRECTION OF THE LEAST SERIOUS EVALUATIONS MADE BY MENTAL HYGIENISTS

	From Schedule 1a	To Schedule 1b	Ratings Made by Mental Hygienists	Critical Ratios Means of 1a and Means of 1b
	Rank-order	Rank-order	Rank-order	
Disobedience	6	8	42	0.72
Destroying school materials	10	14	45	0.69
Impudence, impoliteness	13	17	32	0.84
Disorderliness	14	19	46	0.33
Quarrelsomeness	16	21	31	0.43
Laziness	20	23	36	1.93
Profanity	21	32	47	0.35
Inattention	24	30	34	1.22
Smoking	33	49	49	1.92
Interrupting	35	46	48	1.75
Restlessness	40	45	40	0.47
Whispering	46	50	50	2.16

Parallel results were also observed for six items (set forth in Arrangement Three), to which the ratings of the mental hygienists had ascribed a comparatively intermediate status: truancy, obscene notes, heterosexual activity, silliness, enuresis, and tattling. Although the teachers had regarded the first three of these traits with the utmost seriousness during the first rating procedures, these grave estimates were somewhat lightened when Schedule 1b was filled out, to the extent of a lowering of 4 steps for truancy, 2 for obscene notes, and 1 for heterosexual activity. Silliness and enuresis, to which the teachers had from the outset shown a greater tolerance than had the mental hygienists, under the catalysis of the second questionnaire were now reduced to even lower positions of seriousness by the teachers: so that silliness was displaced from 37th to 42d rank, while enuresis was lowered from 29th to 33d place. Concomitantly, tattling was now deemed to be more serious in the judgments of the teachers than had been the case before, as expressed by its elevation from the lowermost position to one 3 steps higher; a move towards the level of 29th rank assigned to it by the mental hygienists.

Three results were obtained, however, which were quite at variance with the trends thus observed: Slovenly in appearance, which the clinicians had rated as being 35th in order of importance, was now assigned to a *higher* position of seriousness by the teachers, having been shifted upwards from 34th to 25th place. Whereas stubbornness, given 20th place by the judgments of the mental hygienists, thus indicating a comparatively high degree of undesirability, was now *devalued* in the second rating procedure, from 22d to 38th place; and, comparably, nervousness was also *depreciated* by Teachers 1b, showing a downward displacement of 2 steps from its original position of 27th in rank.

ARRANGEMENT THREE

CHANGED RATINGS BY TEACHERS, AND THEIR RELATIONSHIP TO THE RELATIVELY INTERMEDIATE EVALUATIONS MADE BY MENTAL HYGIENISTS

	From Schedule 1a	To Schedule 1b	Ratings Made by Mental Hygienists	Critical Ratios Means of 1a and Means of 1b
	Rank-order	Rank-order	Rank-order	
Truancy	3 → 7		23	0.15
Obscene notes, etc.	8 → 10		28	0.18
Heterosexual activity	1 → 2		26	0.70
Silliness	37 → 42		30	0.23
Enuresis (wetting self)	29 → 33		27	0.38
Tattling	50 → 47		29	1.30

Table VI offers a relative evaluation of the standing of all fifty items, while Table VII offers a statistical check on the reliability of their placement. Taking as an example the item which is fifteenth on both tables, interrupting, one notes that this item is considered to be 35th in point of seriousness by Teachers 1a and 46th by Teachers

TABLE VI

RANK-ORDER OF THE 50 ITEMS, BASED ON THE RATINGS MADE BY SIX GROUPS

	Mental Hygienists	Fathers	Mothers	Teachers 1a	Teachers 1b	Wickman's Teachers
Tardiness	43	35	39	39	36	30
Truancy	23	5	6	3	7	6
Destroying School Materials	45	9	9	10	14	10
Untruthfulness	23	8	4	9	4	5
Imaginative Lying	33	49	49	49	48.5	42
Cheating	23	1	5	15	11	9
Stealing	13.5	1	1	2	1	2
Profanity	47	34	38	21	32	15
Smoking	49	37	34	33	48.5	18
Obscene Notes, Pictures, etc.	28.5	18.5	16	8	10	4
Masturbation	41	10	18	7	9	3
Heterosexual Activity	26	3	3	1	9	1
Disorderliness	46	29	28	14	19	20.5
Whispering	50	50	50	46	50	46.5
Interrupting, Talkativeness	48	48	48	35	46	43.5
Restlessness	41	46	44	40	45	49
Inattention	34	40	33	24	30	26
Lack of Interest in Work	25	23.5	12	17	16	14
Carelessness in Work	37.5	27	30	25	22.5	24.5
Laziness	35.5	31	25	20	22.5	16.5
Unreliable, Irresponsible	21	6	8	12	6	12
Disobedience	41	21	21	6	8	11
Impertinence, Defiance	37.5	12	11	5	5	7
Cruelty, Bullying	6	3	2	4	3	8

Quarrelsomeness	31	20	20	16	21	27
Tattling	28.5	38	37	50	47	46.5
Stubbornness, Contrariness	20	42	41	22	38	32.5
Sullenness	12	33	36	38	37	35
Temper Tantrums	17	23.5	23	11	12	13
Impudence, Rudeness	32	14	22	13	17	16.5
Selfishness	16	13	10	28	20	24.5
Domineering, Overbearing	11	30	15	23	15	32.5
Shyness	13.5	41	43	48	43	50
Sensitiveness	10	45	42	47	39	48
Unsocial, Withdrawing	1	22	24	30	28	40.5
Overcritical of Others	9	32	35	43	35	45
Thoughtlessness	39	39	40	44	40	38
Inquisitiveness	44	43	45	45	44	43.5
Silliness	30	44	46	37	42	39
Unhappy, Depressed	3	7	7	19	18	22.5
Resentfulness	4	25.5	19	26	24	29
Nervousness	18.5	18.5	13	27	29	20.5
Fearfulness	5	16	14	36	34	36
Enuresis (Wetting Self)	27	28	27	29	33	19
Dreaminess	18.5	47	47	42	41	40.5
Slovenly in Appearance	35.5	25.5	31	34	25.5	34
Suspiciousness	2	36	32	41	31	37
Physical Coward	15	15	29	31	27	31
Easily Discouraged	7	11	17	32	25.5	22.5
Suggestible	8	17	26	18	13	28

TABLE VII

CRITICAL RATIOS FOR THE DIFFERENCES BETWEEN THE MEAN RATINGS OF TEACHERS 1a AND TEACHERS 1b

Teachers 1a *versus*	*Teachers 1b*	
	Diff. M.	*C. R.*
Tardiness	−1.10	1.83
Truancy	0.13	0.15
Destroying School Materials	0.52	0.69
Untruthfulness	−1.64	2.13
Imaginative Lying	−0.47	0.71
Cheating	−1.99	2.52
Stealing	−1.62	1.88
Profanity	−0.28	0.35
Smoking	1.65	1.92
Obscene Notes, Pictures, etc.	−0.17	0.18
Masturbation	0.50	0.53
Heterosexual Activity	−0.64	0.70
Disorderliness	−0.22	0.33
Whispering	1.19	2.16
Interrupting, Talkativeness	1.12	1.75
Restlessness	0.32	0.47
Inattention	−0.77	1.22
Lack of Interest in Work	−1.16	1.66
Carelessness in Work	−1.91	2.94
Laziness	−1.29	1.93
Unreliable, Irresponsible	−2.61	3.73
Disobedience	−0.53	0.72
Impertinence, Defiance	−0.83	1.04
Cruelty, Bullying	−1.02	1.19

TABLE VII—*Continued*

Teachers 1a versus	Teachers 1b	
	Diff. M.	C. R.
Quarrelsomeness	−0.31	0.43
Tattling	−0.82	1.30
Stubbornness, Contrariness	0.37	0.58
Sullenness	−1.04	1.65
Temper Tantrums	−0.88	1.05
Impudence, Rudeness	−0.57	0.84
Selfishness	−2.17	3.34
Domineering, Overbearing	−2.50	3.25
Shyness	−1.83	2.90
Sensitiveness	−2.09	3.54
Unsocial, Withdrawing	−1.76	2.29
Overcritical of Others	−1.96	2.97
Thoughtlessness	−1.47	2.30
Inquisitiveness	−0.80	1.33
Silliness	−0.16	0.23
Unhappy, Depressed	−1.17	1.44
Resentfulness	−1.77	2.42
Nervousness	−0.88	1.28
Fearfulness	−1.28	1.78
Enuresis (Wetting Self)	−0.33	0.38
Dreaminess	−0.88	1.33
Slovenly in Appearance	−2.65	4.02
Suspiciousness	−2.33	3.43
Physical Coward	−2.39	3.19
Easily Discouraged	−2.55	3.45
Suggestible	−1.90	2.29

1b. But the question is, to what extent is this a reliable difference, how significant is this difference? In other words, what assurance have we that another test would not produce an opposite trend of results? To answer these questions, statistical treatment was utilized, so that the critical ratio was obtained for this matched set of rating figures by means of the following formulae and computations:

$$\frac{D}{\sigma_d} = \frac{\text{The actual difference obtained}}{\text{Standard error (of the difference between two uncorrelated means)}} = \text{the Critical Ratio}$$

(1) Standard error of the mean, $\sigma^2_m = \dfrac{\sigma^2}{N}$

(2) The standard error of the difference between two uncorrelated means, $\sigma_d = \sqrt{\dfrac{(\sigma_{dis}A)^2}{N_a} + \dfrac{(\sigma_{dis}B)^2}{N_b}}$

By substitution of the proper figures in these calculations we find that the critical ratio for interrupting is 1.75. This means that there are 96 chances in 100 that this result between the two testings is a *stable* one. In other words, the chances are 96 in 100 that when rating the item of interrupting, teachers will, on the average, always give it a lower evaluation under the conditions set forth for Schedule 1*b* than they will under those associated with Schedule 1*a*. But the quotient of 3 obtained from $\dfrac{D}{\sigma_d}$ is customarily taken as giving virtual certainty—there is only 1 chance in 1000 in such case, that the direction of results would be reversed if ratings were made again under similar conditions.

Consultation of Arrangement One or Table VII shows that so far as the upward movements in the direction of mental hygienists' ratings are concerned, we can be virtually certain of more than six of our twelve items, since the difference between each set of paired means yields a critical ratio of more than or close to 3; while within this total array of critical ratios, those for the balance of the items show a gradation down to one of 1.78 for the lowest, which still means that there are 96 chances in 100 that the trend of this differential rating is a stable one, and not due to chance.

Arrangement Two indicates, however, that the teachers do not have as decided convictions about the decreased evaluations they manifested for items which may be subsumed under the general category of classroom and like disorders. Only five items, namely, inattention, interrupting, smoking, laziness, and whispering, show critical ratios of any weight, ranging as they do from 1.22 to 2.16; which means that the stability of these ratings is such that the chances range from 88+ in 100 to 98+ in 100 that the direction of results would be the same if the experiment were repeated with a proper sampling of teachers, under comparable circumstances.

In Arrangement Three we find only one critical ratio of other than very low numerical value and hence, except for this one item, there is no secure assurance that the ratings would not revert to those made under the first set of circumstances if Schedule 1b, and the conditions attendant thereto, were again submitted to a sample group of teachers.

We may definitely conclude, then, that the rated increases in the seriousness of the behavior items presented in Arrangement One—items which are largely categorized as withdrawing, recessive personality traits and personal problems, by Wickman, and which the mental hygienists consider to be among the most serious characteristics—are, by and large, reliable. In other words, when their judgments were made under conditions comparable to those set forth for mental hygienists, that the teachers did evidence a more serious view of these items than they had done previously; and that these elevated ratings were not due to chance.

The items in Arrangement Two show a much less definite trend and, except for the five items already mentioned, do not approach statistical significance; while this lack of statistical warranty obtains for all items, with one qualified exception, in Arrangement Three. However, despite this curtailment, we may still ascribe to these two groupings a certain amount of importance, based on the qualitative and descriptive values they nevertheless possess.

CHAPTER VII

What Do Children
Think of Children's Behavior?

The Purpose of Our Queries

We thus have this partial array of protagonists drawn up, among whom the parents will later be included. But the leading character among this list of dramatis personae is still to be heard from, the child himself. One could call upon retrospection and say, "I know, because I was a child once myself." This view, however, is no more tenable than the supposition that the mere fact of biological procreation leads, per se, to one's being a proper parent—no matter how widely such status has been hailed as a psychological *sine qua non* for the understanding of the young.

No, to understand the child, one must go to the child. By the time the child is going to school, what are his attitudes? For here one could hardly speak of a fixed attitude, a governing set of mind. Is the child the blank tablet that Aristotle has declared him to be, or an impregnated negative susceptible in development to the influence of the reagents of environment which can only bring out what is already there? Analytical studies have shown that children inherit symbolism as a part of their "racial unconscious" heritage. Do they inherit, and if so, to what extent, behavior standards also?

Put in terms of our specific problem: Are children in the "état de neutralité morale . . . à sa naissance" that Durkheim envisions them to be?[1] Counterpoised against this postulate of a natal state of moral neutrality are the views that children never really have a chance to show their natural *reactions,* for the natural *actions* of the newborn are promptly curbed, almost from the moment that they are cribbed. One of the strongest statements in that regard comes from Piaget: "From the hour of its birth certain regularities of conduct are imposed upon the infant by the adult."[2] Social psychology shows no social lag in expounding similar views.[3]

Some of these problems cannot lie within the scope of this investigation—if, indeed, definitively within that of any investigation—for the child of school age is, in a psychological sense, too "old" for such study. But one strong variable, to be found within the milieu of their development, can be studied, and that is: since training is environment, in one sense of the word, we may then attempt to ascertain whose training has had the greatest significance for the child by the time he has reached school age. If Piaget is correct in his declaration that "the baby (at the stage of motor intelligence) is asocial,"[4] we could expect that the untrained child would be completely hedonistic in his outlook. Feral child, brought up in the wilderness and without the benefits of civilization, would in unlimited fashion carry on his limited primitive activities; and would have to await the blessings of civilization for questions about his conduct and for more conduct which would be questionable.

Assuming, then, that children could be expected naturally to have hedonistic views, and that any progress away from this zero point of moral judgment represents the results of training—our raw data, the distances along the ruled scores of the questionnaires filled out by our school children, will furnish us with a measure of this training. In this fashion, the problem of define and allot, of who should concern themselves with the training of children and to what selective extent, is displaced from the somewhat precarious level of a moral issue to the practical and measurable one of statistical considerations.

To this extent, we may thereby answer two concrete questions:

1. Whose views does the child seem to represent most closely, if any one's? Does he agree closest with the teacher or with the parents? Whose views or training has had the greater or greatest effect on the child?

2. To whose influence will he be most amenable in the future, and in what fashion and to what extent?

Questionnaire and Administration

A first step, then, was to elicit absolute findings of children's judgments by administration of appropriate questionnaires. With this in view, a schedule was prepared to be used by school children, Schedule 3 (Appendix A). The schedule itself, for the most part, was the same as the one that had been submitted to our teachers the second time (Schedule 1b), and originally to the mental hygienists, but with one important exception: The investigator here decided that it might be wiser from the standpoint of the children's welfare (and her own!)

to delete the following four items: "obscene notes, etc.," "masturbation," "heterosexual activity," and "enuresis"; and so the children judged forty-six items instead of fifty as the adults had done.

The instructions, however, were considerably simplified in conformity with the status of our new raters. Additionally, endeavor was made to bridge the gap between the instructions that had been given to the teachers originally and those that had been given to the mental hygienists—by avoiding emphasis of either viewpoint and yet including both. This was attempted by stating that we were giving them these questions as part of an effort to study the ways of "helping children to be happy, and successful in school"; and by speaking mainly of the behavior characteristics as being undesirable from that standpoint.

We touched very lightly upon the word "serious," mentioning it in only one comparison: for the connotation is so often, severity of misdeed, and ensuing punishment, which might have affected the ratings. Similarly, we hoped to avert the effects of juvenile crime-and-punishment concepts entering in by avoiding the expressions and ideas of "bad" and of "naughty," but explained, rather, that anything "that is not good for a child" is "undesirable." Cognizance was also taken of the fact that the list inherently resolves itself into two phases, that of active behavior expression as contrasted with a passivity of state of being, and would have to be thus approached. We therefore impressed the word "undesirable" into further service as a binding medium; and at one end of the scale gave the example of stealing as being undesirable, while at the other, the condition of having a cold as being undesirable. In this manner, we attempted to embrace the concepts of undesirable *conduct* and of undesirable states of *being*, as encountered in our list of items: the first being exemplified by overt deeds, such as destroying school materials, and the second being illustrated by the more personal, subjective condition of being unhappy, depressed, dissatisfied, et cetera; and thus lend cohesiveness and the quality of congenerousness to potentially opposing types of traits.

Additionally, at the very beginning and at the very end, emphasis was made that this rating procedure was not a test. And to further ensure the child's candid and honest opinions, instructions to attain these ends were employed, coupled with the assurance that no one except the investigator would see the responses.

After a careful outline of this phase of the investigation had been made and permission of the proper authorities had been obtained, these schedules were administered to boys and girls in grades 4B,

5A, 7A, and 8B, during the academic year of 1944-45. Eventually, the completed schedules of 406 of these boys and girls were utilized; and it is upon the raw data thus obtained that Tables VIII, IX, X, XI, XII, XIII, and, with the exception of nine, part of all the rest are based.

These grades were chosen because of various factors involved. In ethical and moral judgments children tend to show a gradient from age to age, so we essayed to plumb the depths at various levels, as it were, in order to obtain cross-sectional views. Further, unless one were prepared to make as elaborate a survey as was done by Terman and Merrill in carrying out procedures associated with their revision of the Stanford-Binet intelligence scale, it seemed most advisable to keep the general sampling of our school population fairly exhaustive in each case, making certain however that the selection of samples within each group was representative. In the statistical sense, we wanted to make certain that we selected unselected samples. As finally chosen, the school population of each of our groups represented a sufficiently wide range socio-economically, and comparably so, group as against group.

Actual administration of these rating procedures was carried out by means of assembly periods called by the principals of the respective schools, at which time the questionnaires were passed out to the children. The investigator orally then gave the instructions and explanations to the children, and demonstrated the actual operation of the rating methods. Standardized definitions were given by the investigator to the assembled children for some of the more difficult items, such as suggestible, temper tantrums, unreliableness, imaginative lying, and the like. (Definition of "imaginative lying" along the lines of Baby Snooks seemed to furnish a decided fillip to the proceedings in each case.) Any other definitions that were requested, and required answers to any other questions, were promptly given to the pupils individually at their desks—either by the present investigator, a friend who acted as an assistant, or by any of a number of the teachers who had accompanied their classes. In the latter case, though, teachers were asked to give general assistance to the children, not necessarily only to those of their own classes; this was done partially in the interest of obtaining more candid ratings, lest their close presence exercise an unavoidable monitory effect.

No mention was made to the pupils of any time allotment for the completion of this task: on the one hand, a feeling of haste might precipitate precipitate ratings; on the other, experience in giving Binet tests to school children had taught this present writer that if one assured the child that he "need not hurry," some of the more conscientious pupils were apt to change their answers over and over. In the interest of fresher, more spontaneous reactions, this assurance was omitted. However, practically all of the children finished during the period, some well before it was over, while a few were still busily furrowing their brows at the time the bell was about to ring. These were, without undue pressure, allowed to transfer their lines from their foreheads to their papers; and of these, only one or two required a few minutes longer than the period.

In order to obtain the reactions of the very youngest children who could respond to a questionnaire of this type we had, as already pointed out, started with the fourth grade as a tentative point at which to sink our first plumb line. But, the general perturbation of some pupils during the question period, along with specimens of erratic ratings, persuaded us to eliminate this group.

Our statistical treatment and evaluations were, then, based on the 406 children from the other three school groups, boys and girls in Grades 5A, 7A, and 8B; in detail, thus:

1. Grade 5A (low Fifth) was composed of

a) *57 girls,* constituting all the 5A girls enrolled in four public schools of New York City (except for absentees and a few whose schedules had to be discarded).

The distribution was as follows:
     School I* — 8 girls
     School IV —20 girls
     School V —14 girls
     School VII—15 girls

b) *50 boys,* constituting all the 5A boys enrolled in four public schools of New York City.†

The distribution was as follows:
     School I —10 boys
     School IV —14 boys
     School V — 9 boys
     School VII—17 boys

---

* Designations such as "School I," etc., do not refer to the actual numbers of any schools; they are merely symbols which take the place of the real numbers in order to maintain comprehensibility and comparability. So that we may know, for instance, that all the 5A boys and girls were taken from the same schools, designated as "I," "IV," "V," and "VII"; while in the case of the 8B boys, for example, School "VI" had to be added to Schools "IV" and "V" in order to make a group comparable numerically to our 8B girls.

† Except for absentees and a few whose schedules had to be discarded.

2. Grade 7A (low Seventh) was composed of

a) 80 girls, constituting all the 7A girls enrolled in two public schools of New York City.†

The distribution was as follows:

    School IV —24 girls
    School V —56 girls

b) 81 boys, constituting all the 7A boys enrolled in Public School IV and 37 per cent of the 7A boys attending Public School VI, of New York City.†

The distribution was as follows:

    School IV —30 boys
    School VI —51 boys

3. Grade 8B (high Eighth) was represented by

a) 69 girls, constituting all the 8B girls enrolled in two public schools of New York City.†

The distribution was as follows:

    School IV —40 girls
    School V —29 girls

b) 69 boys, constituting all the 8B boys enrolled in Public Schools IV and V and 22 per cent of the 8B boys attending Public School VI, of New York City.†

The distribution was as follows:

    School IV —33 boys
    School V — 2 boys
    School VI —34 boys

General Relationship between the Judgments of the Children, as against Those of the Teachers and Mental Hygienists

Results obtained after statistical treatment of the raw data thus secured are to be found in Tables VIII, IX, X, XI, XII, and XIII, and by reference again to the table of correlations, Table V.

To some extent surprising, but, in the light of other psychological investigations to be anticipated, were the manifestations in the find-

---

† Except for absentees and a few whose schedules had to be discarded.

TABLE VIII

CHILDREN'S RATINGS ON THE SERIOUSNESS OF BEHAVIOR PROBLEMS OF CHILDREN

(Results from Schedule 3, as Filled Out by 57 Girls* in Grade 5A† in Four Public Schools of New York City)

Behavior Problems	Averages	Standard Deviations
Stealing	16.61	4.91
Profanity	15.40	5.54
Destroying School Materials	15.26	5.49
Truancy	15.25	5.79
Impertinence	15.15	5.40
Smoking	14.96	6.29
Cruelty, Bullying	14.82	5.56
Disobedience	14.70	4.90
Impudence, Rudeness	14.00	5.32
Cheating	13.96	5.43
Unreliable, Irresponsible	13.38	5.64
Tattling	13.18	5.67
Untruthfulness	13.11	5.69
Slovenly in Appearance	13.02	5.71
Temper Tantrums	12.93	5.52
Selfishness, Unsportsmanship	12.80	5.67
Domineering, Overbearing	12.70	5.84
Overcritical of Others	12.68	5.88

* The number "57" represents all the 5A girls enrolled in these schools (except for absentees and a few whose schedules had to be discarded), the distribution being as follows: School I–8; School IV–20; School V–14; School VII–15.

† Grade 5A, according to the system of designation used in New York City, is the equivalent of "low Fifth."

Table VIII—Continued

Behavior Problems	Averages	Standard Deviations
Lack of Interest in Work	12.60	5.63
Quarrelsomeness	12.50	5.53
Sullenness, Sulkiness	12.47	5.83
Suggestible	12.07	6.28
Carelessness in Work	12.00	5.52
Easily Discouraged	11.50	5.50
Nervousness	11.46	6.26
Interrupting, Talkativeness	11.35	6.08
Resentfulness	11.35	5.41
Disorderliness	11.18	5.33
Inquisitiveness	11.15	5.71
Laziness	11.15	6.09
Silliness	11.14	5.88
Inattention	11.00	6.01
Thoughtlessness	10.96	6.17
Stubbornness, Contrariness	10.89	5.34
Suspiciousness	10.72	5.57
Whispering	10.70	5.26
Physical Coward	10.46	6.04
Restlessness	10.35	5.37
Imaginative Lying	10.17	5.44
Dreaminess	9.64	5.75
Unsocial, Withdrawing	9.58	5.48
Sensitiveness	9.35	4.86
Unhappy, Depressed	9.08	5.38
Tardiness	9.04	5.44
Fearfulness	9.00	5.87
Shyness	7.80	5.88

TABLE IX

CHILDREN'S RATINGS ON THE SERIOUSNESS OF BEHAVIOR PROBLEMS OF CHILDREN

(Results from Schedule 3, as Filled Out by 50 Boys* in Grade 5A† in Four Public Schools of New York City)

Behavior Problems	Averages	Standard Deviations
Stealing	16.35	6.18
Destroying School Materials	14.67	6.40
Profanity	14.67	5.49
Cruelty, Bullying	14.36	7.36
Disobedience	14.29	6.05
Truancy	14.21	6.47
Smoking	14.13	7.27
Impudence, Rudeness	13.62	6.19
Impertinence, Defiance	13.59	6.90
Lack of Interest in Work	13.59	6.32
Unreliable, Irresponsible	13.31	6.63
Cheating	13.23	6.81
Easily Discouraged	12.93	6.41
Carelessness in Work	12.90	6.30
Disorderliness	12.82	5.67
Physical Coward	12.78	6.48
Quarrelsomeness	12.59	6.28

* The number "50" represents all the 5A boys enrolled in these schools (except for absentees and a few whose schedules had to be discarded), the distribution being as follows: School I–10; School IV–14; School V–9; School VII — 17.

† Grade 5A, according to the system of designation used in New York City, is the equivalent of "low Fifth."

TABLE IX—Continued

Behavior Problems	Averages	Standard Deviations
Sullenness, Sulkiness	12.40	6.60
Untruthfulness	12.39	6.42
Laziness	12.23	5.83
Suggestible	11.98	6.90
Domineering, Overbearing	11.98	7.12
Temper Tantrums	11.96	6.68
Inattention	11.77	6.15
Inquisitiveness	11.74	6.13
Overcritical of Others	11.62	6.92
Selfishness, Unsportsmanship	11.44	6.55
Resentfulness	11.29	6.70
Thoughtlessness	11.25	6.50
Slovenly in Appearance	11.02	6.65
Nervousness	10.87	5.88
Interrupting, Talkativeness	10.63	5.55
Unsocial, Withdrawing	10.61	5.75
Whispering	10.42	5.97
Restlessness	10.30	5.63
Silliness	10.28	7.12
Tattling	10.08	7.25
Stubbornness, Contrariness	9.96	5.55
Unhappy, Depressed	9.73	6.19
Fearfulness	9.28	6.70
Tardiness	9.20	5.54
Sensitiveness	9.14	6.20
Suspiciousness	9.11	6.10
Imaginative Lying	9.09	6.20
Dreaminess	9.05	6.33
Shyness	6.53	5.97

TABLE X

CHILDREN'S RATINGS ON THE SERIOUSNESS OF BEHAVIOR PROBLEMS OF CHILDREN

(Results from Schedule 3, as Filled Out by 80 Girls* in Grade 7A† in Two Public Schools of New York City)

Behavior Problems	Averages	Standard Deviations
Stealing	18.42	4.41
Destroying School Materials	16.64	4.81
Profanity	16.00	4.54
Cruelty, Bullying	15.91	4.94
Truancy	15.62	5.35
Untruthfulness	15.39	4.52
Disobedience	15.34	5.31
Impertinence, Defiance	15.30	5.10
Impudence, Rudeness	15.25	5.09
Cheating	15.10	4.72
Slovenly in Appearance	15.08	4.79
Smoking	14.81	6.91
Selfishness, Unsportsmanship	14.79	4.95
Unreliable, Irresponsible	14.38	5.21
Quarrelsomeness	13.80	5.07
Suggestible	13.74	5.53
Nervousness	13.54	5.95
Laziness	13.50	5.67

* The number "80" represents all the 7A girls enrolled in both schools (except for absentees and a few whose schedules had to be discarded), the distribution being as follows: School IV—24; School V—56.

† Grade 7A, according to the system of designation used in New York City, is the equivalent of "low Seventh."

TABLE X—*Continued*

Behavior Problems	Averages	Standard Deviations
Easily Discouraged	13.44	5.44
Overcritical of Others	13.36	5.34
Lack of Interest in Work	13.22	5.05
Sullenness, Sulkiness	13.16	5.01
Carelessness in Work	13.08	4.94
Resentfulness	13.04	5.45
Disorderliness	12.80	4.85
Physical Coward	12.79	5.71
Domineering, Overbearing	12.75	5.96
Temper Tantrums	12.68	5.49
Interrupting, Talkativeness	12.38	5.16
Inquisitiveness	12.31	5.69
Stubbornness, Contrariness	12.24	5.00
Thoughtlessness	12.21	5.46
Tardiness	12.20	5.71
Tattling	12.18	6.25
Suspiciousness	12.18	5.27
Unsocial, Withdrawing	12.13	5.70
Silliness	12.07	5.64
Inattention	11.79	5.36
Unhappy, Depressed	11.77	5.89
Fearfulness	11.69	6.00
Sensitiveness	10.90	5.83
Whispering	10.13	4.84
Imaginative Lying	9.72	5.89
Restlessness	9.00	5.52
Shyness	8.85	5.89
Dreaminess	8.53	4.93

TABLE XI

CHILDREN'S RATINGS ON THE SERIOUSNESS OF BEHAVIOR PROBLEMS OF CHILDREN

(Results from Schedule 3, as Filled Out by 81 Boys* in Grade 7A† in Two Public Schools of New York City)

Behavior Problems	Averages	Standard Deviations
Stealing	17.09	4.91
Truancy	15.48	5.38
Cruelty, Bullying	15.04	5.89
Destroying School Materials	14.95	5.26
Smoking	14.40	6.72
Profanity	14.31	5.79
Disobedience	14.26	4.76
Impudence, Rudeness	13.97	4.94
Selfishness, Unsportsmanship	13.71	6.16
Impertinence	13.71	5.75
Unreliable, Irresponsible	13.11	5.50
Cheating	13.08	5.53
Lack of Interest in Work	12.91	5.68
Untruthfulness	12.69	5.24
Domineering, Overbearing	12.23	5.54
Silliness	12.16	6.23
Disorderliness	11.97	5.34
Easily Discouraged	11.87	5.33

* The number "81" represents 37% of the 7A boys enrolled in School VI and all the boys enrolled in School IV (except for absentees and a few whose schedules had to be discarded), the distribution being as follows: School IV—30; School VI—51.

† Grade 7A, according to the system of designation used in New York City, is the equivalent of "low Seventh."

TABLE XI—*Continued*

Behavior Problems	Averages	Standard Deviations
Inquisitiveness	11.70	5.73
Overcritical of Others	11.63	5.33
Slovenly in Appearance	11.60	5.97
Temper Tantrums	11.59	5.95
Quarrelsomeness	11.45	5.33
Carelessness in Work	11.28	5.25
Inattention	11.23	5.27
Physical Coward	10.84	6.87
Interrupting, Talkativeness	10.79	5.42
Suggestible	10.70	6.20
Tattling	10.69	6.74
Resentfulness	10.59	5.56
Unhappy, Depressed	10.54	5.96
Sullenness, Sulkiness	10.34	6.04
Unsocial, Withdrawing	10.08	5.98
Stubbornness, Contrariness	9.87	4.49
Laziness	9.78	4.95
Nervousness	9.76	6.17
Suspiciousness	9.71	5.42
Tardiness	9.63	5.03
Thoughtlessness	9.16	5.61
Fearfulness	8.35	5.90
Restlessness	8.22	4.78
Sensitiveness	7.74	5.15
Whispering	7.58	5.43
Dreaminess	7.55	5.08
Imaginative Lying	6.77	5.00
Shyness	4.69	4.62

TABLE XII

CHILDREN'S RATINGS ON THE SERIOUSNESS OF
BEHAVIOR PROBLEMS OF CHILDREN

(Results from Schedule 3, as Filled Out by 69 Girls in
Grade 8B† in Two Public Schools of New York City)*

Behavior Problems	Averages	Standard Deviations
Stealing	18.94	3.56
Profanity	16.87	4.47
Slovenly in Appearance	16.61	4.36
Impudence, Rudeness	16.56	3.78
Disobedience	16.35	4.41
Unreliable, Irresponsible	16.34	4.31
Truancy	16.22	4.68
Cruelty, Bullying	16.03	4.58
Untruthfulness	15.93	4.85
Destroying School Materials	15.91	4.30
Selfishness, Unsportsmanship	15.71	4.66
Smoking	15.61	5.49
Impertinence, Defiance	15.53	4.46
Overcritical of Others	15.46	4.07
Cheating	15.19	4.91
Carelessness in Work	15.12	4.71
Domineering, Overbearing	15.03	5.02
Temper Tantrums	14.88	4.91

* The number "69" represents all the 8B girls enrolled in both schools (except for absentees and a few whose schedules had to be discarded), the distribution being as follows: School IV—40; School V—29.

† Grade 8B, according to the system of designation used in New York City, is the equivalent of "high Eighth."

TABLE XII—*Continued*

Behavior Problems	Averages	Standard Deviations
Suggestible	14.67	5.13
Lack of Interest in Work	14.54	4.85
Easily Discouraged	14.52	5.34
Laziness	14.21	4.92
Quarrelsomeness	14.18	5.20
Disorderliness	14.00	4.78
Physical Coward	13.72	4.75
Sullenness, Sulkiness	13.60	5.04
Inquisitiveness	13.50	4.68
Silliness	13.48	4.74
Inattention	13.37	4.22
Thoughtlessness	13.37	4.60
Suspiciousness	13.31	5.23
Stubbornness, Contrariness	13.31	4.69
Interrupting, Talkativeness	13.22	4.81
Tattling	13.01	6.18
Unsocial, Withdrawing	13.01	5.61
Fearfulness	13.00	5.36
Unhappy, Depressed	12.96	5.26
Nervousness	12.88	5.36
Resentfulness	12.62	5.06
Sensitiveness	12.59	5.08
Dreaminess	11.62	5.40
Imaginative Lying	10.94	5.52
Tardiness	10.93	5.72
Restlessness	10.01	5.09
Shyness	9.51	5.86
Whispering	8.63	4.71

TABLE XIII

CHILDREN'S RATINGS ON THE SERIOUSNESS OF BEHAVIOR PROBLEMS OF CHILDREN

(Results from Schedule 3, as Filled Out by 69 Boys* in Grade 8B† in Three Public Schools of New York City)

Behavior Problems	Averages	Standard Deviations
Stealing	16.51	5.33
Destroying School Materials	15.72	5.55
Truancy	14.83	5.84
Cruelty, Bullying	14.66	5.47
Untruthfulness	13.58	5.47
Selfishness, Unsportsmanship	13.58	6.42
Impudence, Rudeness	13.38	5.52
Profanity	13.25	6.22
Physical Coward	13.00	5.96
Suggestible	12.94	5.67
Cheating	12.94	5.31
Impertinence, Defiance	12.93	5.08
Unreliable, Irresponsible	12.83	5.62
Disobedience	12.76	5.85
Domineering, Overbearing	12.56	5.81
Easily Discouraged	12.55	5.52
Slovenly in Appearance	12.24	6.31
Temper Tantrums	11.82	6.22

* The number "69" represents 22% of the 8B boys enrolled in School VI and all the boys enrolled in Schools IV and V (except for absentees and a few whose schedules had to be discarded), the distribution being as follows: School IV–33; School V–2; School VI–34.

† Grade 8B, according to the system of designation used in New York City, is the equivalent of "high Eighth."

TABLE XIII—*Continued*

Behavior Problems	Averages	Standard Deviations
Sullenness, Sulkiness	11.61	5.75
Silliness	11.54	6.54
Carelessness in Work	11.54	5.44
Lack of Interest in Work	11.51	5.94
Disorderliness	11.46	5.60
Quarrelsomeness	11.26	5.75
Overcritical of Others	11.15	5.22
Smoking	10.98	7.66
Suspiciousness	10.91	5.87
Tattling	10.86	7.71
Inquisitiveness	10.77	5.63
Unhappy, Depressed	10.73	5.64
Nervousness	10.67	6.22
Laziness	10.65	5.89
Thoughtlessness	10.22	6.39
Resentfulness	10.15	5.81
Stubbornness, Contrariness	10.07	5.65
Tardiness	10.00	6.38
Inattention	9.94	5.50
Unsocial, Withdrawing	9.71	5.69
Imaginative Lying	9.46	6.56
Dreaminess	9.42	6.27
Interrupting, Talkativeness	9.21	5.80
Fearfulness	8.85	6.46
Sensitiveness	7.99	5.60
Restlessness	7.74	5.54
Whispering	7.09	5.50
Shyness	6.37	6.02

ings of the extreme "conservatism" of the very young and the extent
to which they corresponded in judgments with their teachers; thus:

Correlations between:

5A boys	.760	Teachers 1a*
5A girls	.655	Teachers 1a
7A boys	.728	Teachers 1a
7A girls	.750	Teachers 1a
8B boys	.719	Teachers 1a
8B girls	.705	Teachers 1a

This technique of correlations, although furnishing evidence of
considerable correspondence between the views of these children
and those of the teachers (before modification), yields even more
information when we compare the ratings of the children with those
of Teachers 1b (whose ratings were made, it will be recalled, under
conditions more comparable with those ordered for the mental hygienists).

Now the children draw away a little from their teachers, with the
following correlations:

Correlations between:

Children versus		Teachers 1b
5A boys	.661	(r is now .099 less)
5A girls	.589	(r is now .066 less)
7A boys	.653	(r is now .075 less)
7A girls	.707	(r is now .043 less)
8B boys	.762	(r is now .043 *more*)
8B girls	.693	(r is now .012 less)

These tables reveal, then, that all the children are *less* in accord
with the Schedule 1b teachers than they had been with Schedule 1a
teachers, with the sole exception of the 8B boys, who show the opposite tendency. And of all these groups, the 5A boys are closest to the
ratings made by the Teachers 1a, as indicated by the correlation figure
of .76; while the 5A girls appear to be the most individualistic, inasmuch as their agreement with the Schedule 1a teachers and Schedule
1b teachers is the lowest in both listings.

---

* That is, the ratings made by teachers when they filled out Schedule 1a.

Whether this general trend of the children's ratings continues further, to its logical conclusion, may best be discerned by another glance at Table V, or this scheme directly below, which is based upon it. Data removed from that table show that the trend continues even more strongly, when the correlations of the children versus the mental hygienists are calculated. Thus we find:

Correlations between:

Children	versus	Mental hygienists
5A boys		−.231
5A girls		−.220
7A boys		−.161
7A girls		−.130
8B boys		+.047
8B girls		−.112

These figures demonstrate that the trend continues in a logical and constant fashion. Except for the 8B boys, all of the correlations are now *negative,* with the 5A boys having the largest negative correlation figure (which corresponds with their having the highest correlation relationship with Teachers 1a). Although these figures do not indicate reversal of ratings, or anything approaching it, they still do express, however, the progressively increasing distance between the viewpoint of the children and that of the mental hygienists, as compared to the initial and relatively high agreement between the children and the teachers when filling out Schedule 1a.

Concomitantly, the 8B boys, with their low but *positive* correlation coefficient, evince less divergence from the degree of correspondence that they had shown with Teachers 1a and 1b than do any of the other children; but still, a definitely lesser degree of consonance than they had evidenced in relationship to the views of Teachers 1a, and even less so than to those of Teachers 1b.

That children, then, think along the same lines that their elders, especially teachers, do, would be a valid conclusion to be drawn from this data. And, according to the correlation coefficients, one may even go further and summarize: In a sense, as the teachers grow more tolerant of behavior disorders the children grow more intolerant. This pattern of out-Heroding Herod was also displayed by the younger children (under 9-10 years of age) that Piaget interrogated.[5]

To What Extent Were These Judgments Acquired *by the Children?*

Study of this data with reference to Aristotle's *tabula rasa* as a standard, leads to the conclusion that training does have an exceedingly important effect on children and that they needs must be expressing an acquired viewpoint: for certainly they would not spontaneously nor naturally think that truancy, for instance, is "bad"; and yet it is rated among the seven highest of the undesirable items in *all* of their lists.

And, indeed, as adults so often do, the child in his thinking may be dealing with practical results of concrete situations. It is hardly to be considered that children, in preponderance, would consider truancy to be undesirable in and of itself only, they are probably also thinking of the consequences in their evaluation of the seriousness of truancy. In most of these items, this same doubleness of ideas may occur (without, nevertheless, any duplicity), so that the question poses itself: Are children thinking of the inherent, innate "badness" of each respective trait listed in the questionnaire, or of the more practical considerations of the undesirability of such conduct so far as *consequences* are concerned, in their fundamental thinking? To some degree, at this stage of childhood development the two aspects may have become inextricably intertwined, but, in any event, to the extent that he accepts the adult's judgment and enforcement that truancy is undesirable and experiences it as part of his own mental operations, to that extent has he absorbed the belief that truancy is really "bad."

But, shifting our example to an item such as cruelty, wherefrom true moral values are more correctly elicited, and to an opposing standpoint, we may wonder to what extent we may subscribe to the existence of Aristotle's "amoral" child.* What opportunity does there exist for the newly born child to evidence any considerable amount of physical activity, let alone spiritual traits? Further, one must wonder if this strong unanimity of rated opinion that was obtained on the seriousness of cruelty would have been evoked from the children unless they had, at least latently, qualities which were there to be developed in the direction of aversion to cruelty, and the like. Profession of belief and its practice do not, of course, necessarily always correlate, nor can the findings of modern psychology be entirely omitted from theoretical consideration, but the overwhelmingly preponderant interpretation

---

* The quotation marks are those of the writer, inasmuch as this term represents an interpretation of Aristotle's discourse on this specific phase of the subject rather than a direct quotation.

must lie in the direction of the validity of the rated expressions of belief as expressed by the children.

However, adherence to the first view, *arguendo*, as the exclusively correct one, that training is the only way wherein the child acquires moral values, leads to the minimization of theoretical overtones and to the possibility of proceeding on a simplified and empiric basis in our attempt to answer the question of the differential and preponderant influence of adults in the training of children.

In the above discussion, the word "elders" was used generically and advisedly, for we still do not know which of the groups of adults that play such predominant roles in the child's developmental life were the more influential causative agents of this discipline on the thinking of the child, and in which cases—whether it was the home or the school, the parents or the teachers.

But before proceeding to the later chapters, dealing with the parents' views and with the selective extent to which the behavior principles of parents and teachers are disseminated down to the children, it might be profitable to study the data obtained from the children in somewhat more specific and absolute fashion.

General Trends Shown by the Ratings of the Children

As the correlations would, partly, have predicted, *we find that most of the school children categorized the problems dealing with schoolroom discipline, class work, and the more aggressive, overt types of behavior as the most serious.*

There were at least three notable variations: All of the children regarded profanity as being more undesirable than their teachers had done, their judgments assigning to it a rank-order which ranged from position 2 to position 8; thus placing it much *higher* in the scale than did the listing derived from the schedules of the teachers. While, contrariwise, except for 5A boys and 7A boys, disorderliness was not viewed so seriously by the children as by the teachers; dropping from the teachers' 11th place to 23d, and lower, in the ratings of the children. Similarly, the judgments of the youngest girls (5A), and the oldest of the boys (7A and 8B), which gave it the position of 30th place, 35th place, and 32d place, respectively, did not accord the weight to laziness that had been attributed to it by the teachers.

And as might also have been anticipated, the converse of the above generalization also held true: *Nine items uniquely associated with mental hygiene, which had to do with the children's personal problems of withdrawal, repression, and inhibition, which showed escaping, re-*

cessive tendencies and which were subjective in quality, were viewed as being of the least importance by the children. Among these, such traits as shyness, fearfulness, sensitiveness, and unsocial were placed in the very lowest section of the list by all of the children's ratings, being among the fourteen lowest items arranged; while the item of unhappy was judged as ranging from 30th to 43d in consequence by all of the boys and girls.

There were three contratrends to this latter course, however: The item of easily discouraged was deemed to be quite serious by all of the children; suggestible found predominant placement among the upper half of scaled importance according to their ratings; while nervousness was taken cognizance of in this manner by two groups only, girls 5A and girls 7A, whose evaluations placed it in the upper half of rated undesirability.

Overcritical and domineering may be considered to constitute borderline types, in a sense, for they are characteristics which may pertain to mental hygiene on the one hand, with ramifications into classroom and home discipline on the other. These were placed almost entirely in the upper half of the graded steps of seriousness by most of the children, the lowest bearing an equivalence of 27th in the scale of undesirability. Similarly, cheating and lack of interest in work, usually manifesting the principal appearance of violation of classroom procedure but often showing underlying adjustment difficulties from the mental hygiene viewpoint, were also evaluated by the children as being in the upper half of the graduated list of serious conduct. It may be assumed fairly safely, however, that the deeper implications of such conduct were not the bases on which these problems were judged by the children but, rather, on the connotation that they constitute schoolroom violations.

Detailed Analysis of Ratings of the Items—Illustrating Uses and Usages of the Tables

An over-all view of the ranking of each individual item by the different groups of children is afforded by Table XIV. It may be noted that the rank-order given for the ratings of the mental hygienists, Teachers 1a, and Teachers 1b in this table will be discrepant for some items in comparison with the placement of these same items in Table VI. Since four characteristics have been deleted from the children's list, leaving forty-six items altogether, this abridgement has decreed that the same removal be made from the listed problems dealt with by the adults; and that these forty-six remaining traits be reranked before any comparisons involving the judgments of children and adults may be made. Hence we find, for example, that whereas the judgments of the fathers grade tardiness as being 35th in importance in Table VI, in this present table (XIV) the evaluations now place it as being 31st in importance. These considerations indicate, then, that Table XIV is most useful for ascertaining the judgments made by the school children and for making possible quickly scanned horizontal comparisons of each of these characteristics, although it does have considerable value so far as presentation of the adults' views is concerned.

The next six tables, Tables XV, XVI, XVII, XVIII, XIX, and XX, successively give the critical ratios for the differences in means of each of the respective items, as obtained in permutative intergroup comparisons between each of the various groups of children; and between each of the various groups of children and Teachers 1a and Teachers 1b, respectively: Table XV furnishes the differences in the means and their critical ratios between 5A girls as against 7A boys, 7A girls, 8B boys, 8B girls, Teachers 1a, and Teachers 1b, respectively, each group being regarded as a separate entity. Table XVI continues on with this, starting with 5A boys as against 5A girls, 7A boys, 7A girls, 8B boys, 8B girls, Teachers 1a, and Teachers 1b, respectively. And so on, so that by successive consultation of the tables, the differences between the means and their critical ratios, for each of the various groups in comparison with any or all of the others, can be ascertained for each of the forty-six items.

If one wishes to obtain information about these groups in differential comparison with the views of the mental hygienists, the results of this statistical treatment are embodied in Table XXI, where the designation of "Mental Hygienists (Wickman's data)" is to be found in the upper left-hand corner, constituting the caption for the first column.

As has already been briefly discussed in Chapter VI, these critical ratios will tell us whether or not the difference in rank-order for any given item, as between any two groups, represents a real difference or one due to chance. Thus all seven of these tables dealing with them serve the purposes of clarifying and acting as a statistical check on our descriptive findings and data. For instance, at the very beginning of our evaluation of findings, on page 82, we demonstrated that the 5A boys were in closest agreement with the 1a teachers, in comparison with all the other children. To what extent does this have meaning? In other words, although the *over-all* agreement between the two listings is .76, for the two groups, how do these *individual* and selfsame items fare in status when they are rated by children in comparison

TABLE XIV

RANK-ORDER OF 46 ITEMS, BASED ON THE RATINGS MADE BY ALL OF OUR GROUPS AND THE MENTAL HYGIENISTS

	Mental Hygienists	Fathers	Mothers	5A Boys	5A Girls	7A Boys	7A Girls	8B Boys	8B Girls	Teachers 1a	Teachers 1b
Tardiness	39	31	35	41	44	38	33	36	43	35	32
Truancy	23	4	5	6	4	2	5	3	7	2	6
Destroying School Materials	41	8	8	2.5	3	4	2	2	10	7	11
Untruthfulness	23	7	3	19	13	14	6	5.5	9	6	3
Imaginative Lying	30	45	45	44	39	45	43	39	42	45	44.5
Cheating	23	3	4	12	10	12	10	10.5	15	12	8
Stealing	13.5	1	1	1	1	1	1	1	1	1	1
Profanity	43	30	34	2.5	2	6	3	8	2	18	29
Smoking	45	33	30	7	6	5	12	26	12	29	44.5
Obscene Notes, Pictures, etc.											
Masturbation											
Heterosexual Activity											
Disorderliness	42	25	24	15	28	17	25	23	24	11	16
Whispering	46	46	46	34	36	43	42	45	46	42	46
Interrupting, Talkativeness	44	44	44	32	26.5	27	29	41	33	31	42
Restlessness	37.5	42	40	35	38	41	44	44	44	36	41
Inattention	31	36	29	24	32	25	38	37	29.5	21	27
Lack of Interest in Work	25	20.5	11	9.5	19	13	21	22	20	14	13
Carelessness in Work	34.5	24	26	14	23	24	23	20.5	16	22	19.5
Laziness	32.5	27	22	20	29.5	35	18	32	22	17	19.5
Unreliable, Irresponsible	21	5	7	11	11	11	14	13	6	9	5
Disobedience	37.5	18	18	5	8	7	7	14	5	5	7
Impertinence, Defiance	34.5	10	10	9.5	5	9.5	8	12	13	4	4

	1	2	3	4	5	6	7	8	9	10	11
Cruelty, Bullying	6	6	2	4	7	3	4	4	8	3	2
Quarrelsomeness	28	17	17	17	20	23	15	24	23	13	18
Tattling	26	34	33	37	12	29	34.5	28	34.5	46	43
Stubbornness, Contrariness	20	38	37	38	34	34	31	35	31.5	19	34
Sullenness	12	29	32	18	21	32	22	19	26	34	33
Temper Tantrums	17	20.5	20	23	15	22	28	18	18	8	9
Impudence, Rudeness	29	12	19	8	9	8	9	7	4	10	14
Selfishness	16	11	9	27	16	9.5	13	5.5	11	25	17
Domineering, Overbearing	11	26	14	21.5	17	15	27	15	17	20	12
Shyness	13.5	37	39	46	46	46	45	46	45	44	39
Sensitiveness	10	41	38	42	42	42	41	43	40	43	35
Unsocial, Withdrawing	1	19	21	33	41	33	36	38	34.5	26	25
Overcritical of Others	9	28	31	26	18	20	20	25	14	39	31
Thoughtlessness	36	35	36	29	33	39	32	33	29.5	40	36
Inquisitiveness	40	39	41	25	29.5	19	30	29	27	41	40
Silliness	27	40	42	36	31	16	37	30.5	28	33	38
Unhappy, Depressed	3	6	6	39	43	31	39	30	37	16	15
Resentfulness	4	22.5	16	28	26.5	30	24	34	39	23	21
Nervousness	18.5	16	12	31	25	36	17	31	38	24	26
Fearfulness	5	14	13	40	45	40	40	42	36	32	30
Enuresis (Wetting Self)											
Dreaminess	18.5	43	43	45	40	44	46	40	41	38	37
Slovenly in Appearance	32.5	22.5	27	30	14	21	11	17	3	30	22.5
Suspiciousness	2	32	28	43	35	37	34.5	27	31.5	37	28
Physical Coward	15	13	25	16	37	26	26	9	25	27	24
Easily Discouraged	7	9	15	13	24	18	19	16	21	28	22.5
Suggestible	8	15	23	21.5	22	28	16	10.5	19	15	10

TABLE XV

CRITICAL RATIOS FOR THE DIFFERENCES BETWEEN THE MEAN RATINGS OF 5A GIRLS VERSUS 7A BOYS, 7A GIRLS, 8B BOYS, 8B GIRLS, TEACHERS 1a, AND TEACHERS 1b

5A Girls versus	7A Boys		7A Girls		8B Boys		8B Girls		Teachers 1a		Teachers 1b	
	Diff. M.	C. R.	Diff. M.	C. R.	Diff. M.	C. R.	Diff. M.	C. R.	Diff. M.	C. R.	Diff. M.	C. R.
Tardiness	−0.59	0.64	−3.16	3.19	−0.96	0.90	−1.89	1.87	1.39	1.70	0.29	0.33
Truancy	−0.23	0.23	−0.37	0.37	0.42	0.40	−0.97	1.01	1.58	1.61	1.71	1.76
Destroying School Materials	0.31	0.32	−1.38	1.48	−0.46	0.46	−0.65	0.71	3.14	3.41	3.66	3.98
Untruthfulness	0.42	0.43	−2.28	2.43	−0.47	0.46	−2.82	2.91	0.77	0.80	−0.87	0.94
Imaginative Lying	3.40	3.66	0.45	0.45	0.71	0.65	−0.77	0.77	4.25	4.89	3.78	4.25
Cheating	0.88	0.92	−1.14	1.27	1.02	1.04	−1.23	1.32	3.25	3.53	1.26	1.38
Stealing	−0.48	0.56	−1.81	2.21	0.10	0.11	−2.33	2.99	2.53	2.75	0.91	1.06
Profanity	1.09	1.11	−0.60	0.67	2.15	2.03	−1.47	1.62	6.25	6.72	5.97	6.42
Smoking	0.56	0.50	0.15	0.13	4.02	3.19	−0.65	0.60	6.92	6.47	8.57	8.49
Obscene Notes, Pictures, etc.												
Masturbation												
Heterosexual Activity												
Disorderliness	−0.79	0.84	−1.62	1.78	−0.28	0.29	−2.82	3.07	0.40	0.48	0.18	0.21
Whispering	3.12	3.28	0.57	0.63	3.61	3.68	2.07	2.25	4.29	5.23	5.48	6.68
Interrupting, Talkativeness	0.56	0.53	−1.03	0.99	2.14	1.93	−1.87	1.80	3.44	3.51	4.56	4.70
Restlessness	2.13	2.34	1.35	1.41	2.61	2.61	0.34	0.36	2.86	3.25	3.18	3.70
Inattention	−0.22	0.23	−0.79	0.78	1.06	1.01	−2.37	2.49	2.02	2.20	1.25	1.36
Lack of Interest in Work	−0.31	0.31	−0.62	0.65	1.09	1.04	−1.94	2.02	2.29	2.52	1.13	1.26
Carelessness in Work	0.72	0.74	−1.08	1.15	0.46	0.46	−3.12	3.32	3.03	3.52	1.12	1.23
Laziness	1.37	1.36	−2.35	2.24	0.50	0.45	−3.06	3.00	1.56	1.64	0.27	0.28
Unreliable, Irresponsible	0.27	0.27	−1.00	1.01	0.55	0.53	−2.96	3.15	2.10	2.28	−0.51	0.55
Disobedience	0.44	0.51	−0.64	0.71	1.94	1.98	−1.65	1.94	1.67	1.92	1.17	1.41

Impertinence, Defiance	1.41	1.41	−0.15	0.16	2.22	2.34	−0.38	0.41	2.05	2.20	1.22	1.33
Cruelty, Bullying	−0.22	0.22	−1.09	1.16	0.16	0.16	−1.21	1.30	1.60	1.65	0.58	0.61
Quarrelsomeness	1.05	1.07	−1.30	1.35	1.24	1.19	−1.68	1.68	1.89	2.05	1.58	1.72
Tattling	2.49	2.31	1.00	0.96	2.32	1.93	0.17	0.16	7.52	8.55	6.70	7.53
Stubbornness, Contrariness	1.02	1.15	−1.35	1.45	0.82	0.82	−2.42	2.60	1.85	2.13	2.22	2.61
Sullenness	2.13	2.05	−0.69	0.71	0.86	0.82	−1.13	1.13	4.80	5.33	3.76	4.18
Temper Tantrums	1.34	1.33	0.25	0.26	1.11	1.05	−1.95	2.05	1.42	1.48	0.54	0.58
Impudence, Rudeness	0.03	0.03	−1.25	1.33	0.62	0.62	−2.56	2.94	3.15	3.54	2.58	2.97
Selfishness	−0.91	0.88	−1.99	2.07	−0.78	0.72	−2.91	3.03	3.98	4.42	1.81	2.01
Domineering, Overbearing	0.47	0.46	−0.05	0.05	0.14	0.13	−2.33	2.33	3.69	3.84	1.19	1.23
Shyness	3.11	3.24	−1.05	1.01	1.43	1.32	−1.71	1.60	1.78	1.93	−0.05	0.05
Sensitiveness	1.61	1.83	−1.55	1.65	1.36	1.43	−3.24	3.56	2.95	3.78	0.86	1.09
Unsocial, Withdrawing	−0.50	0.50	−2.55	2.58	−0.13	0.13	−3.43	3.43	1.10	1.20	−0.66	0.73
Overcritical of Others	1.05	1.03	−0.68	0.67	1.53	1.49	−2.78	2.93	5.70	6.20	3.74	3.98
Thoughtlessness	1.80	1.70	−1.25	1.19	0.74	0.65	−2.41	2.41	4.16	4.43	2.69	2.80
Inquisitiveness	−0.55	0.54	−1.16	1.14	0.38	0.37	−2.35	2.45	4.50	5.06	3.70	4.25
Silliness	−1.02	0.97	−0.93	0.91	−0.40	0.35	−2.34	2.41	3.41	3.67	3.25	3.49
Unhappy, Depressed	−1.46	1.46	−2.69	2.69	−1.65	1.63	−3.88	3.96	−0.80	0.85	−1.97	2.12
Resentfulness	0.76	0.79	−1.69	1.74	1.20	1.19	−1.27	1.34	2.40	2.70	0.63	0.72
Nervousness	1.70	1.52	−2.08	1.89	0.79	0.69	−1.42	1.33	2.52	2.55	1.64	1.69
Fearfulness	0.65	0.61	−2.69	2.49	0.15	0.13	−4.00	3.81	1.26	1.30	−0.02	0.02
Enuresis (Wetting Self)												
Dreaminess	2.09	2.13	1.11	1.13	0.22	0.20	−1.98	1.89	2.58	2.80	1.70	1.85
Slovenly in Appearance	1.42	1.37	−2.06	3.43	0.78	0.71	−3.59	3.74	5.06	5.62	2.41	2.62
Suspiciousness	1.01	1.03	−1.46	1.51	−0.19	0.18	−2.59	2.59	3.52	3.91	1.19	1.32
Physical Coward	−0.38	0.33	−2.33	2.22	−2.54	2.31	−3.26	3.26	2.37	2.47	−0.02	0.02
Easily Discouraged	−0.37	0.39	−1.94	2.00	−1.05	1.06	−3.02	3.05	3.44	3.87	0.89	0.97
Suggestible	1.37	1.26	−1.67	1.58	−0.87	0.80	−2.60	2.48	1.89	1.83	−0.01	0.01

TABLE XVI

CRITICAL RATIOS FOR THE DIFFERENCES BETWEEN THE MEAN RATINGS OF 5A BOYS VERSUS 5A GIRLS, 7A BOYS, 7A GIRLS, 8B BOYS, 8B GIRLS, TEACHERS 1a, AND TEACHERS 1b

5A Boys versus	5A Girls		7A Boys		7A Girls		8B Boys		8B Girls		Teachers 1a		Teachers 1b	
	Diff. M.	C. R.	Diff. M.	C. R.	Diff. M.	C. R.	Diff. M.	C. R.	Diff. M.	C. R.	Diff. M.	C. R.	Diff. M.	C. R.
Tardiness	0.16	0.15	−0.43	0.44	−3.00	2.91	−0.80	0.72	−1.73	1.65	1.55	1.78	0.45	0.49
Truancy	−1.04	0.86	−1.27	1.14	−1.41	1.26	−0.62	0.53	−2.01	1.84	0.53	0.48	0.67	0.61
Destroying School Materials	−0.59	0.50	−0.28	0.26	−1.97	1.84	−1.05	0.92	−1.24	1.18	2.55	2.41	3.07	2.90
Untruthfulness	−0.72	0.59	−1.30	1.16	−3.00	2.78	−0.19	0.16	−3.54	3.19	0.05	0.05	−1.59	1.47
Imaginative Lying	−1.08	0.92	2.32	2.17	−0.63	0.56	−0.37	0.31	−1.85	1.64	3.17	3.14	2.70	2.62
Cheating	−0.73	0.59	0.15	0.13	−1.87	1.65	0.29	0.24	−1.96	1.69	2.52	2.19	0.53	0.47
Stealing	−0.26	0.24	−0.74	0.70	−2.07	2.03	−0.16	0.14	−2.59	2.62	2.27	2.06	0.65	0.62
Profanity	−0.73	0.67	0.36	0.35	−1.33	1.39	1.42	1.28	−2.20	2.27	5.52	5.58	5.24	5.29
Smoking	−0.83	0.61	−0.27	0.20	−0.68	0.51	3.15	2.20	−1.48	1.17	6.09	4.83	7.74	6.40
Obscene Notes, Pictures, etc.														
Masturbation														
Heterosexual Activity														
Disorderliness	1.64	1.48	0.85	0.81	0.02	0.02	1.36	1.25	−1.18	1.15	2.04	2.13	1.82	1.84
Whispering	−0.28	0.25	2.84	2.68	0.29	0.28	3.33	3.06	1.79	1.72	4.01	4.22	5.20	5.47
Interrupting, Talkativeness	−0.72	0.61	−0.16	0.16	−1.75	1.77	1.42	1.33	−2.59	2.62	2.72	2.92	3.84	4.22
Restlessness	−0.05	0.05	2.08	2.08	1.30	1.25	2.56	2.37	0.29	0.28	2.81	2.90	3.13	3.29
Inattention	0.77	0.64	0.54	0.50	−0.02	0.02	1.83	1.62	−1.60	1.55	2.79	2.79	2.02	2.02
Lack of Interest in Work	0.99	0.84	0.68	0.60	0.37	0.34	2.08	1.79	−0.95	0.88	3.28	3.18	2.12	2.06
Carelessness in Work	0.90	0.76	1.62	1.47	−0.18	0.17	1.36	1.21	−2.22	2.07	3.93	3.93	2.02	1.94
Laziness	1.08	0.92	2.45	2.38	−1.27	1.18	1.58	1.41	−1.98	1.90	2.64	2.72	1.35	1.38
Unreliable, Irresponsible	−0.07	0.06	0.20	0.18	−1.07	0.96	0.48	0.41	−3.03	2.81	2.03	1.92	−0.58	0.54
Disobedience	−0.41	0.37	0.03	0.03	−1.05	0.99	1.53	1.35	−2.06	2.02	1.26	1.22	0.76	0.76

Behavior														
Impertinence, Defiance	-1.56	1.23	-0.12	0.10	-1.71	1.43	0.66	0.55	-1.94	1.64	0.49	0.41	-0.34	0.29
Cruelty, Bullying	-0.46	0.35	-0.68	0.53	-1.55	1.25	-0.30	0.23	-1.67	1.36	1.14	0.90	0.12	0.10
Quarrelsomeness	0.09	0.08	1.14	1.05	-1.21	1.13	1.33	1.17	-1.59	1.45	1.98	1.92	1.67	1.62
Tattling	-3.10	2.38	-0.61	0.47	-2.10	1.67	-0.78	0.56	-2.93	2.27	4.42	3.91	3.60	3.16
Stubbornness, Contrariness	-0.93	0.86	0.09	0.10	-2.28	2.33	-0.11	0.10	-3.35	3.42	0.92	1.00	1.29	1.42
Sullenness	-0.07	0.06	2.06	1.75	-0.76	0.68	0.79	0.66	-1.20	1.05	4.73	4.46	3.69	3.48
Temper Tantrums	-0.97	0.80	0.37	0.31	-0.72	0.63	0.14	0.11	-2.92	2.58	0.45	0.39	-0.43	0.38
Impudence, Rudeness	-0.38	0.33	-0.35	0.34	-1.63	1.55	0.24	0.22	-2.94	2.97	2.77	2.77	2.20	2.20
Selfishness	-1.36	1.12	-2.27	1.96	-3.35	3.10	-2.14	1.77	-4.27	3.92	2.62	2.54	0.45	0.43
Domineering, Overbearing	-0.72	0.55	-0.25	0.21	-0.77	0.62	-0.58	0.47	-3.05	2.54	2.97	2.56	0.47	0.40
Shyness	-1.27	1.09	1.84	1.84	-2.32	2.15	0.16	0.14	-2.98	2.68	0.51	0.53	-1.32	1.38
Sensitiveness	-0.21	0.19	1.40	1.32	-1.76	1.59	1.15	1.03	-3.45	3.19	2.74	2.80	0.65	0.66
Unsocial, Withdrawing	1.03	0.94	0.53	0.50	-1.52	1.45	0.90	0.83	-2.40	2.24	2.13	2.15	0.37	0.38
Overcritical of Others	-1.06	0.81	-0.01	0.01	-1.74	1.45	0.47	0.39	-3.84	3.34	4.64	4.14	2.68	2.35
Thoughtlessness	0.29	2.25	2.09	1.77	-0.96	0.82	1.03	0.82	-2.12	1.88	4.45	4.16	2.98	2.73
Inquisitiveness	0.59	0.50	0.04	0.04	-0.57	0.51	0.97	0.85	-1.76	1.64	5.09	5.09	4.29	4.33
Silliness	-0.86	0.67	-1.88	1.54	-1.79	1.49	-1.26	0.97	-3.20	2.76	2.55	2.26	2.39	2.13
Unhappy, Depressed	0.65	0.57	-0.81	0.73	-2.04	1.84	-1.00	0.89	-3.23	2.96	-0.15	0.14	-1.32	1.26
Resentfulness	-0.06	0.50	0.70	0.61	-1.75	1.51	1.14	0.96	-1.33	1.17	2.34	2.15	0.57	0.53
Nervousness	-0.59	0.49	1.11	1.00	-2.67	2.45	0.20	0.18	-2.01	1.88	1.93	1.95	1.05	1.08
Fearfulness	0.28	0.22	0.93	0.78	-2.41	1.99	0.43	0.34	-3.72	3.15	1.54	1.39	0.26	0.24
Enuresis (Wetting Self)														
Dreaminess	-0.59	0.48	1.50	1.34	0.52	0.46	-0.37	0.30	-2.57	2.18	1.99	1.88	1.11	1.05
Slovenly in Appearance	-2.00	1.60	-0.58	0.49	-4.06	3.63	-1.22	0.98	-5.59	5.04	3.06	2.81	0.41	0.38
Suspiciousness	-1.61	1.36	-0.60	0.55	-3.07	2.82	-1.80	1.55	-4.20	3.75	1.91	1.85	-0.42	0.41
Physical Coward	2.32	1.83	1.94	1.55	-0.01	0.01	-0.22	0.18	-0.94	0.83	4.69	6.33	2.30	2.07
Easily Discouraged	1.43	1.19	1.06	0.95	-0.51	0.45	0.38	0.33	-1.59	1.38	4.87	4.55	2.32	2.11
Suggestible	-0.09	0.07	1.28	1.06	-1.76	1.50	-0.96	0.80	-2.69	2.30	1.80	1.57	-0.10	0.09

TABLE XVII

CRITICAL RATIOS FOR THE DIFFERENCES BETWEEN THE MEAN RATINGS OF 7A GIRLS VERSUS 8B BOYS, 8B GIRLS, TEACHERS 1a, AND TEACHERS 1b

7A Girls versus	8B Boys		8B Girls		Teachers 1a		Teachers 1b	
	Diff. M.	C. R.	Diff. M.	C. R.	Diff. M.	C. R.	Diff. M.	C. R.
Tardiness	2.20	2.16	1.27	1.32	4.55	5.99	3.45	4.21
Truancy	0.79	0.85	−0.60	0.71	1.95	2.27	2.08	2.48
Destroying School Materials	0.92	1.06	0.73	0.96	4.52	5.87	5.04	6.63
Untruthfulness	1.81	2.13	−0.54	0.68	3.05	3.96	1.41	1.91
Imaginative Lying	0.26	0.25	−1.22	1.28	3.80	4.75	3.33	4.01
Cheating	2.16	2.57	−0.09	0.12	4.39	5.63	2.40	3.16
Stealing	1.91	2.33	−0.52	0.79	4.34	5.29	2.72	3.63
Profanity	2.75	2.99	−0.87	1.18	6.85	8.90	6.57	8.53
Smoking	3.83	3.09	−0.80	0.76	6.77	6.51	8.42	8.59
Obscene Notes, Pictures, etc.								
Masturbation								
Heterosexual Activity								
Disorderliness	1.34	1.52	−1.20	1.48	2.02	2.85	1.80	2.40
Whispering	3.04	3.53	1.50	1.90	3.72	5.47	4.91	7.33
Interrupting, Talkativeness	3.17	3.45	−0.84	1.01	4.47	5.96	5.59	7.66
Restlessness	1.26	1.35	−1.01	1.15	1.51	1.86	1.83	2.38
Inattention	1.85	2.03	−1.58	2.00	2.81	3.75	2.04	2.72
Lack of Interest in Work	1.71	1.84	−1.32	1.59	2.91	3.78	1.75	2.30
Carelessness in Work	1.54	1.77	−2.04	2.55	4.11	5.87	2.20	2.89
Laziness	2.85	2.91	−0.71	0.79	3.91	4.83	2.62	3.20
Unreliable, Irresponsible	1.55	1.68	−1.96	2.45	3.10	4.03	0.49	0.62
Disobedience	2.58	2.74	−1.01	1.26	2.31	2.85	1.81	2.35

Impertinence, Defiance	2.37	2.79	−0.23	0.28	2.20	2.65	1.37	1.67
Cruelty, Bullying	1.25	1.42	−0.12	0.15	2.69	3.20	1.67	2.01
Quarrelsomeness	2.54	2.79	−0.38	0.44	3.19	4.14	2.88	3.74
Tattling	1.32	1.13	−0.83	0.81	6.52	7.86	5.70	6.79
Stubbornness, Contrariness	2.17	2.41	−1.07	1.32	3.20	4.27	3.57	4.96
Sullenness	1.55	1.72	−0.44	0.52	5.49	7.63	4.45	6.18
Temper Tantrums	0.86	0.87	−2.20	2.53	1.17	1.31	0.29	0.34
Impudence, Rudeness	1.87	2.10	−1.31	1.75	4.40	5.71	3.83	5.11
Selfishness	1.21	1.26	−0.92	1.15	5.97	8.29	3.80	5.21
Domineering, Overbearing	0.19	0.19	−2.28	2.48	3.74	4.30	1.24	1.41
Shyness	2.48	2.51	−0.66	0.67	2.83	3.49	1.00	1.27
Sensitiveness	2.91	3.06	−1.69	1.86	4.50	5.76	2.41	3.05
Unsocial, Withdrawing	2.42	2.52	−0.88	0.94	3.65	4.29	1.89	2.22
Overcritical of Others	2.21	2.48	−2.10	2.66	6.38	8.51	4.42	5.67
Thoughtlessness	1.99	1.99	−1.16	1.36	5.41	7.03	3.94	4.99
Inquisitiveness	1.54	1.60	−1.19	1.35	5.66	7.08	4.86	6.23
Silliness	0.53	0.51	−1.41	1.62	4.34	5.29	4.18	5.16
Unhappy, Depressed	1.04	1.08	−1.19	1.28	1.89	2.12	0.72	0.83
Resentfulness	2.89	3.01	0.42	0.47	4.09	4.87	2.32	2.83
Nervousness	2.87	2.79	0.66	0.69	4.60	5.35	3.72	4.43
Fearfulness	2.84	2.65	−1.31	1.35	3.95	4.44	2.67	3.10
Enuresis (Wetting Self)	−0.89	0.90	−3.09	3.40	1.47	1.96	0.59	0.79
Dreaminess	2.84	3.02	−1.53	1.96	7.12	10.03	4.47	6.04
Slovenly in Appearance	1.27	1.35	−1.13	1.27	4.98	6.47	2.65	3.40
Suspiciousness	−0.21	0.21	−0.93	1.06	4.70	5.66	2.31	2.69
Physical Coward	0.89	0.98	−1.08	1.19	5.38	6.73	2.83	3.37
Easily Discouraged	0.80	0.86	−0.93	1.04	3.56	4.14	1.66	1.93
Suggestible								

TABLE XVIII

CRITICAL RATIOS FOR THE DIFFERENCES BETWEEN THE MEAN RATINGS OF 7A BOYS VERSUS 7A GIRLS, 8B BOYS, 8B GIRLS, TEACHERS 1a, AND TEACHERS 1b

7A Boys versus	7A Girls		8B Boys		8B Girls		Teachers 1a		Teachers 1b	
	Diff. M.	C. R.	Diff. M.	C. R.	Diff. M.	C. R.	Diff. M.	C. R.	Diff. M.	C. R.
Tardiness	−2.57	2.95	−0.37	0.39	−1.30	1.46	1.98	2.96	0.88	1.19
Truancy	−0.14	0.16	0.65	0.70	−0.74	0.89	1.81	2.13	1.94	2.34
Destroying School Materials	−1.69	2.09	−0.77	0.86	−0.96	1.22	2.83	3.54	3.35	4.19
Untruthfulness	−2.70	3.42	−0.89	1.00	−3.24	3.86	0.35	0.43	−1.29	1.63
Imaginative Lying	−2.95	3.35	−2.69	2.74	−4.17	4.74	0.85	1.18	0.38	0.51
Cheating	−2.02	2.46	0.14	0.15	−2.11	2.48	2.37	2.79	0.38	0.46
Stealing	−1.33	1.77	0.58	0.67	−1.85	2.61	3.01	3.50	1.39	1.76
Profanity	−1.69	2.04	1.06	1.06	−2.56	3.01	5.16	5.93	4.88	5.61
Smoking	−0.41	0.37	3.42	2.83	−1.21	1.20	6.36	6.30	8.01	8.52
Obscene Notes, Pictures, etc.										
Masturbation										
Heterosexual Activity										
Disorderliness	−0.83	1.00	0.51	0.56	−2.03	2.42	1.19	1.59	0.97	1.24
Whispering	−2.55	3.07	0.49	0.54	−1.05	1.24	1.17	1.60	2.36	3.23
Interrupting, Talkativeness	−1.59	1.87	1.58	1.68	−2.43	2.86	2.88	3.74	4.00	5.26
Restlessness	−0.78	0.93	0.48	0.55	−1.79	2.16	0.73	0.97	1.05	1.46
Inattention	−0.56	0.65	1.29	1.42	−2.14	2.68	2.25	3.00	1.48	1.95
Lack of Interest in Work	−0.31	0.36	1.40	1.44	−1.63	1.85	2.60	3.17	1.44	1.77
Carelessness in Work	−1.80	2.17	−0.26	0.29	−3.84	4.57	2.31	3.12	0.40	0.51
Laziness	−3.72	4.23	−0.87	0.94	−4.43	5.27	0.19	0.25	−1.10	1.45
Unreliable, Irresponsible	−1.27	1.46	0.28	0.30	−3.23	3.94	1.83	2.32	−0.78	0.96
Disobedience	−1.08	1.33	1.50	1.65	−2.09	2.71	1.23	1.58	0.73	0.99

Impertinence, Defiance	-1.59	1.77	0.78	0.87	-1.82	2.09	0.61	0.69	-0.22	0.25
Cruelty, Bullying	-0.87	0.98	0.38	0.40	-0.99	1.13	1.82	1.98	0.80	0.88
Quarrelsomeness	-2.35	2.80	0.19	0.20	-2.73	3.10	0.84	1.05	0.53	0.67
Tattling	-1.49	1.42	-0.17	0.14	-2.32	2.15	5.03	5.72	4.21	4.73
Stubbornness, Contrariness	-2.37	3.08	-0.20	0.24	-3.44	4.53	0.83	1.20	1.20	1.79
Sullenness	-2.82	3.23	-1.27	1.30	-3.26	3.54	2.67	3.26	1.63	1.99
Temper Tantrums	-1.09	1.17	-0.23	2.25	-3.29	3.62	0.08	0.09	-0.80	0.90
Impudence, Rudeness	-1.28	1.58	0.59	0.68	-2.59	3.60	3.12	4.22	2.55	3.49
Selfishness	-1.08	1.27	0.13	0.13	-2.00	2.35	4.89	5.89	2.72	3.24
Domineering, Overbearing	-0.52	0.56	-0.33	0.35	-2.80	3.18	3.22	3.88	0.72	0.86
Shyness	-4.16	4.89	-1.68	1.87	-4.82	5.42	-1.33	1.90	-3.16	4.65
Sensitiveness	-3.16	3.55	-0.25	0.28	-4.85	5.64	1.34	1.86	-0.75	1.04
Unsocial, Withdrawing	-2.05	2.16	0.37	0.38	-2.93	3.02	1.60	1.82	-0.16	0.18
Overcritical of Others	-1.73	1.99	0.48	0.54	-3.83	4.85	4.65	6.12	2.69	3.41
Thoughtlessness	-3.05	3.32	-1.06	1.05	-4.21	4.89	2.36	2.99	0.89	1.10
Inquisitiveness	-0.61	0.66	0.93	0.97	-1.80	2.07	5.05	6.39	4.25	5.52
Silliness	0.09	0.09	0.62	0.58	-1.32	1.47	4.43	5.15	4.27	5.02
Unhappy, Depressed	-1.23	1.29	-0.19	0.20	-2.42	2.60	0.66	0.74	-0.51	0.58
Resentfulness	-2.45	2.69	0.44	0.46	-2.03	2.28	1.64	1.98	0.13	0.16
Nervousness	-3.78	3.78	-0.91	0.88	-3.12	3.22	0.82	0.93	-0.06	0.70
Fearfulness	-3.34	3.37	-0.50	0.48	-4.65	4.89	0.61	0.71	-0.67	0.80
Enuresis (Wetting Self)										
Dreaminess	-0.98	1.18	-1.87	1.81	-4.07	4.47	0.49	0.66	-0.39	0.52
Slovenly in Appearance	-3.48	3.95	-0.64	0.63	-5.01	5.76	3.64	4.49	0.99	1.18
Suspiciousness	-2.47	2.84	-1.20	1.25	-3.60	4.00	2.51	3.18	0.18	0.23
Physical Coward	-1.95	1.89	-2.16	2.00	-2.88	2.94	2.75	2.93	0.36	0.37
Easily Discouraged	-1.57	1.80	-0.68	0.76	-2.65	2.94	3.81	4.82	1.26	1.54
Suggestible	-3.04	3.23	-2.24	2.31	-3.97	4.27	0.52	0.57	-1.38	1.52

TABLE XIX

CRITICAL RATIOS FOR THE DIFFERENCES BETWEEN THE MEAN RATINGS OF 8B GIRLS VERSUS TEACHERS 1a AND TEACHERS 1b

8B Girls versus	Teachers 1a		Teachers 1b	
	Diff. M.	C. R.	Diff. M.	C. R.
Tardiness	3.28	4.21	2.18	2.60
Truancy	2.55	3.07	2.68	3.31
Destroying School Materials	3.79	5.12	4.31	5.82
Untruthfulness	3.59	4.38	1.95	2.50
Imaginative Lying	5.02	6.20	4.55	4.84
Cheating	4.48	5.53	2.49	3.15
Stealing	4.86	6.23	3.24	4.63
Profanity	7.72	9.77	7.44	9.42
Smoking	7.57	8.05	9.22	10.60
Obscene Notes, Pictures, etc.				
Masturbation				
Heterosexual Activity				
Disorderliness	3.22	4.41	3.00	3.95
Whispering	2.22	3.17	3.41	4.94
Interrupting, Talkativeness	5.31	7.08	6.43	8.81
Restlessness	2.52	3.15	2.84	3.69
Inattention	4.39	6.46	3.62	5.31
Lack of Interest in Work	4.23	5.49	3.07	3.99
Carelessness in Work	6.24	8.91	4.33	5.70
Laziness	4.62	6.00	3.33	4.32
Unreliable, Irresponsible	5.06	7.13	2.45	3.36
Disobedience	3.32	4.31	2.82	3.86
Impertinence, Defiance	2.43	3.08	1.60	2.05

TABLE XIX—*Continued*

8B Girls versus	Teachers 1a		Teachers 1b	
	Diff. M.	C. R.	Diff. M.	C. R.
Cruelty, Bullying	2.81	3.39	1.79	2.18
Quarrelsomeness	3.57	4.41	3.26	4.02
Tattling	7.35	8.45	6.53	7.42
Stubbornness, Contrariness ..	4.27	5.77	4.64	6.44
Sullenness	5.93	7.80	4.89	6.43
Temper Tantrums	3.37	3.92	2.49	3.04
Impudence, Rudeness	5.71	8.40	5.14	7.79
Selfishness	6.89	9.44	4.72	6.47
Domineering, Overbearing ...	6.02	7.43	3.52	4.29
Shyness	3.49	4.11	1.66	1.98
Sensitiveness	6.19	8.25	4.10	5.39
Unsocial, Withdrawing	4.53	5.21	2.77	3.18
Overcritical of Others	8.48	12.66	6.52	9.31
Thoughtlessness	6.57	9.25	5.10	6.99
Inquisitiveness	6.85	9.51	6.05	8.64
Silliness	5.75	7.47	5.59	7.36
Unhappy, Depressed	3.08	3.54	1.91	2.25
Resentfulness	3.67	4.48	1.90	2.38
Nervousness	3.94	4.75	3.06	3.78
Fearfulness	5.26	6.19	3.98	4.85
Enuresis (Wetting Self)				
Dreaminess	4.56	5.43	3.68	4.38
Slovenly in Appearance	8.65	12.36	6.00	8.22
Suspiciousness	6.11	7.54	3.78	4.67
Physical Coward	5.63	7.31	3.24	4.05
Easily Discouraged	6.46	7.78	3.91	4.55
Suggestible	4.49	5.22	2.59	3.01

TABLE XX

CRITICAL RATIOS FOR THE DIFFERENCES BETWEEN THE MEAN RATINGS OF 8B BOYS VERSUS 8B GIRLS, TEACHERS 1*a*, AND TEACHERS 1*b*

8B Boys versus	8B Girls		Teachers 1a		Teachers 1b	
	Diff. M.	C. R.	Diff. M.	C. R.	Diff. M.	C. R.
Tardiness	—0.93	0.89	2.35	2.73	1.25	1.37
Truancy	—1.39	1.54	1.16	1.25	1.29	1.42
Destroying School Materials .	—0.19	0.22	3.60	4.19	4.12	4.79
Untruthfulness	—2.35	2.64	1.24	1.41	—0.40	0.47
Imaginative Lying	—1.48	1.42	3.54	3.85	3.07	3.27
Cheating	—2.25	2.59	2.23	2.56	0.24	0.28
Stealing	—2.43	3.12	2.43	2.64	0.81	0.94
Profanity	—3.62	3.89	4.10	4.32	3.82	4.02
Smoking	—4.63	3.99	2.94	2.56	4.59	4.21
Obscene Notes, Pictures, etc. .						
Masturbation						
Heterosexual Activity						
Disorderliness	—2.54	2.85	0.68	0.84	0.46	0.55
Whispering	—1.54	1.75	0.68	0.88	1.87	2.43
Interrupting, Talkativeness ..	—4.01	4.36	1.30	1.53	2.42	2.92
Restlessness	—2.27	2.44	0.25	0.29	0.57	0.69
Inattention	—3.43	4.08	0.96	1.20	0.19	0.23
Lack of Interest in Work	—3.03	3.22	1.20	1.36	0.04	0.05
Carelessness in Work	—3.58	4.11	2.57	3.29	0.66	0.80
Laziness	—3.56	3.20	1.06	1.23	—0.23	0.26
Unreliable, Irresponsible	—3.51	4.03	1.55	1.85	—1.06	1.23
Disobedience	—3.59	3.99	—0.27	0.30	—0.77	0.89
Impertinence, Defiance	—2.60	3.21	—0.17	0.20	—1.00	1.22

TABLE XX—*Continued*

8B Boys versus	8B Girls		Teachers 1a		Teachers 1b	
	Diff. M.	C. R.	Diff. M.	C. R.	Diff. M.	C. R.
Cruelty, Bullying	−1.37	1.57	1.44	1.58	0.42	0.47
Quarrelsomeness	−2.92	3.11	0.65	0.76	0.34	0.40
Tattling	−2.15	1.79	5.20	5.10	4.38	4.25
Stubbornness, Contrariness ..	−3.24	3.64	1.03	1.24	1.40	1.73
Sullenness	−1.99	2.16	3.94	4.81	2.90	3.54
Temper Tantrums	−3.06	3.19	0.31	0.32	−0.57	0.61
Impudence, Rudeness	−3.18	3.88	2.53	3.05	1.96	2.39
Selfishness	−2.13	2.22	4.76	5.29	2.59	2.88
Domineering, Overbearing ..	−2.47	2.66	3.55	3.99	1.05	1.12
Shyness	−3.14	3.08	0.35	0.41	−1.48	1.74
Sensitiveness	−4.60	5.00	1.59	2.01	−0.50	0.63
Unsocial, Withdrawing	−3.30	3.37	1.23	1.38	−0.53	0.60
Overcritical of Others	−4.31	5.32	4.17	5.35	2.21	2.73
Thoughtlessness	−3.15	3.32	3.42	3.89	1.95	2.17
Inquisitiveness	−2.73	3.03	4.12	5.02	3.32	4.10
Silliness	−1.94	1.96	3.81	4.01	3.65	3.84
Unhappy, Depressed	−2.23	2.37	0.85	0.94	−0.32	0.36
Resentfulness	−2.47	2.63	1.20	1.35	−0.57	0.66
Nervousness	−2.21	2.21	1.73	1.90	0.85	0.96
Fearfulness	−4.15	3.99	1.11	1.16	−0.17	0.18
Enuresis (Wetting Self)						
Dreaminess	−2.20	2.08	2.36	2.57	1.48	1.59
Slovenly in Appearance	−4.37	4.65	4.28	4.81	1.63	1.79
Suspiciousness	−2.40	2.47	3.71	4.26	1.38	1.59
Physical Coward	−0.72	0.77	4.91	5.52	2.52	2.77
Easily Discouraged	−1.97	2.10	4.49	5.41	1.94	2.26
Suggestible	−1.73	1.86	2.76	3.07	0.86	0.96

TABLE XXI

CRITICAL RATIOS FOR THE DIFFERENCES BETWEEN THE MEAN RATINGS OF MENTAL HYGIENISTS VERSUS EACH OF OUR TEN GROUPS

Mental Hygienists (Wickman's data) versus	Fathers		Mothers		5A Boys		5A Girls		7A Boys		7A Girls		8B Boys		8B Girls		Teachers 1a		Teachers 1b	
	Diff. M.	C.R.	Diff. M.	C.R.	Diff. M.	C.R.	Diff. M.	C.R.	Diff. M.	C.R.	Diff. M.	C.R.	Diff. M.	C.R.	Diff. M.	C.R.	Diff. M.	C.R.	Diff. M.	C.R.
Tardiness	−3.40	3.91	−3.84	5.82	−3.60	3.91	−3.44	3.95	−4.03	5.45	−6.60	8.05	−4.40	4.84	−5.33	6.35	−2.05	3.42	−3.15	4.70
Truancy	−4.30	4.57	−5.35	6.45	−3.91	3.34	−4.95	4.71	−5.18	5.57	−5.32	5.66	−4.53	4.53	−5.92	6.51	−3.37	3.62	−3.24	3.52
Destroying School Materials	−8.60	8.78	−9.75	12.50	−9.57	8.70	−10.16	1.05	−9.85	11.45	−11.54	13.90	−10.62	11.54	−10.81	13.35	−7.02	8.56	−6.50	7.93
Untruthfulness	−3.48	3.74	−6.01	9.11	−2.09	1.94	−2.81	2.99	−2.39	3.03	−5.09	6.79	−3.28	3.86	−5.63	7.13	−2.04	2.62	−3.68	4.97
Imaginative Lying	2.02	1.54	1.43	1.16	−1.59	1.10	−2.67	1.98	0.73	0.57	−2.22	1.69	−1.96	1.41	−3.44	2.63	1.58	1.30	1.11	0.90
Cheating	−5.16	4.30	−5.81	8.25	−2.93	2.27	−3.66	3.33	−2.78	2.70	−4.80	4.90	−2.64	2.54	−4.89	4.84	−0.41	0.41	−2.40	2.45
Stealing	−4.88	5.38	−6.05	9.45	−3.85	3.60	−4.11	4.72	−4.59	5.67	−5.92	7.69	−4.01	4.61	−6.44	8.94	−1.58	1.82	−3.20	3.95
Profanity	−6.20	6.53	−6.75	9.00	−11.77	12.39	−12.50	14.20	−11.41	13.91	−13.10	18.45	−10.35	11.37	−13.97	19.14	−6.25	8.22	−6.53	8.59
Smoking	−6.26	6.39	−8.10	10.80	−11.83	10.38	−12.66	13.76	−12.10	14.24	−12.51	14.06	−8.68	8.51	−13.31	17.29	−5.74	7.55	−4.09	6.10
Obscene Notes, Pictures, etc.	−3.07	2.44	−4.48	4.27													−3.90	3.48	−4.07	3.73
Masturbation	−7.04	6.23	−6.65	6.93													−6.36	6.63	−6.86	7.15
Heterosexual Activity	−6.68	8.02	−7.10	7.40													−4.19	3.88	−4.83	4.64
Disorderliness	−7.25	8.15	−8.08	11.22	−9.42	9.33	−7.78	8.74	−8.57	10.58	−9.40	12.21	−8.06	9.37	−10.60	13.59	−7.38	10.70	−7.60	10.56
Whispering	−3.38	5.28	−4.44	9.25	−9.62	10.93	−9.90	13.20	−6.78	10.43	−9.33	16.09	−6.29	8.99	−7.83	12.84	−5.61	12.75	−4.42	10.05
Interrupting, Talkativeness	−3.43	4.18	−3.63	5.76	−7.83	8.60	−8.55	8.81	−7.99	10.51	−9.58	13.12	−6.41	7.72	−10.42	14.27	−5.11	7.98	−3.99	6.44
Restlessness	−0.81	0.74	−1.40	1.44	−3.90	3.33	−3.95	3.62	−1.82	1.84	−2.60	2.52	−1.34	1.25	−3.61	3.50	−1.09	1.12	−0.77	0.82
Inattention	−0.60	0.59	−3.28	4.00	−4.47	4.03	−3.70	3.56	−3.93	4.37	−4.49	5.04	−2.64	3.18	−6.07	7.68	−1.68	2.13	−2.45	3.10
Lack of Interest in Work	−1.68	1.43	−4.57	4.48	−3.99	3.12	−3.00	2.52	−3.31	2.96	−3.62	3.32	−1.91	1.63	−4.94	4.53	−0.71	6.83	−1.87	1.82
Carelessness in Work	−4.08	4.34	−4.32	5.84	−5.80	5.42	−4.90	5.21	−4.18	5.04	−5.98	7.48	−4.44	5.10	−8.11	10.14	−1.87	2.67	−3.78	4.97
Laziness	−3.28	2.83	−4.87	5.24	−5.03	4.45	−3.95	3.56	−2.58	2.72	−6.30	6.30	−3.45	3.32	−7.01	7.30	−2.39	2.73	−3.68	4.13
Unreliable, Irresponsible	−3.68	3.54	−5.08	6.12	−2.91	2.47	−2.98	2.81	−2.71	2.85	−3.98	4.28	−2.43	2.45	−5.94	6.75	−0.88	1.02	−3.49	4.01

Behavior																				
Disobedience	-5.30	5.64	-6.30	8.63	-7.89	7.74	-8.30	9.76	-7.86	10.21	-8.94	11.18	-6.38	7.15	-9.95	13.27	-6.63	8.72	-7.13	9.90
Impertinence, Defiance	-6.00	6.19	-7.37	9.33	-6.49	5.41	-8.05	8.47	-6.61	7.34	-8.20	9.65	-5.83	6.86	-8.43	10.41	-6.00	7.23	-6.83	8.33
Cruelty, Bullying	-2.24	2.36	-4.13	5.36	-0.86	0.66	-1.32	1.29	-1.54	1.59	-2.41	2.68	-1.16	1.21	-2.53	2.84	0.28	0.30	-0.74	0.80
Quarrelsomeness	-3.45	3.48	-4.45	5.36	-4.29	3.83	-4.30	4.12	-3.15	3.46	-5.50	6.18	-2.96	3.05	-5.88	6.32	-2.31	2.72	-2.62	3.12
Tattling	0.27	0.22	-0.97	0.83	-1.28	0.88	-4.38	3.42	-1.89	1.48	-3.38	2.73	-2.06	1.49	-4.21	3.31	3.12	2.81	2.32	2.07
Stubbornness, Contrariness	3.11	3.27	2.19	2.52	0.94	0.88	0.01	0.01	1.03	1.18	-1.34	1.46	0.83	0.84	-2.41	2.65	1.86	2.19	2.23	2.65
Sulleness	3.06	3.40	2.74	3.47	0.20	0.18	0.13	0.13	2.26	2.48	-0.56	0.67	0.99	1.08	-1.00	1.16	4.93	8.57	3.89	5.19
Temper Tantrums	0.44	0.40	-0.87	0.91	-0.26	0.21	-1.23	1.13	0.11	0.10	-0.98	0.96	-0.12	0.11	-3.18	3.18	0.19	0.19	-0.69	0.70
Impudence, Rudeness	-5.22	4.92	-5.07	5.76	-6.02	5.23	-6.40	6.10	-6.37	6.85	-7.65	8.05	-5.78	5.78	-8.96	10.18	-3.25	3.65	-3.82	4.34
Selfishness	-1.17	1.19	-2.86	3.53	0.36	0.31	-1.00	0.97	-1.91	1.97	-2.99	3.40	-1.78	1.73	-3.91	4.44	2.98	3.68	0.81	0.99
Domineering, Overbearing	2.45	2.15	-0.48	0.49	1.02	0.77	0.30	0.26	0.77	0.74	0.25	0.23	0.44	0.41	-2.03	1.99	3.99	4.07	1.49	1.51
Shyness	4.68	4.22	4.56	4.61	5.97	4.98	4.70	4.05	7.81	7.89	3.65	3.41	6.13	5.52	2.99	2.72	6.48	6.75	4.65	4.95
Sensitiveness	5.79	5.46	4.80	4.95	3.96	3.27	3.75	3.57	5.36	5.31	2.20	2.08	5.31	4.96	0.51	0.50	6.70	7.28	4.61	5.01
Unsocial, Withdrawing	5.63	5.74	5.08	6.35	6.69	6.50	7.72	8.04	7.22	7.78	5.17	5.74	7.59	8.07	4.29	4.66	8.82	10.63	7.06	8.61
Overcritical of Others	3.64	3.50	3.23	3.55	1.58	1.25	0.52	0.48	1.57	1.65	0.16	0.17	2.05	2.11	-2.26	2.57	6.22	7.32	4.26	4.84
Thoughtlessness	-1.22	1.24	-2.28	2.71	-4.45	3.74	-4.16	3.89	-2.36	2.51	-5.41	5.82	-3.42	3.35	-6.57	7.47	0.00	0.00	-1.47	1.79
Inquisitiveness	-2.46	2.44	-2.34	2.54	-6.44	5.50	-5.85	5.47	-6.40	6.46	-7.01	7.01	-5.47	5.36	-8.20	8.72	-1.35	1.55	-2.15	2.50
Silliness	0.97	0.82	1.92	1.83	-1.78	1.32	-2.64	2.22	-3.66	3.24	-3.57	3.25	-3.04	2.53	-2.98	2.81	0.77	0.75	0.61	0.60
Unhappy, Depressed	2.35	2.40	0.64	0.79	6.47	5.94	7.12	7.27	5.66	6.09	4.43	4.82	5.47	5.82	3.24	3.56	6.32	7.26	5.15	6.06
Resentfulness	2.89	3.01	1.09	1.25	2.81	2.36	2.75	2.72	3.51	3.68	1.06	1.10	3.95	3.91	1.48	1.56	5.15	5.79	3.38	3.89
Nervousness	-0.57	0.44	-2.54	2.13	0.43	0.32	-0.16	0.12	1.54	1.20	-2.24	1.78	0.63	0.48	-1.58	1.27	2.36	2.02	1.48	1.28
Fearfulness	1.41	1.28	0.27	0.26	4.72	3.60	5.00	4.17	5.65	5.09	2.31	2.08	5.15	4.36	1.00	0.90	6.26	6.14	4.98	4.98
Enuresis (Wetting Self)	-1.94	1.56	-2.32	2.37													0.42	0.44	0.09	0.09
Dreaminess	4.12	3.81	4.85	5.05	2.25	1.80	1.66	1.47	3.75	3.79	2.77	2.80	1.88	1.66	-0.32	0.30	4.24	4.56	3.36	3.61
Slovenly in Appearance	-4.01	3.26	-4.13	3.69	-3.82	2.79	-5.82	4.66	-4.40	3.73	-7.88	7.10	-5.04	4.10	-9.41	8.48	-0.76	0.71	-3.41	3.16
Suspiciousness	7.61	7.61	5.49	6.24	7.29	6.39	5.68	5.51	6.69	7.19	4.22	4.59	5.49	5.49	3.09	3.25	9.20	10.95	6.87	8.08
Physical Coward	-0.76	0.75	0.56	0.63	-0.78	0.65	1.54	1.41	1.16	1.08	-0.79	0.81	-1.00	0.98	-1.72	1.98	3.91	4.49	1.52	1.69
Easily Discouraged	0.06	0.06	0.13	0.16	0.47	0.42	1.90	1.98	1.53	1.76	-0.04	0.05	0.85	0.93	-0.12	0.13	5.34	6.68	2.79	3.36
Suggestible	1.06	1.03	1.30	1.51	1.32	1.13	1.23	1.16	2.60	2.77	-0.44	0.49	0.36	0.39	-1.37	1.54	3.12	3.63	1.22	1.40

to their status when they are judged by Teachers 1*a*, and how truly
do they do so? Also, since the r of .76 conversely shows that the 5A
boys and Teachers 1*a* differ from each other by .24 (1−.76), to what
extent are there *differences* in rating of these individual traits and to
what extent are they true differences?

Let us then continue on with our 5A boys, as an example to illustrate
several of the many types of conclusions that may be deduced from
these tables. As we have seen, list as against list, their judgments
correspond to the extent of .76 with those made by Teachers 1*a*. Reference to Table XIV gives the comparative rank-order of each of the
individual items for the 5A boys versus Teachers 1*a*. Scanning of this
table, going down the appropriate column of listed items, and stopping
at the sixteenth one, brings us to restlessness as an example. The third
column beyond, headed by the caption "5A boys," takes us to the rating
"35"; thus informing us that the 5A boys' evaluation of restlessness
places it as 35th in the scale of seriousness. Perusal of each column in
turn, towards the right, in the same row (16), displays the ratings
made by the other groups for that characteristic, and reveals that the
5A boys assigned a higher value to restlessness than any of the other
children did, but only one step above that of the results obtained from
the teachers. Restlessness, thus, was given the placement of 35 by
the 5A boys and 36 by the teachers. Is this statistically significant?
—in other words, is this difference reliable in direction of rating?

Table XVI, with its critical ratios, informs us that there is close
to virtual certainty that this raw unit of one step in difference does
represent a true difference. Again looking down the column of listed
items until the sixteenth one, restlessness, is reached (having noted
that this table compares 5A boys with all the other groups), and
going across to the twelfth column, headed by the caption "Teachers
1*a*," with its subheadings of "Diff. M." and "C.R.," one notes that the
numerical difference between these two means is 2.81 and that the
critical ratio is 2.90. Although the figure of 3.0 is required for virtual
certainty, this figure of 2.90 is very close to it and denotes that there
are 99.8 chances in 100 that this difference in rating is a reliable one;
that is, if the experiment were repeated the boys of 5A would again
rate restlessness more seriously than the 1*a* teachers do.

Starting from the very top of this column, now, and going down
the list systematically, thus ascertaining what the critical ratios are for
5A boys as against Teachers 1*a*, we find that, of the forty-six problems,
twenty-three have critical ratios ranging from 2.40 upwards. Which
means that for these items the chances are anywhere from 99.2 in 100

to 99.9$^+$ in 100 that these trends are stable, that doing the experiment over again would give us the same direction of rating in each case. In other words, that for items such as destroying school materials (c.r., 2.41), imaginative lying (c.r., 3.14), profanity (c.r., 5.58), etc., the same relative position of each would again be maintained by the 5A boys as against the Teachers 1a.

Six other characteristics range from 2.06 up: which means that in these instances there are at least 98 chances in 100 that there would be no reversal of relative position with further sampling and experimentation.

Careful study of the table reveals, then, that *twenty-nine items out of the forty-six* have critical ratios ranging from good reliability to virtual certainty: so that the respective ratings given them by the 5A boys (higher or lower, as the case may be) would always bear the same directional relationship to the rankings assigned to them by Teachers 1a, in conformity with the results obtained in this case.

But, in addition to informing ourselves as to the stability of the direction of our differential listings, these tables offer a more concrete way of analyzing the meaning of our correlation figure of .76 obtaining between 5A boys and Teachers 1a. (Still proceeding with these two groups as our example groups.) Resuming the study of Table XIV and comparing the rated series, item by item, shows that for the most part the 5A boys, like the teachers who filled out Schedule 1a, consider overt conduct, school work violations, disorders of conduct, extravagant personality characteristics, and the like, to be among the most undesirable forms of behavior difficulties: whereas, on the whole, the shy, withdrawing, inhibited, unsocial forms of behavior were regarded by them as being among the least serious.

In some cases they went beyond the teachers in rating the importance of traits: so that they considered smoking to be 7th in seriousness, as contrasted with the teachers' evaluation of 29th; carelessness in work was given 14th place as against the teachers' rating of 22d down the list; sullenness, 18th versus 34th; overcritical of others, 26th versus 39th; inquisitiveness, 25th versus 41st; physical coward, 16th versus 27th; and easily discouraged, 13th versus 28th.

On the other hand, three items which had evoked considerable concern on the part of the mental hygienists and which the Teachers 1a had also deemed important enough to be located in the upper half of the series—namely, stubbornness, temper tantrums, and unhappy—are depreciated in the views of the 5A boys: so that stubbornness has been reduced to 38th, unhappy to 39th, and the characteristic of temper tantrums to 23d place down the scale of seriousness. Nervousness, ranked 24th by Teachers 1a, is deemed by the 5A boys to be 31st in undesirability.

And so, by and large, inspection of the tables here corroborates and substantiates the statistical figure of .76 obtained for the 5A boys in comparison with Teachers 1a.

Similarly, reference to Table XIV furnishes some rather striking particulars as to the background of the *negative* correlation of .231 obtained between the 5A boys and the mental hygienists. As has already been pointed out, a negative .231 would not indicate complete reversal nor anything approximating complete reversal, but it might be expected to foretoken that the children deviate from the mental hygiene viewpoint even more than they do from that held by their teachers, for some of the most salient mental hygiene items. This expectation is borne out: We find that the traits considered among the topmost in seriousness by the mental hygienists, such as unsocial, suspiciousness, unhappy, resentful, fearfulness, and suggestible, and which the Teachers 1a reduce in importance, are further reduced in undesirability by the estimates of the 5A boys. The same is true of other high-ranking items in the same category, such as nervousness, dreaminess, and shyness.

This rather detailed excursion into the various possibilities of the tables, using boys 5A as our guiding example, may serve as a generic prototype of procedure whereby to obtain answers to similar questions so far as all of the groups are concerned: supplemented by the information embodied in Tables XXI-XXV, information is thus available for Wickman's mental hygienists and for all of the ten groups dealt with in this present study.

The Extent to Which Children Agree in Their Ratings Item by Item

So that our excursion shall not have taken us too far afield, it may be time to return to all of our groups of children, and to point out (Table V) that the ratings of all of the children agree quite closely with each other in general—their correlations ranging from .796 to .895. And now, as has already been suggested, inspection of Table XIV will also afford us a picture of how the children agree or disagree with each other on the individual items, within the framework of their high correlations.

For the majority of the items, there is close agreement, item by item. So that unhappy, for instance, ranges in positions: 39-43-31-39-

30-37; fearfulness, 40-45-40-40-42-36. In the other direction, stealing is rated 1st by all of the children (in fact, by *all* of the groups, children and adults, with the sole exception of the mental hygienists). Untruthfulness, although ranging from 5th down to 19th in placement, is still well within the same general category of being regarded as an important problem. In total fashion, *twenty-eight of the forty-six items show this closeness of agreement.*

The remaining eighteen items, where there is wider variation so that one or more of the groups of children enter by average into differing categories of judgment of degree of seriousness, reveal some rather noteworthy dissenting groups. All of the children, for instance, consider smoking to be very serious; except the 8B boys, who see in it a moderated undesirability, with a rank-order of 26. Tattling is judged as being moderately to relatively unimportant by five of the six groups of children. For some reason, however, the 5A girls deem it to be very serious, ranking it 12th in importance. Laziness is regarded with considerable tolerance by the 7A and 8B boys, and also by the 5A girls; while the opposite, so to speak, the rather energetic item of temper tantrums, is viewed with the most concern by two of these groups of raters, the 5A girls and 8B boys (along with the 8B girls). Only the 5A boys consider selfishness to be of relatively moderate consequence. Nervousness is rated high by the 7A girls and high-moderate by the 5A girls, the rest of the children taking a less serious view of it. Slovenly, with the exception of one dissentient group, is deemed important by all of the children, but there appears to be a relationship with age and sex: so that the 8B girls rank it as high as 3d in the scale, while the 5A boys rank it as low as 30th. In the intervening positions, the girls assign to it higher values than do the boys. Physical coward, as might be anticipated, is found to range in status from high-moderate to rather unimportant by the girls, while the 8B boys regard it as being very undesirable. For some unknown reason, the 5A boys also rate it as serious (16th rank) while the 7A boys consider it to be of only high-moderate importance.

Patterns Established when Our Data Are Represented by Graphs

Subjecting our data to graphic treatment (Figures 1-49, Appendix B), presents a series of pictures not readily obtainable through other means of statistical procedure. We note, for instance, that out of the total of forty-six items in question, *the ratings made by the girls show a higher numerical level for thirty-one of the items.* And that for the fifteen remaining items, except for the 5A boys, the girls rate higher in fourteen cases; while the characteristic of silliness has the 7A boys as the sole group exception to the higher evaluation made by the girls for this item also.

This finding would seem to be at variance with Piaget's investigation concerning the social development of children as evidenced by their games. Comparing the practices employed by boys in games of marbles with those manifested by girls in analogous ones, Piaget concludes that "in the main the legal sense is far less developed in little girls than in boys. We did not succeed in finding a single collective game played by girls in which there were as many rules and, above all, as fine and consistent an organization and codification of these rules as in the game of marbles examined above."[6]

The only obvious interpretation that suggests itself on the basis of this expressed and probably innate lack of desire for codification and rules is the corollary one that girls are more individualistic and flexible in their standards of disciplines. To what extent this relates to a truly ethical sense, in sooth a truly moral sense, is a fine point and a debatable one; and does not necessarily indicate a discrepancy with our present findings: that the girls regard behavior disorders of children with a greater degree of seriousness than the boys do, to an overwhelming preponderance.

It may mean that, although one would expect that well-developed standards would automatically come into force in any situation where social interrelationships were involved, games do not bear for girls the ethical and moral connotations that they do for boys, assuming that such is the basis for the legalistic formalities imposed by the boys —or, at any rate, not to the extent that these principles are called into play by the latter. Or, that Piaget's girls, individualistic and unformed so far as the code imposed upon themselves by themselves is concerned would, nevertheless, show the same healthy regard for standards imposed from above, by the adult world, that our girls do in their ratings.

This could lead to many interesting speculations. Do girls naturally have less regard for rules and desire to codify their conduct than boys display, but, being more fearful or suggestible, are therefore more ready to accept dogma laid down by authority? In other words, are there two sets of paradoxes here, when we compare Piaget's results with our own? That is, when left to their own devices boys are more legalistic, but once confronted with rules laid down from above, they are more individualistic and more independent in their attitudes? While girls, seemingly more individualistic in their own milieu, become the conformists when outward authority is imposed upon them?

Or, as has already been suggested, is it that girls, even in their tender stages, reveal that sense of realism so often attributed to their sex and regard rules of games as a form of pomposity more suitable for the masculine spirit; whereas situations of real life evoke from them a more studied, respectful attitude?

Be that as it may, one of the most striking aspects of this present study is the manifestation that, by and large, item for item, coming from widely diverse backgrounds and without previous coaching or preparation of any sort, the ratings of the boys made common cause while those of the girls showed the same general homogeneity of outlook so far as crossing each other's orbit was concerned.

Earlier in this study, mention was made of the gradient pattern of response to be looked for in the evaluations made by our children.

We found this expectation sustained to a surprising extent, particularly so in regard to the judgments made by the girls. *For thirty-five out of our forty-six items, we find that the higher the grade of the girls, the greater is the tendency to give a higher rating for the seriousness of behavior disorders.* And of these, the plotted lines for thirteen items show a perfect or nearly perfect upward gradient, while twenty-two show irregularly rising curves. There is only one characteristic where the evaluations of the girls charted a progressively downward trend—and that appears in the item of whispering and note-writing.

Four items rated by the girls—imaginative lying, smoking, dreaminess, and temper tantrums—produced the lowest rankings at grade 7A and the highest at grade 8B; while two others—tattling and restlessness—exhibited the lowest at the seventh but the highest at the fifth grade. Four others—tardiness, nervousness, resentfulness, and destroying school materials—called forth the lowest evaluations from the girls in grade 5A and the highest from those in grade 7A.

Our *boys* evidenced much less uniformity. There are only eight traits which developed an upward gradient, regular or irregular. Thirteen items show a declivity of seriousness of judgments: four of these fashioning a perfect or almost perfect downward gradient, while nine are irregular in their descent. Ten items described a rise to the seventh grade as the highest point and then a decline: in five of these cases, the ratings of the eighth-grade boys going below those of the fifth graders, while in the other five the decline was halted to a point where the eighth-grade boys are second highest in their rated evaluations of the items judged.

The remaining fifteen characteristics are those concerning which the lowest evaluations were made by our 7A boys: ten of these items having started from the topmost points as produced by the ratings of the 5A boys, while the balance reached the most elevated positions through the respective rankings assigned to them by the 8B boys.

Before leaving these graphs, it seemed desirable to compare our findings with others in the literature. The study made by Marie Cecilia McGrath, in 1923, on the moral development of children,[7] appeared to offer some slight source of similarity, so that three of our questions could thus be placed side by side in analogy, even if not in direct comparison. In McGrath's study, the numerical evaluations were ascertained on the basis of the number of affirmative answers received and then transformed into *percentages* of children polled; while in our case, as has been well established by now, the children ascribed degrees of importance, respectively, to items offered to them for inspection, presented in such fashion as to make possible transmutation of verbal values into numerical ones.

One of McGrath's questions reads: "Is it a sin to talk in school?"[8] as compared with our prescribed instructions to evaluate the seriousness of "Whispering and note-writing." We thereupon made a graph of McGrath's obtained percentages[9] and compared it with ours. (Figures 47 and 11.) In both studies (except for the thirteen-year-old girls in the former) the girls show higher numerical ratings for the seriousness of talking; in our present case by higher ratings and in the older study by the higher percentage of girls deeming it to be a sin.

Also, in both investigations, there are marked, though irregular, downward gradients representing a *decrease* in judgmental attribution of seriousness as accompaniment to an *increase* in the child's grade and year. In the case of McGrath's study, the steep decline in the percentages of the girls was markedly slowed down between the ages of thirteen and fourteen, while the percentage ratings of the boys described a plateau between the ages of twelve to thirteen.

In broad terms, then, the results of these two studies, carried out more than twenty years apart, may be described as roughly comparable for this item.

A second question that seemed suitable for selection was McGrath's "Would it be wrong to take a nickel out of your mother's pocketbook without asking her?"[10] as a point of comparison for our item of "Stealing." There was a certain dubiety in the propriety of so doing, however, since McGrath's question was subject to various types of interpretation, ranging from simple thoughtlessness, disobedience, up to and including deliberate stealing. However, upon noting the high percentage of "yes" answers returned by the children,[11] it seemed proper to assume that the connotation of stealing was a component of the children's judgmental context and hence was comparable to our trait of stealing.

Study of the graphs (Figures 7 and 48), shows that our girls go higher all the way in their judgments of seriousness than do our boys; with the graphic representation of the former describing an irregular, upward gradient, while that of our boys starts from the lowest point of the fifth graders and reaches the summit at the seventh-grade level.

In McGrath's case, the ten-year-old boys and girls start on the same high level of 98.6% of these children deeming that characteristic to be wrong: the twelve- and thirteen-year-old girls show a higher percentage of affirmation than do the boys; while the fourteen-year-old boys reach the highest level of affirmation with their 99.2%, thereby exceeding the percentage elicited from the girls of the same age group and equalling the percentage obtained from the thirteen-year-old girls.[12] In like fashion, the plotted lines display accompanying irregularities—with the girls starting from a percentage of 98.6, then downward to the twelve-year-old level, upward again and downward for the lowest point, the fourteen-year-old level (97.6%). The boys show a steep decline from the initial figure of 98.6% to the twelve-year-old level, then climb upward irregularly but markedly to reach the highest point of 99.2% at age fourteen.

But on the whole, very little comparison between the two studies is possible for this problem of appropriation or stealing.

The third item compared, expressed in McGrath's study as "Is it a sin to cheat?"[13] yielded some points of similarity.[14] (Figures 6 and 49.)

In both investigations the girls maintained a higher level for this item than did the boys. In our case the ratings of the girls are represented by an irregular, upward gradient, while those of the boys are expressed by a rather regular downward gradient. In McGrath's inquiry, the plotted lines of the percentages of both the girls and the boys describe a sharp descent from the ten-year-old level to the twelve-year-old level, then upward rises: those of the girls, in irregular gradient fashion, but never again reaching the high point of the ten-year-old level; while those of the boys demonstrate a fairly smooth upward progression, exceeding the ten-year-old percentage at both the thirteen- and fourteen-year-old levels.

The similarity which the two studies bear for cheating is thus twofold:

1. The progressive rise evinced by all of our girls in seriousness of evaluation as compared to the increasing percentages of affirmation expressed by the thirteen- and fourteen-year-old girls in McGrath's study.

2. And the fact that the girls in both instances consistently show higher levels than do the boys for this characteristic.

How Our Groups of Children Relate to Each Other

As a subsidiary point of information, it might be profitable to study the table of correlations again, briefly, to obtain a descriptive account of how our groups of children relate to *each other* (as expressed through their ratings) *grade by grade* and *age by age* and *sex by sex*, in addition to what has already been described.

We find, for instance, that the grade-by-grade correlations are:

5A boys ...... .837 ...... 5A girls
7A boys ...... .845 ...... 7A girls
8B boys ...... .883 ...... 8B girls

Although inspection of the actual items would reveal that instances of the greatest deviations of rating are to be found in frequencies of 17, 15, and 15, respectively, for these three grade groups; while instances of the least deviations are to be found in frequencies of 18, 18, and 16, respectively, for these three grade groups—the correlation coefficients do not appear, by and large, to reflect these trends perfectly, nor are they necessarily expected to do so; but do point out that, for the most part, there is a great deal of agreement between the boys and girls of each grade as to the relative importance of the various behavior items. *And that such intragrade agreement increases with the increase of age of the groups.*

Surveying all the correlation figures for an *intergroup* picture, it is to be noted that the least amount of correspondence is shown by the 5A boys contra the 8B boys, and by the 5A girls as against the 8B boys; while the highest correlation of all was obtained by statistical treatment of the data elicited from the 7A boys versus the 8B girls, with a coefficient of .895.

We note also that *girls appear to agree closer with each other's judgments than the boys do:* so that the groups of 5A girls and 7A girls concur with each other to an extent which produces a correlation of .893, while the views of the 7A girls and 8B girls also correspond with each other to the identical degree, .893 again. There is, however, a slight dropping of consonance between 5A girls and 8B girls, so that the correlation is .880 there.

Boys start on a somewhat lower level of correspondence, with a coefficient of correlation of .866 between the 5A boys and 7A boys.

Then, these two groups of boys respectively show a somewhat lessening concurrence with the 8B boys than they do with each other: so that the 5A boys agree to an extent of .866 with the 7A boys but only to that of .796 with the 8B boys; and similarly, the 7A boys agree to an extent of .866 with the 5A boys, but to that of .859 with the 8B boys. Thus, as was noted in the case of the girls, the 5A boys also draw away to a slight but perceptible degree from the oldest of their own sex.

Two of these schemata of correlations collaborate with the findings already represented, that: As the teachers milden their views (in their status of Teachers 1b), those of the 8B boys show a greater correspondence with them than do those of the other groups of children; that the 8B boys likewise evidence the closest consonance with the mental hygienists; that they also display the greatest agreement with fathers and mothers: to present a rather clear picture of the 8B boys, on the average, drawing away from all the other groups of children and, so far as four of the five adult sets of evaluations are concerned, in the direction of more adult reasoning.

This is somewhat analogous to the findings made by Piaget, wherein he demonstrates that towards the age of 10-11 boys feel free to modify and adapt the rules of the game (marbles)[15] and which he characterizes as belonging to "consciousness of autonomy."[16]

The time lag that appears in our case, of our 8B boys manifesting an increased independence (compared to the other children) at a rather later age, may be ascribed to the nature of the activity in question. So far as standards of playing marbles are concerned, the pressure of older children upon them has ceased operating some time ago; whereas judgments which operate in the realm of adult suzerainty would still, even now, exercise considerable of the force they had exerted earlier in their development. As Piaget expresses it, in reference to his investigation: "A child of 10 will, for example, show signs of autonomy in his application of the rules of the game of marbles, but will give proof of heteronomy in the extent to which he is conscious of these rules and in his application of rules relating to lying and justice."[17]

The correlation coefficients of .866 and .859 for *5A boys versus 7A boys and 7A boys versus 8B boys* would appear to indicate that sameness of sex is slightly more important in promoting agreement of views than age or being in the same grade, so far as grades 5A and 7A are concerned (5A boys versus 5A girls, .837; 7A boys versus 7A girls, .845); but that age and being in the same grade play stronger relative roles for the boys in grade 8B (8B boys versus 8B girls, .883):

and even more so when the correlation coefficients related to sex alikeness are attenuated by the increased age gap existent between the 5A boys and the 8B boys, where the correlation coefficient is .796.

In like manner and more inclusively, in relationship to *5A girls versus 7A girls and 7A girls versus 8B girls* (whose correlations are .893 and .893), sex sameness seems to be rather more effective than age or being in the same grade, so far as closeness of agreement is concerned. (5A boys versus 5A girls, .837; 7A boys versus 7A girls, .845; 8B boys versus 8B girls, .883.) But when the 5A girls are compared with the 8B girls (correlation coefficient of .880) and there is thus a relatively wide gap in age, then being in the eighth grade and of the same approximate age is a whit more important for consonance, but almost imperceptibly so, than being of the same sex. (The correlation coefficient for 8B boys versus 8B girls being .883.)

However, even though diverse and finely exemplicative of important aspects, these coefficients of correlation are not far removed from each other in numerical value but, along with the other material presented in this chapter, allow the conclusion that: *The ratings show variations in differing ways but they are variations within a general theme of rather close correspondence of views manifested by these school children of grades 5A, 7A, and 8B.*

REFERENCES

1. DURKHEIM, ÉMILE. *L'Éducation Morale.* Paris: Librairie Félix Alcan, 1925. P. 167.
2. PIAGET, JEAN. *The Moral Judgment of the Child.* London: Kegan Paul, Trench, Trubner & Co. Ltd., 1932. P. 82.
3. MURPHY, GARDNER, MURPHY, LOIS BARCLAY, and NEWCOMB, THEODORE M. *Experimental Social Psychology.* New York: Harper, 1937 (revised). P. 414.
4. PIAGET, *op. cit.,* p. 79.
5. PIAGET, *op. cit.,* p. 130.
6. PIAGET, *op. cit.,* p. 69.
7. McGRATH, M. C. "A Study of the Moral Development of Children," *Psychological Monographs,* XXXII, 1923, No. 2.
8. *Ibid.,* p. 84.
9. *Ibid.,* p. 86.
10. *Ibid.,* p. 111.
11. *Ibid.,* p. 113.

12. *Ibid.*, p. 113.
13. *Ibid.*, p. 94.
14. *Ibid.*, p. 95.
15. PIAGET, *op. cit.*, pp. 56-63.
16. PIAGET, *op. cit.*, p. 66.
17. PIAGET, *op. cit.*, p. 79 n.

CHAPTER VIII

How Parents View the Behavior of Children
(With a Side View towards a Successful Life)

The groundwork thus laid, we are now ready to present the judgments of, perhaps, the most important of all the groups of adults. Their findings are, in some ways, the most interesting of all thus far put forth: for here we deal not only with parents' observations on the conduct of children but, in a sense, with parents' views of life.

Upon entering this phase of our investigation, the possibility of polling the parents of the selfsame children whose opinions we had already obtained, school by school, was explored; but, unfortunately, this exploration led to a cul-de-sac, it was not considered feasible to do so. Hence the next best approach was made. Mrs. Bess B. Lane, Educational Director of the United Parents Associations of New York City, approved of the project, and her kind offices made it possible for us to solicit the views of the members of the association. Permission was granted for this present writer and a friend to attend a meeting of delegates and to pass out the literature. Thus, an introductory sheet, entitled "Parent Opinion," bearing the imprint of sponsorship of the association and Mrs. Lane's collaboration in composing it, was distributed to the fathers and mothers who attended this meeting on the evening of February 7, 1945.

Along with this, "Schedule 2" was also distributed to each of the delegates present that evening. This schedule consisted of five sheets, three of which magnified and extended the instructions and explanations given in "Parent Opinion," and two of which consisted of the rating sheets themselves. "Parent Opinion" and "Schedule 2" are reproduced in full in Appendix A.

At the beginning of this assembly, Mrs. Lane addressed the entire group, read some of the explanations and directions, and clarified the purpose and procedural technique of these questionnaires. Particular mention was made of the fact that these schedules were to be filled out separately by fathers and mothers, designation for which was supplied by a box in the upper left-hand corner of each rating sheet. Before the session was over, extra sets of this questionnaire material were handed out to all who wished to take them home to their respective wives or husbands, as the case might be. Self-addressed, stamped envelopes were also issued for the convenience of these parents.

In all, 460 parents received the schedules, the predominant majority of those attending the meeting and accepting the material being mothers; and eventually, 166 of these schedules were completed and returned.

Of these 166 schedules, some could not be utilized, for various reasons, one of the most prevalent being the collaboration that had taken place between fathers and mothers in jointly rating the items: this leading to the regretful but necessary discarding of 24 sets of schedules. Finally, then, 40 questionnaires answered by fathers were employed in this study, while the number of usable forms filled out by the mothers totalled 102.

These parents came from all the five boroughs of New York City and represented a statistically satisfying socio-economic range. In one respect, obviously, the very fact of their membership, of their delegacy, and attendance on a cold winter's evening would bespeak that these were a superior group, not only as parents but experimentally. Due to the exigencies and paradoxes of scientific investigation, such advantage might conceivably and under unfavorably favorable circumstances turn out to be a disadvantage. Here, however, since the most forward view of ascertained devotion to welfare was the objective in mind, this superiority was not only noted but gratefully acknowledged as, indeed, bringing the completion of data within the reach of accomplishment.

It will be noted that several additional techniques of eliciting comprehensive views were employed, inasmuch as the specialized approaches to the teachers and to the mental hygienists had appeared to have in them desirable but, to partial extent, mutually exclusive features. Generally, the attempt was made to present the child to the parent within the framework of regarding him "not only as your son (or daughter) in terms of your affection and concern for him, but as a young person in his own right," etc. Within this frame of reference, then, the instructions were intended to depersonalize the relationship, so that mention was made of judging these characteristics when they appeared in any child. This judicious blending was employed to prevent the parent from embarking too far off on the tangent of abstract considerations. There is a vast difference between "my child" and "any child," and the effort was thus made to keep the drawbridge up between the two concepts so that the parents could span the distance between them with comfort; keeping some of the detachment called forth by "any child" for "my child" and, it was hoped, some of the warmth usually attached to "my child" for "any child." In short, parallel with the two sets of questionnaires submitted to the teachers, in this instance the designation of "my child" was utilized to evoke emotion, while that of "any child" was made use of to call forth an intellectual approach.

And, further, so that the viewing glass might be as stereoscopic as possible in depth of comprehension, the parents were further adjured:

"4. You may take as much time as you require for making *careful* ratings, bearing in mind the consequences of these undesirable characteristics in children from the standpoint of the child and the society in which he lives; his present happiness, educability, adjustments; and his future adjustment—socially, vocationally, and emotionally— as an adult."

These elaborate instructions were, theoretically, avoidable on the basis that the parents might naturally weight the importance of each trait if no specific instructions were offered; but, on the other hand, when such procedural guidance is omitted, the raters might only too naturally weight these items in unstandardized fashion, in line with preconceived ideas, or incomplete understanding of their respective tasks. As members of a parents' association, seeing their children primarily in their capacity of pupils, their ratings might be decisively different than when approached as parents of individuals whose pupilage is only one phase of a larger and more diverse role.

In a way, this list again has a bifold view. Even with this comprehensive approach, experimentally, the items still appear to pose themselves into two sets: outward success as against inward success; getting ahead, even on a juvenile scale, as against personal contentment. For, implicit in the issue of what is undesirable is the issue of what is success, what is the successful life for the child and for the later adult which he is to become. And yet the problem answers itself, empirically even if somewhat indirectly, and goes back to the meaning of ultimate values. In other words, our quest is not one that occupies itself exclusively with academic school problems, but one whose ramifications extend into every phase of juvenile and adult life. If the parent deems contentment and personal happiness to be the criteria of a successful life, then we may confidently assume that he will evaluate unhappiness as being very high in undesirability. But, if achievement, getting ahead is very important in his personal creed, then this parent will be bound to rate schoolroom violations, of various types, as ranking very high in comparative seriousness.

These two sets of questions, then, derived and deduced from this list, instead of posing a problem incapable of resolution actually bring about a further source of enlightenment as they furnish information whereby to answer the query: Which is more important, getting ahead or personal contentment? What do parents consider success, for their children—achievement or happiness?

Shall we not, however, eventually conclude that it is only for artificial situations that one can thus accept similitudes of life realities suspended for the moment in space of time on white sheets of questionnaire paper, situations which have meaning only because a daguerreotype fixity allows the opportunity to study characteristics whose features inevitably change with the viability that life gives to its processes? In other words, in the actual dynamics of real life, are the two necessarily and mutually exclusive, achievement as against happiness? Shall we not go beyond this static concept and find that these equations—happiness equals success, achievement equals success—have their fundamental usefulness only in making possible the more accurate appraisal of these rated traits while they are in a state of suspension, at a point fixed in animation when they are not in the act of reacting, each upon the other?

For, in real life we may assuredly feel—if one may borrow the nomenclature from a sister science—that the reaction embodied in the concept of the reversible equation holds the most logical and complete answer:

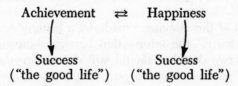

$$\text{Achievement} \rightleftarrows \text{Happiness}$$

$$\text{Success} \qquad \text{Success}$$
$$\text{("the good life")} \quad \text{("the good life")}$$

That achievement and happiness are the respective reagents on either side of this reversible equation, that achievement leads to happiness and that happiness in its turn reacts back again and leads to achievement (one may start with either end of the equation), that the two elements are solubly reactive with each other; and, allowing for differences in the individual reactions that, by and large, the reagents which compose the solution in this imaginary beaker will also determine the solution of each person's success in life.

These theoretical observations are, obviously, a simplification of a very complicated and exigent problem, one which reaches even into the relatively mundane and concrete field of vocational guidance, for example. There, the selection of criteria to validate aptitude tests presents one of the greatest difficulties, simply because criteria for professional or trade success are so hard to obtain reliably. To start with, the term, success, varies with the individual: some will think of earnings in their definition, others of how much time their vocation allows them to spend with their family; some will think of the mental aspects, others of the physical. In one sense, it is an absolute term, and hence immeasurable; at the same time, and paradoxically, the concept of success is one which deals in relativities and dynamic relationships to an extent surpassed by few other areas of human existence.

A list such as this, then, has a major value in that the items can be evaluated and judged while they are in a state of rest, a necessary prelude to gauging them from the standpoint of their reactive consequences. And, with this more meaningful conceptual background, that of ascertaining what are the basic requirements for a successful life for a child, and contrariwise, what traits are undesirable for the attaining of such goal, the rated views of the parents were treated statistically, and set up in Tables XXII and XXIII, for mothers' ratings and fathers' ratings, respectively.

As a preliminary to further discussion it may be mentioned that one of the many interesting and stimulating points made in Wickman's book was the statement on page 119 that "it is our opinion, unsupported by evidence, that the stress laid on school accomplishment is the chief and perhaps the only characteristic that distinguishes teachers' attitudes from generally prevailing attitudes toward behavior problems of children."[1]

In the light of this statement made by a leading educator, "unsupported by evidence," the information hereby obtained, even after a gap of almost two decades, should still contain in it a great deal of pertinency. What then was the prevailing attitude towards behavior problems of children, as shown by our, later, evidence? That is, as manifested by this third great segment of the adult population, the parents, which, together with the other two already reported upon, may fairly be said to constitute a full complement of adult views.

Even if they did so at that time (1927), did teachers in 1945 still stand out from the rest by their stress on school accomplishment? Conversely: did parents emphasize such accomplishment to a much less degree than was true of school teachers? Did they tend to agree more with the mental hygienists in their appraisal of the undesirable items of conduct?

Again, for a quick preview of results, Table V, of correlations, acts as a form of statistical shorthand. We find that fathers agree to the extent of .789 with Teachers 1*a*, and to the extent of .880 with Teachers 1*b*. Mothers and fathers agree very closely with each other; in fact, they show the closest correspondence of all the groups, with a fathers-versus-mothers correlation figure of .945. It was not surprising, therefore, to find that the mothers also agree closely with the teachers, so that the correlation of their ratings with those of Teachers 1*a* is .801 and with those of Teachers 1*b* is .885.

In the case of both parents, then, the correlations were slightly higher between fathers versus Teachers 1*b* and mothers versus Teachers 1*b* than they were between fathers versus Teachers 1*a* and mothers versus Teachers 1*a*. (Teachers 1*b*, it will be remembered, were the same groups of our teachers who had filled out Schedule 1*a* and, later on, Schedule 1*b*; and who had shown more of a "mental hygiene" approach in filling out the questionnaires the second time than they had in their first appraisals.)

This shift in the direction of Teachers 1*b* on the part of the parents would seem to augur the possibility of close accordance between the parents and the mental hygienists. Surprisingly, however, *the correlation coefficient between the ratings of the fathers and mental hygienists was low, being only .330; and that between the mothers and mental hygienists was only a very little larger, being .357.* In fact, as the table shows, the parents were not markedly in more outstanding agreement with the mental hygienists than were Teachers 1*b*, whose views corresponded with those of the mental hygienists to the extent of .229.

So far, then, there does not seem to be any support for the hypothesis that the teachers are unique in their stress on school accomplishment as compared to the "generally prevailing attitudes"; it is, rather, the mental hygienists who appear to differ decisively from the generally held views.

Here, however, as before, we are aware that a blanket statement, based on correlations, may cover many of the finer and possibly more rewarding facts that have been secured. Recourse to Tables III, I, IV, and VI, along with the more immediate tables, XXII and XXIII (which follow), affords the more detailed information to enhance the meaningfulness of our correlation figures. Opportunity may also be taken at this point to introduce Table XXIV, in which are given the numerical differences between means and their critical ratios, so far as fathers versus all the other groups questioned in this study are concerned. Similarly, mothers versus eight of the other groups,

TABLE XXII

MOTHERS' RATINGS ON THE SERIOUSNESS OF BEHAVIOR PROBLEMS OF CHILDREN

(Results from Schedule 2, as Filled Out by 102 Mothers of Public School Children of New York City) *

Behavior Problems	Averages	Standard Deviations
Stealing	18.55	2.57
Cruelty, Bullying	17.63	3.35
Heterosexual Activity	17.00	4.36
Untruthfulness	16.31	3.96
Cheating	16.11	4.47
Truancy	15.65	4.22
Unhappy, Depressed	15.56	5.04
Unreliable, Irresponsible	15.48	4.28
Destroying School Materials	14.85	4.70
Selfishness, Unsportsmanship	14.66	4.46
Impertinence	14.47	5.04
Lack of Interest in Work	14.17	4.50
Nervousness	13.84	5.48
Fearfulness	13.73	5.78
Domineering, Overbearing	13.48	5.13
Obscene Notes, Pictures, etc.	13.28	5.56
Easily Discouraged	13.27	5.21
Masturbation	13.05	6.49
Resentfulness	13.01	5.06
Quarrelsomeness	12.95	4.90

* This schedule was given out to 460 parents, the predominant majority of whom were mothers. 166 of these were filled out and returned, by fathers and mothers.

As some schedules could not be used, the number of questionnaires made out by mothers, that were finally utilized in this survey, was 102.

TABLE XXII —*Continued*

Behavior Problems	Averages	Standard Deviations
Disobedience	12.70	5.04
Impudence, Rudeness	12.67	4.68
Temper Tantrums	12.57	5.21
Unsocial, Withdrawing	12.22	5.07
Laziness	12.07	5.53
Suggestible	12.00	5.80
Enuresis	11.52	6.37
Disorderliness	11.48	4.83
Physical Coward	11.44	5.32
Carelessness in Work	11.42	4.73
Slovenly in Appearance	11.33	5.64
Suspiciousness	10.91	5.42
Inattention	10.58	4.78
Smoking	10.40	6.27
Overcritical of Others	9.97	5.43
Sullenness, Sulkiness	9.86	5.14
Tattling	9.77	5.82
Profanity	9.65	5.60
Tardiness	9.44	4.61
Thoughtlessness	9.08	4.91
Stubbornness, Contrariness	8.71	5.06
Sensitiveness	8.30	5.27
Shyness	7.94	5.27
Restlessness	7.80	5.25
Inquisitiveness	7.64	5.35
Silliness	6.58	5.43
Dreaminess	6.45	5.13
Interrupting, Talkativeness	6.43	4.60
Imaginative Lying	6.07	4.81
Whispering	5.24	4.36

TABLE XXIII

FATHERS' RATINGS ON THE SERIOUSNESS OF BEHAVIOR PROBLEMS OF CHILDREN

(Results from Schedule 2, as Filled Out by 40 Fathers of Public School Children of New York City) *

Behavior Problems	Averages	Standard Deviations
Stealing	17.38	4.45
Heterosexual Activity	16.58	4.48
Cruelty, Bullying	15.47	4.10
Cheating	15.46	5.44
Truancy	14.60	3.90
Unreliable, Irresponsible	14.08	4.84
Unhappy, Depressed	13.85	4.61
Untruthfulness	13.78	4.85
Destroying School Materials	13.70	4.82
Masturbation	13.44	5.61
Easily Discouraged	13.34	5.07
Impertinence, Defiance	13.10	4.83
Selfishness, Unsportsmanship	12.97	4.43
Impudence, Rudeness	12.82	4.66
Physical Coward	12.76	4.38
Fearfulness	12.59	4.14
Suggestible	12.24	4.99
Nervousness	11.87	4.74
Obscene Notes, Pictures, etc.	11.87	5.49
Quarrelsomeness	11.75	4.57

* This schedule was given out to 460 parents, the predominant majority of whom were mothers. 166 of these were filled out and returned, by fathers and mothers.

As some schedules could not be used, the number of questionnaires made out by fathers, that were finally utilized in this survey, was 40.

TABLE XXIII —*Continued*

Behavior Problems	Averages	Standard Deviations
Disobedience	11.70	4.91
Unsocial, Withdrawing	11.67	4.77
Temper Tantrums	11.26	4.83
Lack of Interest in Work	11.26	4.43
Resentfulness	11.21	4.02
Slovenly in Appearance	11.21	4.76
Carelessness in Work	11.18	4.73
Enuresis	11.14	5.91
Disorderliness	10.65	4.54
Domineering, Overbearing	10.55	4.88
Laziness	10.48	5.57
Overcritical of Others	9.56	4.44
Sullenness, Sulkiness	9.54	4.17
Profanity	9.10	5.13
Tardiness	9.00	4.61
Suspiciousness	8.79	4.54
Smoking	8.56	5.66
Tattling	8.53	4.39
Thoughtlessness	8.02	4.44
Inattention	7.90	4.79
Shyness	7.82	4.57
Stubbornness, Contrariness	7.79	3.88
Inquisitiveness	7.76	4.22
Silliness	7.53	4.80
Sensitiveness	7.31	4.22
Restlessness	7.21	4.55
Dreaminess	7.18	4.45
Interrupting, Talkativeness	6.23	4.37
Imaginative Lying	5.48	4.18
Whispering	4.18	3.82

TABLE XXIV

CRITICAL RATIOS FOR THE DIFFERENCES BETWEEN THE MEAN RATINGS OF THE FATHERS VERSUS EACH OF OUR OTHER NINE GROUPS

Fathers versus	Mothers		5A Boys		5A Girls		7A Boys		7A Girls		8B Boys		8B Girls		Teachers 1a		Teachers 1b	
	Diff. M.	C. R.	Diff. M.	C. R.	Diff. M.	C. R.	Diff. M.	C. R.	Diff. M.	C. R.	Diff. M.	C. R.	Diff. M.	C. R.	Diff. M.	C. R.	Diff. M.	C. R.
Tardiness	−0.44	0.51	−0.20	0.19	−0.04	0.04	−0.63	0.68	−3.20	0.32	−1.00	0.94	−1.93	1.93	1.35	1.65	0.25	0.29
Truancy	−1.05	1.48	0.39	0.35	−0.65	0.66	−0.88	1.02	−1.02	1.17	−0.23	0.24	−1.62	1.93	0.93	1.08	1.06	1.25
Destroying School Materials	−1.15	1.29	−0.97	0.82	−1.56	1.46	−1.25	1.29	−2.94	3.13	−2.02	1.98	−2.21	2.40	1.58	1.70	2.10	2.26
Untruthfulness	−2.53	2.94	1.39	1.14	0.67	0.61	1.09	1.12	−1.61	1.71	0.20	0.20	−2.15	2.22	1.44	1.50	−0.20	0.22
Imaginative Lying	−0.59	0.72	−3.61	3.22	−4.69	4.74	−1.29	1.48	−4.24	4.51	−3.98	3.83	−5.46	5.81	−0.44	0.55	−0.91	1.11
Cheating	−0.65	0.66	2.23	1.69	1.50	1.33	2.38	2.22	0.36	0.35	2.52	2.31	0.27	0.26	4.75	4.57	2.76	2.68
Stealing	−1.17	1.56	1.03	0.91	0.77	0.80	0.29	0.32	−1.04	1.20	0.87	0.91	−1.56	1.90	3.30	3.44	1.68	1.87
Profanity	−0.55	0.56	−5.57	4.89	−6.30	5.78	−5.21	5.01	−6.90	7.19	−4.15	3.74	−7.77	8.01	−0.05	0.05	−0.33	0.33
Smoking	−1.84	1.66	−5.57	3.98	−6.40	5.20	−5.84	4.95	−6.25	5.17	−2.92	2.23	−7.05	6.24	0.52	0.46	2.17	2.05
Obscene Notes, Pictures, etc.	−1.41	1.34													−0.83	0.74	−1.00	0.92
Masturbation	0.39	0.35													0.68	0.61	0.18	0.16
Heterosexual Activity	−0.42	0.49													2.49	2.49	1.85	1.95
Disorderliness	−0.83	0.95	−2.17	1.94	−0.53	0.52	−1.32	1.40	−2.15	2.36	−0.81	0.82	−3.35	3.64	−0.13	0.15	−0.35	0.40
Whispering	−1.06	1.41	−6.24	5.94	−6.52	6.21	−3.40	3.91	−5.95	7.26	−2.91	3.23	−4.45	5.36	−2.23	3.10	−1.04	1.44
Interrupting, Talkativeness	−0.20	0.24	−4.40	4.15	−5.12	4.65	−4.56	4.90	−6.15	6.41	−2.98	3.01	−6.99	7.68	−1.68	2.02	−0.56	0.68
Restlessness	−0.59	0.66	−3.09	2.81	−3.14	3.05	−1.01	1.10	−1.79	1.86	−0.53	0.53	−2.80	2.92	−0.28	0.31	0.04	0.05
Inattention	3.48	3.82	−3.87	3.28	−3.10	2.79	−3.33	3.40	−3.89	3.97	−2.04	2.00	−5.47	5.95	−1.08	1.21	−1.85	2.08
Lack of Interest in Work	2.91	3.46	−2.33	2.03	−1.34	1.29	−1.65	1.72	−1.96	2.13	−0.25	0.25	−3.28	3.57	0.95	1.09	−0.21	0.24
Carelessness in Work	−0.24	0.27	−1.72	1.46	−0.82	0.77	−0.10	0.10	−1.90	2.02	−0.36	0.36	−3.94	4.19	2.21	2.60	0.30	0.33
Laziness	−1.59	1.53	−1.75	1.43	−0.67	0.56	0.70	0.66	−3.02	2.75	−0.17	0.15	−3.73	3.49	0.89	0.89	−0.40	0.40
Unreliable, Irresponsible	−1.40	1.59	0.77	0.63	0.70	0.64	0.97	0.98	−0.20	0.21	1.25	1.21	−2.21	2.43	2.80	3.11	0.19	0.21
Disobedience	−1.00	1.09	−2.59	2.21	−3.00	2.94	−2.56	2.67	−3.64	3.71	−1.06	1.00	−4.65	4.95	−1.33	1.40	−1.83	1.99

Impertinence, Defiance	-1.37	1.49	-0.49	0.38	-2.45	2.31	-0.61	0.60	-2.20	2.27	0.17	0.18	-2.43	2.59	0.00	0.00	-0.83	0.87
Cruelty, Bullying	-1.89	2.55	1.38	1.08	0.92	0.93	0.70	0.74	-0.17	0.20	1.08	1.15	-0.29	0.34	2.52	2.80	1.50	1.69
Quarrelsomeness	-1.20	1.48	-0.84	0.73	-0.75	0.71	0.30	0.32	-2.05	2.20	0.49	0.49	2.43	2.53	1.14	1.30	0.83	0.94
Tattling	-1.24	1.38	-1.55	1.23	-4.65	4.51	-2.16	2.08	-3.65	3.69	-2.33	2.01	-4.48	4.31	2.87	3.50	2.05	2.47
Stubbornness, Contrariness	-0.92	1.14	-2.17	2.15	-3.10	3.23	-2.08	2.57	-4.45	5.24	-2.28	2.45	-5.52	6.49	-1.25	1.58	-0.88	1.14
Sullenness	-0.32	0.38	-2.86	2.44	-2.93	2.84	-0.80	0.83	-3.62	4.11	-2.07	2.16	-4.06	4.46	1.87	2.34	0.83	1.04
Temper Tantrums	-1.31	1.41	-0.70	0.56	-1.67	1.56	-0.33	0.32	-1.42	1.42	-0.56	0.52	-3.52	3.59	-0.25	0.25	-1.13	1.18
Impudence, Rudeness	0.15	0.17	-0.80	0.70	-1.18	1.12	-1.15	1.24	-2.43	2.56	-0.56	0.56	-3.74	4.25	1.97	2.21	1.40	1.59
Selfishness	-1.69	2.01	1.53	1.31	0.17	0.16	-0.74	0.75	-1.82	2.00	-0.61	0.58	-2.74	3.01	4.15	4.94	1.98	2.33
Domineering, Overbearing	-2.93	3.12	-1.43	1.10	-2.15	1.92	-1.68	1.66	-2.20	2.10	-2.01	1.90	-4.48	4.48	1.54	1.60	-0.96	1.00
Shyness	-0.12	0.13	1.29	1.15	0.02	1.85	3.13	3.48	-1.03	1.04	1.45	1.41	-1.69	1.66	1.80	2.07	-0.03	3.53
Sensitiveness	-0.99	1.15	-1.83	1.65	-2.04	2.15	-0.43	0.48	-3.59	3.78	-0.68	0.71	-5.28	5.74	0.91	1.15	-1.18	1.48
Unsocial, Withdrawing	-0.55	0.60	1.06	0.95	2.09	1.97	1.59	1.54	-0.46	0.46	1.96	1.88	-1.34	1.31	3.19	3.39	1.43	1.52
Overcritical of Others	-0.41	0.46	-2.06	1.65	-3.12	2.89	-2.07	2.20	-3.80	4.04	-1.59	1.66	-5.90	6.78	2.58	3.07	0.62	0.72
Thoughtlessness	-1.06	1.22	-3.23	2.67	-2.94	2.70	-1.14	1.18	-4.19	4.36	-2.20	2.10	-5.35	5.94	1.22	1.47	-0.25	0.28
Inquisitiveness	0.12	0.14	-3.98	3.52	-3.39	3.32	-3.94	4.19	-4.55	4.80	-3.01	3.10	-5.74	6.52	1.11	1.37	0.31	0.39
Silliness	0.95	1.01	-2.75	2.17	-3.61	3.28	-4.63	4.45	-4.54	4.54	-4.01	3.61	-5.95	6.20	-0.20	0.22	-0.36	0.40
Unhappy, Depressed	-1.71	1.92	4.12	3.58	4.77	4.59	3.31	3.31	2.08	2.10	3.12	3.09	0.89	0.91	3.97	4.22	2.80	3.01
Resentfulness	-1.80	2.20	-0.08	0.07	-0.14	0.15	0.62	0.68	-1.83	2.01	1.06	1.10	-1.41	1.57	2.26	2.72	0.49	0.60
Nervousness	-1.97	2.10	1.00	0.88	0.41	0.38	2.11	2.03	-1.67	1.62	1.20	1.12	-1.01	1.01	2.93	3.22	2.05	2.30
Fearfulness	-1.14	1.30	3.31	2.81	3.59	3.42	4.24	4.42	0.90	0.93	3.74	3.60	-0.41	0.44	4.85	5.71	3.57	4.35
Enuresis (Wetting Self)	-0.38	0.32													2.36	2.02	2.03	1.72
Dreaminess	0.73	0.82	-1.87	1.56	-2.46	2.30	-0.37	0.40	-1.35	1.45	-2.24	2.09	-4.44	4.44	0.12	0.14	-0.76	0.88
Slovenly in Appearance	-0.12	0.13	0.19	0.15	-1.81	1.61	-0.39	0.38	-3.87	4.12	-1.03	0.95	-5.40	5.74	3.25	3.69	0.60	0.66
Suspiciousness	-2.12	2.33	-0.32	0.28	-1.93	1.84	-0.92	0.96	-3.39	3.57	-2.12	2.06	-4.52	4.66	1.59	1.83	-0.74	0.85
Physical Coward	1.32	1.47	-0.02	0.02	2.30	2.11	1.92	1.79	-0.03	0.03	-0.24	0.24	-0.97	1.05	4.67	5.31	2.28	2.51
Easily Discouraged	0.07	0.07	0.41	0.33	1.84	1.67	1.47	1.44	-0.10	0.10	0.79	0.75	-1.18	1.11	5.28	5.50	2.73	2.76
Suggestible	0.24	0.24	0.26	0.20	0.17	0.15	1.54	1.44	-1.50	1.46	-0.70	0.66	-2.43	2.38	2.06	2.06	0.16	0.16

TABLE XXV

CRITICAL RATIOS FOR THE DIFFERENCES BETWEEN THE MEAN RATINGS OF THE MOTHERS VERSUS 5A BOYS, 5A GIRLS, 7A BOYS, 7A GIRLS, 8B BOYS, 8B GIRLS, TEACHERS 1a, AND TEACHERS 1b

Mothers versus	5A Boys		5A Girls		7A Boys		7A Girls		8B Boys		8B Girls		Teachers 1a		Teachers 1b	
	Diff. M.	C.R.	Diff. M.	C.R.	Diff. M.	C.R.	Diff. M.	C.R.	Diff. M.	C.R.	Diff. M.	C.R.	Diff. M.	C.R.	Diff. M.	C.R.
Tardiness	0.24	0.26	0.40	0.46	-0.19	0.26	-2.76	3.41	-0.56	0.62	-1.49	1.80	1.79	3.03	0.69	1.05
Truancy	1.44	1.41	0.40	0.45	0.17	0.23	0.03	0.41	0.82	1.00	-0.57	0.80	1.98	2.68	2.11	2.93
Destroying School Materials	0.18	0.17	-0.41	0.47	-0.10	0.13	-1.79	2.49	-0.87	1.06	-1.06	1.51	2.73	3.85	3.25	4.58
Untruthfulness	3.92	3.81	3.20	3.68	3.62	5.03	0.92	1.39	2.73	3.50	0.38	0.54	3.97	5.67	2.33	3.53
Imaginative Lying	-3.02	2.93	-4.10	4.61	-0.70	0.93	-3.65	4.40	-3.39	3.61	-4.87	5.87	0.17	0.26	-0.32	0.46
Cheating	2.88	2.64	2.15	2.53	3.03	3.94	1.01	1.44	3.17	4.01	0.92	1.24	5.40	7.50	3.41	4.87
Stealing	2.20	2.37	1.94	2.77	1.46	2.35	0.13	0.23	2.04	2.91	-0.39	0.78	4.47	6.39	2.85	4.67
Profanity	-5.02	5.07	-5.75	6.18	-4.66	5.36	-6.35	8.25	-3.60	3.79	-7.22	9.26	0.50	0.62	0.22	0.27
Smoking	-3.73	2.98	-4.56	4.30	-4.00	4.00	-4.41	4.28	-0.58	0.51	-5.21	5.60	2.36	2.57	4.01	4.72
Obscene Notes, Pictures, etc.													0.58	0.67	0.41	0.49
Masturbation													0.29	0.31	-0.19	0.20
Heterosexual Activity													2.91	3.51	2.27	2.95
Disorderliness	-1.34	1.35	0.30	0.34	-0.49	0.62	-1.32	1.76	0.02	0.02	-2.52	3.32	0.70	1.06	0.48	0.69
Whispering	-5.18	5.34	-5.46	6.50	-2.34	3.08	-4.89	6.99	-1.85	2.31	-3.39	4.71	-1.17	1.98	0.02	0.03
Interrupting, Talkativeness	-4.20	4.57	-4.92	5.02	-4.36	5.66	-5.95	8.04	-2.78	3.31	-6.79	9.18	-1.48	2.28	-0.36	0.57
Restlessness	-2.50	2.55	-2.55	2.87	-0.42	0.55	-1.20	1.48	0.06	0.07	-2.21	2.73	0.31	0.42	0.63	0.91
Inattention	-1.19	1.17	-0.42	0.45	-0.65	0.83	-1.21	1.55	0.64	0.77	-2.79	3.99	1.60	2.46	0.83	1.26
Lack of Interest in Work	0.58	0.57	1.57	1.78	1.26	1.59	0.95	1.28	2.66	3.13	-0.37	0.50	3.86	5.76	2.70	4.09
Carelessness in Work	-1.48	1.45	-0.58	0.65	0.14	0.18	-1.66	2.24	-0.12	0.15	-3.70	5.00	2.45	3.89	0.54	0.78
Laziness	-0.16	0.16	0.92	0.93	2.29	2.86	-1.43	1.66	1.42	1.56	-2.14	2.61	2.48	3.44	1.19	1.63
Unreliable, Irresponsible	2.17	2.09	2.10	2.36	2.37	3.12	1.10	1.49	2.65	3.27	-0.86	0.89	4.20	4.47	1.59	1.66

Disobedience	-1.59	1.57	-2.00	2.41	-1.56	2.08	-2.64	3.38	-0.06	0.07	-3.65	5.00	-0.33	0.44	-0.83	1.19
Impertinence, Defiance	0.88	0.76	-0.68	0.76	0.76	0.90	-0.83	1.06	1.54	1.97	-1.06	1.41	1.37	1.78	0.54	0.71
Cruelty, Bullying	3.27	2.84	2.81	3.43	2.59	3.41	1.72	2.61	2.97	3.96	1.60	2.46	4.41	6.30	3.39	4.91
Quarrelsomeness	0.36	0.35	0.45	0.49	1.50	1.92	-0.85	1.12	1.69	1.99	-1.23	1.54	2.34	3.30	2.03	2.90
Tattling	-0.31	0.26	-3.41	3.55	-0.92	0.96	-2.41	2.65	-1.09	1.00	-3.24	3.41	4.11	5.71	3.29	4.45
Stubbornness, Contrariness	-1.25	1.33	-2.18	2.45	-1.16	1.61	-3.53	4.58	-1.36	1.60	-4.60	6.05	-0.33	0.48	0.04	0.05
Sullenness	-2.54	2.33	-2.61	2.78	-0.48	0.56	-3.30	4.29	-1.75	2.03	-3.74	4.68	2.19	3.22	1.15	1.69
Temper Tantrums	0.61	0.55	-0.36	0.40	0.98	1.14	-0.11	0.13	0.75	0.82	-2.31	2.92	1.06	1.31	0.18	0.23
Impudence, Rudeness	-0.95	0.96	-1.33	1.51	-1.30	1.78	-2.58	3.44	-0.71	0.87	-3.89	5.89	1.82	2.68	1.25	1.89
Selfishness	3.22	3.13	1.86	2.09	0.95	1.14	-0.13	0.18	1.08	1.21	-1.05	1.46	5.84	9.13	3.67	5.65
Domineering, Overbearing	1.50	1.30	0.78	0.82	1.25	1.54	0.73	0.85	0.92	1.06	-1.55	1.94	4.47	6.04	1.97	2.63
Shyness	1.41	1.41	0.14	0.15	3.25	4.33	-0.91	1.07	1.57	1.74	-1.57	1.76	1.92	2.74	0.09	0.13
Sensitiveness	-0.84	0.82	-1.05	1.25	0.56	0.71	-2.60	3.02	0.31	0.36	-4.29	5.23	1.90	2.84	-0.19	0.28
Unsocial, Withdrawing	1.61	1.66	2.64	2.93	2.14	2.49	0.09	0.11	2.51	2.89	-0.79	0.93	3.74	4.99	1.98	2.68
Overcritical of Others	-1.65	1.41	-2.71	2.82	-1.66	2.02	-3.39	4.13	-1.18	1.40	-5.49	7.42	2.99	4.27	1.03	1.41
Thoughtlessness	-2.17	1.97	-1.88	1.94	-0.08	0.10	-3.13	3.86	-1.14	1.24	-4.29	5.72	2.28	3.45	0.81	1.19
Inquisitiveness	-4.10	3.90	-3.51	3.73	-4.06	4.83	-4.67	5.49	-3.13	3.56	-5.86	7.51	0.99	1.43	0.19	2.84
Silliness	-3.70	3.25	-4.56	4.75	-5.58	6.34	-5.49	6.54	-4.96	5.11	-6.90	8.73	-1.15	1.55	-1.31	1.79
Unhappy, Depressed	5.83	5.72	6.48	7.28	5.02	5.02	3.79	3.79	4.83	4.78	2.60	2.65	5.68	6.04	4.51	4.85
Resentfulness	1.72	1.59	1.66	1.89	2.42	2.95	-0.03	0.04	2.86	3.29	0.39	0.49	4.06	5.56	2.29	3.23
Nervousness	2.97	2.94	2.38	2.36	4.08	4.53	0.30	0.34	3.17	3.37	0.96	1.13	4.90	6.53	4.02	5.58
Fearfulness	4.45	3.90	4.73	4.73	5.38	5.97	2.04	2.22	4.88	4.98	0.73	0.83	5.99	7.58	4.71	6.20
Enuresis (Wetting Self)													2.74	3.04	2.41	2.64
Dreaminess	-2.60	2.39	-3.19	3.36	-1.10	1.41	-2.08	2.63	-2.97	3.13	-5.17	5.94	-0.61	0.87	-1.49	2.13
Slovenly in Appearance	0.31	0.28	-1.69	1.71	-0.27	0.30	-3.75	4.74	-0.91	0.96	-5.28	6.68	3.37	4.68	0.72	0.96
Suspiciousness	1.80	1.70	0.19	0.20	1.20	1.45	-1.27	1.55	0.00	0.00	-2.40	2.82	3.71	5.08	1.38	1.87
Physical Coward	-1.34	1.22	0.98	1.00	0.60	0.63	-1.35	1.59	-1.56	1.73	-2.28	2.92	3.35	4.59	0.96	1.25
Easily Discouraged	0.34	0.31	1.77	1.97	1.40	1.75	-0.17	0.21	0.72	0.85	-1.25	1.49	5.21	7.24	2.66	3.50
Suggestible	0.02	0.02	-0.07	0.07	1.30	1.44	-1.74	2.02	-0.94	1.04	-2.67	3.14	1.82	2.22	-0.08	0.10

may be studied by consulting Table XXV in the same manner. For such information concerning mental hygienists versus all the other groups, Table XXI is again referred to, and should be consulted by locating, first of all, the caption, "Mental Hygienists (Wickman's data)," which will be found in the upper left-hand corner of the page.

In order to facilitate assimilation of the data, all of the fifty* items have been classified into three self-explanatory categories and therein ranked in accordance with the relative standing of importance assigned to them by the ratings of three groups, namely, mothers, fathers, and Teachers 1b. As follows:

CHART I

REPRESENTATIONS OF POSITIONS IN RATING FOR ALL THE ITEMS

CATEGORY I – SCHOOL ITEMS

	Mothers	*Fathers*	*Teachers 1b*
Seriously regarded	Cheating Truancy Destroying school materials Lack of interest in work Obscene notes	Cheating Truancy Destroying school materials Suggestible Obscene notes Lack of interest in work	Truancy Obscene notes Cheating Suggestible Destroying school materials Lack of interest in work Disorderliness Carelessness in work
High-moderately regarded in seriousness	Suggestible Disorderliness Carelessness in work Inattention	Carelessness in work Disorderliness Tardiness	Inattention
Least seriously regarded	Tardiness Restlessness Silliness Dreaminess Interrupting Whispering	Inattention Silliness Restlessness Dreaminess Interrupting Whispering	Tardiness Dreaminess Silliness Restlessness Interrupting Whispering

* Additively there will seemingly be fifty-one items involved, since the characteristic suggestible appeared to be eminently suitable for inclusion in two categories.

CATEGORY II – MENTAL HYGIENE ITEMS

	Mothers	Fathers	Teachers 1b
Seriously regarded	Unhappy Nervousness Fearfulness Easily discouraged Unsocial	Unhappy Easily discouraged Fearfulness Suggestible Nervousness Unsocial	Suggestible Unhappy
High-moderately regarded in seriousness	Suggestible Suspiciousness	Easily discouraged Unsocial Nervousness Suspiciousness Fearfulness	
Least seriously regarded	Shyness Sensitiveness	Suspiciousness Shyness Sensitiveness	Sensitiveness Shyness

CATEGORY III – HOME-SCHOOL ITEMS

	Mothers	Fathers	Teachers 1b
Seriously regarded	Stealing Cruelty Heterosexual activity Untruthfulness Unreliableness Selfishness Impertinence Domineering Masturbation Resentfulness Quarrelsomeness Disobedience Impudence Temper tantrums	Stealing Heterosexual activity Cruelty Unreliableness Untruthfulness Masturbation Impertinence Selfishness Impudence Physical coward Quarrelsomeness Disobedience Temper tantrums	Stealing Heterosexual activity Cruelty Untruthfulness Impertinence Unreliableness Disobedience Masturbation Temper tantrums Domineering Impudence Selfishness Quarrelsomeness Laziness Resentfulness
High-moderately regarded in seriousness	Laziness Enuresis Physical coward Slovenly Smoking Overcritical	Resentfulness Slovenly Enuresis Domineering Laziness Overcritical Sullenness Profanity	Slovenly Physical coward Profanity Enuresis Overcritical

CATEGORY III—*Continued*

	Sullenness	Smoking	Sullenness
	Tattling	Tattling	Stubbornness
Least	Profanity	Thoughtlessness	Thoughtlessness
seriously	Thoughtlessness	Stubbornness	Inquisitiveness
regarded	Stubbornness	Inquisitiveness	Tattling
	Inquisitiveness	Imaginative lying	Imaginative lying
	Imaginative lying		Smoking

Comparing, respectively, the mothers and the fathers with Teachers 1*b*, this latter group of ratings again being utilized in order to present the minimal and thus bring out in boldest relief the differences which may manifest themselves in the views of the parents as against those of the teachers, we find that there is a difference of opinion about some selected salient traits, while for most of them the general over-all agreement between parents and teachers prevails. These traits are graphically set forth below:

CHART II

REPRESENTATION OF POSITIONS IN RATING FOR SELECTED SALIENT ITEMS

MENTAL HYGIENE ITEMS

	Mothers	*Fathers*	*Teachers 1b*
Seriously regarded	Unhappy	Unhappy	Unhappy
	Nervousness	Easily discouraged	
	Fearfulness	Fearfulness	
	Easily discouraged	Nervousness	
High-moderately regarded in seriousness	Suspiciousness		Easily discouraged
			Nervousness
			Suspiciousness
			Fearfulness
Least Seriously regarded		Suspiciousness	

HOME-SCHOOL ITEMS

	Mothers	*Fathers*	*Teachers 1b*
Seriously regarded	Stealing	Stealing	Stealing
	Untruthfulness	Unreliableness	Untruthfulness
	Unreliableness	Untruthfulness	Impertinence
	Impertinence	Impertinence	Unreliableness
	Disobedience	Disobedience	Disobedience
	Temper tantrums	Temper tantrums	Temper tantrums

SCHOOL ITEMS

	Mothers	Fathers	Teachers 1b
Seriously regarded	Cheating Truancy Destroying school materials Lack of interest in work	Cheating Truancy Destroying school materials Suggestible Lack of interest in work	Truancy Cheating Suggestible Destroying school materials Lack of interest in work Disorderliness Carelessness in work
High-moderately regarded in seriousness	Suggestible Disorderliness Carelessness in work	Carelessness in work Disorderliness	

The following descriptive observations about these salient items may be of interest. From a mental hygiene standpoint, unhappiness, nervousness, fearfulness, easily discouraged, and suspiciousness are considered to be among the most distinctive characteristics symptomatic of maladjustment.

Unhappiness was regarded very gravely by the mothers, the item of unhappy being assigned to 7th place by their ratings; considerably higher than those of the teachers which placed it into 18th rank. Nervousness was also considered among the most serious items by the mothers (13th place); as contrasted with the teachers' comparative discounting of its importance (29th place). Again, fearfulness was ranked as being among the most undesirable traits by the mothers (14th place); an even greater deviation than so far obtaining between these two groups was evidenced by the teachers' lower estimation of its importance, which relegated it to a position among the least serious items, with a rank-order of 34. Easily discouraged also showed considerable, but less, difference in viewpoint; so that the judgments of the mothers assigned it to a position in the upper third of ranked undesirability (17th in position), while the teachers rated it as high-moderate, with a rank-order of 26 in the scale of importance.

Suspiciousness which, in clinical application, may have a significance over and beyond its usual manifestations and expression, both from an interpretative and behavioral standpoint, was regarded as comparatively unimportant both by mothers and teachers (although clinicians had given it as their specialists' judgment that suspiciousness ranks second in seriousness). Mothers evaluated this item as 32d, while teachers rated it as 31st, in importance.

Fathers, with their following rankings: unhappy, 7; nervousness, 18; fearfulness, 16; easily discouraged, 11; and suspiciousness, 36; generally agreed quite closely with the views of the mothers on these various items, with very minor variations. So that they put the same high evaluation on being unhappy that mothers did; somewhat less stress on the importance of nervousness, fearfulness, and suspiciousness, but somewhat more stress on being easily discouraged. The small discrepancy in outlook manifested for this lattermost trait perhaps reflects the masculine view, the need to accomplish missions or tasks once they are embarked upon; it is possible, but in consideration of the other items, rather unlikely, that the fathers here regarded easily discouraged from the mental hygiene viewpoint. In like fashion, rating suspiciousness with even more casualness than mothers did, may show the masculine viewpoint again: their attenuated estimate of its undesirability indicating the obverse possibility that there could be a certain advantageousness in possessing a certain amount of the quality of suspiciousness, taken in the context of intelligent skepticism and wariness.

On another axis—items of behavioral adjustment—are located the traits which bespeak the type of objective, overt, aggressive conduct that school teachers regard as being the most serious in nature. But as we scan the complete list and note some of the various types of conduct that may be subsumed under this category, we observe that such characteristics as stealing, untruthfulness, unreliableness, impertinence, disobedience, and temper tantrums are also traits that would evidence themselves with equal undesirability when displayed in behavior at home. Hence the general finding revealed by the tables, that *these items are all among the upper half of rank-order listings for seriousness* and that *their positions represent the judgment of the parents as well as of the teachers,* does not lend any surprise evidence to the general picture. For classification purposes, these have been termed "home-school" items by the writer.

However, the problems of truancy, cheating, lack of interest in work, carelessness in work, suggestible (insofar as suggestibility pertains to incitement to mischievous behavior, as contrasted with the mental hygienists' emphasis on the more subjective aspect), destroying school materials, and disorderliness—remembering, also, that each of these as well as suggestible has its objective and subjective possibilities, the emphasis on the former aspect keeping them within this prescribed designation—may be considered, more restrictively, as schoolroom violations and the like, and have therefore been termed "school items."

Of these, truancy, cheating, and destroying school materials evoked a marked amount of disapproval from the parents as well as from the teachers; indeed, *they received a somewhat higher ranking by the parents than had been assigned to them by the teachers.*

Lack of interest in work and carelessness in work show some amusing differences. Whereas mothers agree closely with teachers that lack of interest in work is quite undesirable, the fathers' rating, giving it the equivalency of 24th in rank, practically reduces that item to only high-moderate status. But so far as carelessness in work is concerned: although neither parent considers it of more than high-moderate significance (the teachers rating it a little higher, placing it 22d in rank-order), the fathers regard carelessness in work as being of somewhat more relative importance than do the mothers. Put somewhat differently, this would mean that fathers do not put the same emphasis on lack of interest in work that mothers express; but that, once a task is attempted, they would be more insistent on its being carried out properly than would be true of the latter.

REFERENCES

1. WICKMAN, E. K. *Children's Behavior and Teachers' Attitudes.* New York: The Commonwealth Fund, 1928. P. 119.

CHAPTER IX

Whose Influence, if Any, Is Strongest with the Child?

And so, some 57 correlations and 3572 sigmas and 2570 critical ratios later, the crux of the investigation is reached. Much farther back, the investigator had been led to believe that one could head this chapter in a clear-cut fashion, but analysis of the data shows that the ideal of the typical researcher, of biddable figures ranking themselves into neat columns, ranged against opposite and sometimes apposite sides of definite and groundbreaking (along with record-breaking and perhaps backbreaking) conclusions, will not altogether be realized in this case. Format must yield to facts. But this loss to hypothesis is, in essence, happily a hypothetical one, since what is lost in dogmatic values shows a more than compensating gain in human values. For we find that there is nowhere the divergency of influence on the child that had been anticipated; that, on the contrary, the parents and teachers have shown themselves, by and large, to be truly protagonists and not the antagonists that newspaper accounts and other Dresden tempests would have us sporadically believe them to be.

Before proceeding, it may be well to present our "shorthand" information again, in the form of the correlations existing between children and their teachers; and adding those of children as against parents:

	Teachers 1a	Teachers 1b	Fathers	Mothers
Boys 5A	.760	.661	.625	.583
Girls 5A	.655	.589	.542	.542
Boys 7A	.728	.653	.630	.613
Girls 7A	.750	.707	.711	.671
Boys 8B	.719	.762	.752	.689
Girls 8B	.705	.693	.632	.584

In her comprehensive "Child Development," Elizabeth B. Hurlock cites a study made by Hartshorne, May, and Shuttleworth in 1930, concerning scores involving moral knowledge. In that instance, the correlation coefficient obtained for parents versus children was .55, and that between Sunday-school teachers and children was .35. Upon the basis of these, and other, background facts, Hurlock suggests that parents have greater influence on the child, so far as moral judgments are concerned, than do his teachers.[1] Our correlation figures, generally high but predominantly showing considerably smaller differences between the coefficients for parents (fathers, mothers) and children, as against those for teachers and children, would not allow any similarly general inference to be drawn for our groups.

In any event, whether pro or con, as has been noted elsewhere in this study, a more detailed transcription is often more revealing than the rather cryptic stenography of statistics; and, accordingly, a rather detailed and elaborated study of our findings forms the substance of this present chapter. Analysis and grouping of our data makes allowable their categorization into three large, and four small, groups; along with a fourfold chart to make their representation more graphic.

Group I is self-explanatory: "s" following some of the items merely signifies "school" items, whereas the symbol "H-s" following the others means that those are "home-school" problems. Close study of our rank-order list, Table XIV, makes it possible for us to conclude that for thirteen of the forty-six characteristics listed for adults and children, both the Teachers 1a and the parents hold very close views as to their undesirability or *lack* of seriousness. These thirteen items thus embodied in Group I are not ranked in order of their seriousness, but were selected as one scanned the columns from top to bottom; for comparisons here were made on a *crosswise* basis, the object being to ascertain the standing of *each* item according to the positions given to it by the respective groups. Selection was made on a rather arbitrary but practical basis, so that where there was a difference of four or less in placement between the Teachers 1a and both of the parents, it was considered that the groups were virtually of one mind in ranking. Any larger differences, between either or both parents as against Teachers 1a, were listed in one of the other two large groups or in the smaller groups, IV, V, VI, or VII.

It may also be explained that, although the teachers rated rather differently when filling out the two schedules, the assumption is made here that their actual practicing procedures with the children had, for the most part, been more in accordance with the views expressed in Schedule 1a than with those expressed in Schedule 1b.

GROUP I

INSTANCES WHEREIN FATHERS, MOTHERS, AND TEACHERS 1a AGREE VERY CLOSELY IN RATED SERIOUSNESS OF ITEMS

(So closely that children's selective predilections would, for the most part, be unascertainable)

Tardiness s*
Truancy s
Destroying school materials s
Untruthfulness H-s†
Imaginative lying H-s
Stealing H-s
Smoking H-s

Whispering s
Careless in work s
Unreliableness H-s
Cruelty H-s
Quarrelsomeness H-s
Inquisitiveness H-s

Group I thus contains thirteen items which show marked closeness in ratings for seriousness (or lack of it) by fathers, mothers, and Teachers 1a. Five of these items lend themselves to the title of "school" items, inasmuch as tardiness, truancy, destroying school materials, whispering, and carelessness in work would, in emphasis, be more of a problem in the classroom than anywhere else. Regarding three of these traits with concern, the teacher can rest confident that her views are staunchly backed by the disapproval of the parents at home.

Similarly, characteristics such as untruthfulness, stealing, cruelty, and quarrelsomeness are problems in the home as well as in the school, and may conveniently be called "home-school" items. Parental training of the young in social mores and eschewal of behavior traits expressed in these items, is reinforced by the similarity of attitude that teachers of school children also hold in reference to them.

In fact, of such efficacy is this combination of effort, that it results in the younger members of society sometimes holding them in even greater disapproval than their elders do, as witness their sterner judgments regarding destroying school materials, smoking, and inquisitiveness, in comparison with those expressed by their elders.

One is always aware of the mental reservation that while, in many cases, teachers and parents may act more severely than they *think*, children would more consistently think more severely than they *act*

---

* The symbol *s* stands for school item; that is, an item which is more apt to be of consequence in the schoolroom milieu than anywhere else.

† The symbol *H-s* stands for home-school item: that is, an item which is apt to be considered important in the home as well as in the school; and sometimes to an even greater degree.

(no doubt!). What we can most reliably learn from their ratings is what children think they *ought* to think, the goals we set for them, and the standards that they are in turn setting up for themselves. And if the usual description of an ideal is: to set up a code of standards towards which we strive, but at which we do not always arrive, we may say that the conduct of children will bear out the assumption that they are, indeed, striving towards ideals. While in this state of ethical flux, it is not surprising therefore that the following formulation by Piaget is, partially at least, applicable to our children subjects also "—an attitude of respect for the letter of the law and of waywardness in its application."[2]

Any discrepant attitudes that they may harbor inwardly are thus often revealed by their conduct; which in its turn offers a substantive basis upon which to estimate how short they are of attaining their expressed goals, whether it be happiness or school activities, and a point of reference from which to start looking for the causes of such divergencies.

The next tabulated grouping, Group II, follows below:

GROUP II

INSTANCES WHEREIN THE CHILDREN AGREE MORE CLOSELY WITH TEACHERS 1a THAN THEY DO WITH PARENTS, IN RATED SERIOUSNESS OF ITEMS

—*	Cheating s	(All groups)
+†	Profanity H-s	(All groups)
+	Interrupting s	(Five groups)
+	Disobedience H-s	(Five groups)
—	Shyness MH‡	(All groups)
—	Unsocial MH	(All groups)
+	Silliness s	(Five groups)
—	Unhappy MH	(All groups)
—	Nervousness MH	(Five groups)
—	Fearfulness MH	(All groups)
—	Suspiciousness MH	(Four groups)
+	Impudence H-s	(All groups)

* The minus sign (—) preceding an item means that this trait is viewed less seriously by the Teachers 1a than it is by the parents.

† The plus sign (+) before an item means that this characteristic is viewed more seriously by the Teachers 1a than it is by the parents.

‡ The symbol *MH* after an item indicates that it belongs heavily in the domain of mental health and correspondingly in that of mental hygiene.

Here we see that for twelve traits the children appear to be influenced more by the views of the teachers, whether it be of more serious rating or less serious rating than given by the parents, than they are by those of the parents. Perhaps, it would be more accurate to state for the time being, that the children demonstrate a closer agreement with the teachers' ratings, leaving the question of ascendancy temporarily in abeyance.

As the footnotes to the table indicate, the items preceded by a plus sign are those which were given a higher evaluation of importance by the teachers than by the parents; similarly, those preceded by a minus sign are traits which were regarded less seriously by the teachers than by the parents. Here, too, the symbol "s" stands for "school" item; the symbol "H-s" for "home-school" item; while the symbol "MH" signifies a mental hygiene type of trait.

Thus, there are five characteristics to which the children as well as the teachers attribute a greater degree of importance than do the parents: profanity, interrupting, disobedience, silliness, and impudence. Interrupting and silliness are apt to be felt more as a factor in school progress than elsewhere, while profanity, disobedience, and impudence would be troublesome at home as well as in the school milieu. In all five instances the teacher tends to reinforce home training in her attitudes; and the children evidence an even closer consonance with the opinions of their teachers than they do with the parents' rated judgments.

Cheating, preceded by a minus sign, presents a double anomaly. For not only do the 1a teachers rate it as being 12th in importance, compared with the parents' enhanced ranking to 3d and 4th place, but the children also give it this lower standing in seriousness. The fact that the same teachers raise its status as a problem to 8th in placement when filling out Schedule 1b suggests that cheating, in this context, represents to the teachers a mental hygiene item; or, at least, one having less direct bearing on the child's immediate welfare than on his composite welfare, and one that offers more of a threat to the child's total personality than to his personality and welfare as a pupil. Nor would the parents' theoretical approach be apt to express itself very forcibly or frequently in practical training, for cheating, in its pure manifestations, would hardly rise as an issue in the home situation except under most exceptional circumstances.

All of the others in this group (II) are mental hygiene items, associated primarily with personal happiness, such as the qualities of fearfulness, nervousness, etc.; and here, too, the children regard them, along with their teachers, as being of less consequence than the parents do. However, these latter evaluations do not exemplify a positive result of training or example by the teachers or parents, but rather, a lack of stress, a negative composed of two parts: That is, unlike other expressions of behavior which are discouraged upon manifestation, the child rarely if ever is admonished against being unhappy, adjured not to be nervous; these are not in the realm of forbidden expressions of feeling or conduct. Nor can the parents, notwithstanding their greater concern about these traits, stress this concern through discipline, or in any other manner which customarily attempts to impress upon a child a positive code of conduct. In addition to this negative, there is the second one, that the child himself is not yet prepared to fill these deficiencies. As will be discussed more fully later, the child at that age usually lacks sufficient retrospective and introspective faculties to wholly realize that he is unhappy, for example; and if he does, is insufficiently articulate to channelize these emotions to full awareness and express them through the medium of language. These two negatives do not lead to positive evaluation on the part of the child.

The fact that parents do, however, perhaps more in practice than precept, attempt to modify such characteristics when manifested in their children, has evidently not activated the reality of these traits in the minds of the children to the point of emotional tangibility; and especially when overweighed by the galvanizing properties confronting them in the form of the more vital and charged misbehavior items such as disobedience, etc., which possess so much more imminence and immediacy than the relatively dormant and quiescent properties of personal unhappiness.

The third classification demonstrates that the more serious view taken by parents than by Teachers 1a for *plus* items such as tattling, selfishness, overcritical, thoughtlessness, easily discouraged, sullenness, and slovenly has the concurrence of the children. Excluding selfishness, which is perhaps of less special pertinency in school activities than it is at home and elsewhere, and easily discouraged, which is related more strongly to mental hygiene, these items—the remaining ones thus being tattling, overcritical, thoughtlessness, sullenness, and slovenly—may perhaps be most properly considered as home-school problems, showing equal possibilities of disturbance for home and school. Here, then, the teachers' more lenient views are more than reinforced in the direction of less leniency, by the parents; and, one

GROUP III

INSTANCES WHEREIN THE CHILDREN AGREE MORE CLOSELY WITH PARENTS THAN THEY DO WITH TEACHERS 1a, IN RATED SERIOUSNESS OF ITEMS

−*	Disorderliness s	(Four groups)
−	Restlessness s	(Four groups)
−	Inattention s	(Four groups)
−	Laziness H-s	(Five groups)
−	Impertinence H-s	(Five groups)
+†	Tattling H-s	(All groups)
−	Stubborness H-s	(All groups)
−	Temper tantrums H-s	(All groups)
+	Selfishness H-s	(All groups except 5A boys)
+	Overcritical H-s	(All groups)
+	Thoughtlessness, forgetting H-s	(Five groups)
+	Easily discouraged MH	(Three groups, and two more closest with mothers alone)
−	Dreaminess s	(Four groups)
+	Sullenness H-s	(Five groups)
+	Slovenly H-s	(Five groups)

may say, the parent is supported by the child in the direction of less clemency in rating.

A numerically superior aggregation of items in this Group III are the ones prefaced with a *minus* sign. Of these eight items, disorderliness, restlessness, inattention, and dreaminess may most practically be labelled *school* items; and in these instances a contrary trend has been established: where the parents tend to regard these schoolroom dis-

---

* The minus sign (−) preceding an item means that this trait is viewed with less seriousness by the parents than it is by the Teachers 1a.

† The plus sign (+) before an item means that this characteristic is viewed with more seriousness by the parents than it is by the Teachers 1a.

orders less severely than the teachers do, and the children evidence similar lenity. These four traits are not only looked upon with less concern by the parents but, further, do not represent home situations to any prevalent degree. Hence, one may deduce that the teachers' more disapproving attitudes are not strengthened by those of the parents, and may partly account for the failure of these more severe views to impose themselves upon the pupils to a commensurate degree.

An analogous situation obtains when the four negatively marked *home-school* items of this group are studied:

Laziness is also looked upon with greater tolerance by the parents (although with seriousness) than by the teachers. Further, for the urban child home life ordinarily does not lend as much exigency to the accomplishment of home chores as it does to the performance of school tasks, and hence, here too, the attitudes evinced by the teachers are not reinforced sufficiently to influence the child in like direction.

Impertinence offers an enigma. There is undoubtedly a great deal of background support from the parents as to its relative undesirability, along with the obviousness of the fact that a behavior characteristic rated fourth in importance by teachers would be impressed upon the child as being objectionable in nature. There is the possibility, however, that this in a sense represents direct dealing with adults, where the results are directly known, and where the greater fear of temporarily unrealized and unknown punishment does not work upon the imagination. With the relatively milder punitive measures employed by modern parents for this offense, the child realizes that transgressions of this type do not create consequences that are very fearful. With this experience behind him, there is less tendency to reflect the teachers' more drastic judgments.

Stubbornness again shows that the influence of the parents is stronger, in the sense that lack of severity, manifested by the parents' lower ranking for stubbornness (38th and 37th as contrasted with the teachers' 19th in placement), expresses itself in the child's marked nonacceptance of the sterner outlook.

Temper tantrums. There, also, the parents' views contained a lesser amount of disapprobation than did those of the teachers. Also, temper tantrums are not typically a schoolroom problem nor one associated with children of school age; hence, the teachers' theoretical principles in this regard are rarely translated into concrete remedial measures. The ratings of the pupils here, too, may thus be possibly traced to a lesser degree of severity of parental attitude, even if this type of situation is no longer commonly prone to arise.

In brief summary then:

Children's Judgments Agree More Closely with the Lower Rankings
Made by the Parents

Disorderliness ⎫		Laziness ⎫	
Restlessness	*School items*	Impertinence	*Home-school items*
Inattention		Stubbornness	
Dreaminess ⎭		Temper tantrums ⎭	

(Less apt to arise as home problems)   (Disciplines presumably follow the more
                                              tolerant attitudes of the parents)

This rather detailed analysis allows us to conclude that when the two groups of adults do not reinforce each other's views and disciplines, those of the parents may well be the prevailing ones, even if in a negative and indirect fashion; and that all eight items bear the greater impress of the parents' influence than of the teachers', forasmuch as we find that the child's evaluations reflect the parental discounting of importance.

Chart III represents these arrangements graphically: The solid circle (●) next to an item indicates those cases wherein the children agreed more closely with the opinions expressed by the group mentioned first in a given caption than they did with the other. The unfilled circle (○) indicates those instances wherein the children agreed more closely with the other group of raters than they did with the one captioned as the first group in the heading of the pertinent quadrant.

This chart embodies the findings for the twelve items of Group II, along with the fifteen traits of Group III, and does so in two ways, so that fifty-four items appear to be listed instead of twenty-seven. In the upper left-hand quadrant (labelled A) are listed the problems that are regarded with more seriousness by teachers than they are by the parents. Below these items, on the same left-hand side (B) and suitably headed, are listed the traits that are looked upon with less seriousness by the teachers than they are by the parents. Similar comparisons are made on the right-hand side of this chart, upper and lower quadrants.

This mirror-image type of presentation was devised to offer a more detailed and vivid account than would be possible if only the upper sections were portrayed. However, *should this duality be found confusing, the lower two sections of this chart may be safely ignored.* A few examples, for usage, may not come amiss: In the upper left-hand section, the first item listed is *profanity*. And this has a *filled* circle at its right. This means that profanity is deemed to be of greater undesirability by the teachers than by the parents; and that the ratings of the children are in greater consonance with the judgments made by the teachers than they are with those made by the parents. Five items lower down we find *disorderliness,* listed in the same left-hand column, followed by a *blank* circle. This signifies that disorderliness evokes more disapproval from the teachers than from the parents, but that the children do not give it a similar rating, tending rather to be in accord with parents in this regard. The lower *right-hand* section, entitled, "Characteristics Viewed Less Seriously by the Parents than by Teachers 1*a,*" in reverse presentation bears the interpretation that the item *disorderliness* is assigned less importance by the parents than by Teachers 1*a,* and that the children agree more closely with the parents than with this other group. Inasmuch as this chart only relates children to parents and to Teachers 1*a,* this double representation may seem redundant, but it does have certain advantages in furnishing some types of information more directly and pointedly.

One possible pitfall in logic born of statistics may be mentioned here in connection with some of the items: Even a temporary lapse in recognition that any consonance in rating between children and parents (or teachers) was based upon completely independent procedures of judging, or any assumption that such agreement is necessarily of a positive nature, would lead to the fallacious premise that such concordance is based upon the adult's actually inculcating such sentiments into the children's attitudes—and thus to absurdities. If such were the case, one might reach the conclusion that teachers deliberately trained children to cheat and that parents designedly instructed their children in the fine art of being inattentive, say, in the classroom.

The most we can say, in so many of these above cases, is that the influence of the parents (sometimes that of the teachers) is insufficient or was not exerted to the extent requisite to make possible the deterring effects which were potentially available in such exercise. However, this observation is not meant as unfavorable criticism. It would be a shattering thing if children had constantly impressed upon them from all sides the undesirability of so many as forty-six items. And modern psychology is coming, to a greater extent than ever before, to view a little salutary neglect as a very desirable factor in child training.

CHART III

RELATIONSHIP OF CHILDREN'S ATTITUDES TO:

(A)
CHARACTERISTICS VIEWED MORE SERIOUSLY BY TEACHERS 1a THAN BY THE PARENTS*

Profanity ●	Disorderliness ○
Interrupting ●	Restlessness ○
Disobedience ●	Inattention ○
Silliness ●	Laziness ○
Impudence ●	Impertinence ○
	Stubbornness ○
	Temper tantrums ○
	Dreaminess ○

(B)
CHARACTERISTICS VIEWED LESS SERIOUSLY BY TEACHERS 1a THAN BY THE PARENTS*

Cheating ●	Tattling ○
Shyness ●	Selfishness ○
Unsocial ●	Overcritical ○
Unhappy ●	Thoughtlessness ○
Nervousness ●	Easily discouraged ○
Fearfulness ●	Sullenness ○
Suspiciousness ●	Slovenly ○

* ● Indicates items wherein the children agree more closely with the group mentioned first in the above caption than they do with the other.

○ Indicates items wherein the children agree *less* closely with the group mentioned first in the above caption than they do with the other.

On the other hand, there are considerations which militate against point-by-point identity or even closer approximation of ratings, as between the children and either or both of these adult groups:

1. Among the most important is the discrepancy often existing between the adult's inward evaluation of an undesirable trait and the outward measures taken to correct its manifestations when the need arises. Slovenliness, say, is not looked upon with a *great* amount of disquiet by mothers or teachers as being inimical to the child's welfare (fathers, interestingly, rank it somewhat higher than either mothers or teachers do), yet considerable pressure is put upon the child in this regard, especially by mothers and teachers; and it is this outward action that is impressed upon the child rather than the private views

CHART III — *Continued*

(C)
CHARACTERISTICS VIEWED MORE SERIOUSLY BY
THE PARENTS THAN BY TEACHERS 1a*

Tattling ●	Cheating ○
Selfishness ●	Shyness ○
Overcritical ●	Unsocial ○
Thoughtlessness ●	Unhappy ○
Easily discouraged ●	Nervousness ○
Sullenness ●	Fearfulness ○
Slovenly ●	Suspiciousness ○

(D)
CHARACTERISTICS VIEWED LESS SERIOUSLY BY
THE PARENTS THAN BY TEACHERS 1a*

Disorderliness ●	Profanity ○
Restlessness ●	Interrupting ○
Inattention ●	Disobedience ○
Laziness ●	Silliness ○
Impertinence ●	Impudence ○
Stubbornness ●	
Temper tantrums ●	
Dreaminess ●	

---

* ● Indicates items wherein the children agree more closely with the group mentioned first in the above caption than they do with the other.

○ Indicates items wherein the children agree *less* closely with the group mentioned first in the above caption than they do with the other.

of either group of adults. So much so, that most of the children rate it as being quite high in importance. Smoking and profanity are two other typical items which may bring forth even more energetic measures of correction.

2. Relationship of ratings and nondisciplinal nature of charactertistic. To give a rather extreme example: Although being unhappy is regarded gravely by parents, the question of punitory correction would not enter; which, as has already been suggested, may be one of the reasons for the children's preponderantly low evaluation of it.

3. A third factor is the range *within* separate groups of the numerical values yielded by the ratings and the variability *between* the various groups. We find among the children, for instance, that girls in

grade 8B have an enhanced platform of judging, so that the item they consider least serious has an average of 8.63, while the most important one has the estimation of 18.94. These figures contrast strikingly with those of Teachers 1a, whose highest and lowest averages are 14.09 and 5.66, respectively.

Groups IV, V, VI, and VII show interesting differences of opinion between the fathers and mothers for the balance of our forty-six items, six in number, and are fairly self-explanatory.

Although no effective categorization along the lines already laid out would be possible here, it is clear that the oldest and youngest groups of boys agree with the fathers in evaluated seriousness of being a physical coward, but that all the girls, and 7A boys, concur with the mothers and Teachers 1a in taking a much less weighty view of this item. As to sensitiveness, the gentler attitude espoused by the mothers is eschewed by the children in favor of the more tough-minded one, which diminishes its importance, evidenced by the fathers and Teachers 1a.

Suggestible produces an almost equally divided cleavage: the two youngest groups of children, and 7A boys, agree with the mothers' lesser views of its significance; two groups of children, the 7A girls and the 8B boys, show alignment with the fathers and Teachers 1a in ascribing to it greater importance; while the 8B girls are to be found midway between the mothers on the one hand, and the fathers and Teachers 1a on the other.

GROUP IV

INSTANCES WHEREIN THE CHILDREN AGREE MORE CLOSELY WITH THE FATHERS, AS AGAINST TEACHERS 1a AND THE MOTHERS, IN RATED SERIOUSNESS OF ITEMS

— * Lack of interest in work s   (Four out of the six groups of children)

+† Physical coward H-s   (Only the 5A and 8B boys)

---

* The minus sign (—) before an item denotes that this characteristic is viewed with less seriousness by the fathers than it is by Teachers 1a and the mothers.

† The plus sign (+) before an item denotes that this characteristic is viewed with more seriousness by the fathers than it is by Teachers 1a and the mothers.

GROUP V

INSTANCES WHEREIN THE CHILDREN AGREE MORE CLOSELY WITH THE FATHERS AND TEACHERS 1a, AS AGAINST THE MOTHERS, IN RATED SERIOUSNESS OF ITEMS

−* Sensitiveness MH	(All groups)
− Resentfulness H-s	(All groups)
+† Suggestible s-MH‡	(The 7A girls and 8B boys do so; while the 8B girls occupy a position equidistant between the fathers and Teachers 1a, and the mothers)

GROUP VI

AN INSTANCE WHEREIN THE CHILDREN AGREE MORE CLOSELY WITH THE MOTHERS, AS AGAINST TEACHERS 1a AND THE FATHERS, IN RATED SERIOUSNESS OF ITEMS

−§ Suggestible s-MH	(Three groups — the 5A boys and 5A girls and 7A boys — do so; while the 8B girls occupy a position equidistant between the mothers on one hand, and the fathers and Teachers 1a on the other)

---

* The minus sign (−) before an item indicates that this trait is viewed less seriously by the fathers and Teachers 1a than it is by the mothers.

† The plus sign (+) before an item indicates that this trait is viewed more seriously by the fathers and Teachers 1a than it is by the mothers.

‡ The symbol *s-MH* stands for school-and-mental hygiene item: that is, a trait which is apt to be of consequence in the school but may also be of equal or greater importance in the domain of mental hygiene.

§ The symbol of the minus sign (−) before an item denotes that this trait is viewed with less seriousness by the mothers, as against Teachers 1a and the fathers.

GROUP VII

INSTANCES WHEREIN THE CHILDREN AGREE MORE CLOSELY WITH THE MOTHERS AND TEACHERS 1a, AS AGAINST THE FATHERS, IN RATED SERIOUSNESS OF ITEMS

−* Physical coward H-s

(The 7A boys, and all the girls, agree with the mothers and Teachers 1a in their discounting of its importance)

++ Domineering H-s

(Five groups of the children)

Further summary and discussion of these findings follow in Chapter X, entitled, "The Anthropomorphism of Statistics."

---

* The symbol of the minus sign (−) before an item signifies that this characteristic is viewed less seriously by the mothers and Teachers 1a than it is by the fathers.

† The symbol of the plus sign (+) before an item denotes that this trait is viewed with more seriousness by the mothers and Teachers 1a than it is by the fathers.

REFERENCES

1. HURLOCK, ELIZABETH B. *Child Development*. 1st edition. New York: McGraw-Hill Book Company, Inc., 1942. P. 335.

2. PIAGET, JEAN. *The Moral Judgment of the Child*. London: Kegan Paul, Trench, Trubner & Co. Ltd., 1932. P. 399.

CHAPTER X

The Anthropomorphism of Statistics

Define and Allot

In this chapter we convert our statistical values into human values. Throughout this report there have been intimations of the basic culmination of this study, references to allot and define, which, in more complete form, may be expanded into the formula: define functions and allot responsibility and duties.

From time to time, among other developments there will be a journalistic flurry lending color to a frequent misconception that there exists some basic conflict between parents on the one hand, and the Board of Education and teachers on the other; now augmented by the experimentally reached conclusion of Wickman's, already cited, that there is also a divergence of views between teachers and mental hygienists. If so, these divergences must exist primarily in the realm of methods and not of final objectives. This position is lent further credence by this present investigator's experiences in obtaining the necessary cooperation for this research: From the appropriate officials at the Board of Education, participating principals of schools, teachers, parents—down to the youngest of the 5A pupils—the mentioning of a project to aid in the understanding of children and thereby to help them, with few exceptions acted as an open-sesame, evoking heartening, enthusiastic participation and earnest consideration.

Rather than a conflict of authority, of interest, there is evidently a situation reproduced here which is in some ways analogous to that existing in the case of the Constitution of the United States in its relationship to the laws of the several States. Not conflict but rather a twilight zone exists, a form of no man's land of unmarked authority. (Inasmuch as teachers have been more involved in this sphere than any other groups, perhaps one could more pertinently say, a no woman's land.)

So far as these characteristics of children, particularly these personal subjective ones, are concerned, as a community we have not analyzed their implications clearly enough nor have we decided who should deal with them, *in toto* or selectively. When problems of children (which are not necessarily children's problems!) come up, there is a rankling of irritation because there is an awareness of responsibility, a realization that someone is remiss somewhere; but not knowing how, and in our anxiety to help the child, the natural tendency is to blame one another; not knowing where to place the blame, we spread it all over, as is the habit with diffuse emotions. And so it has come about that the school, which no longer whips the boy has now, in many instances, become the whipping boy!

Even Caroline Zachry, inclined to bear rather heavily upon the obligations of the school for the development of the adolescents in its charge,[1] has subscribed to the wider concept that the community, through the parent as a citizen and through other representatives, must also make its contributions to the betterment of the educative processes and to the milieu in which they take place.[2] While Mrs. Hugh Bradford (former president, National Congress of Parents and Teachers, Sacramento, California), widens the role of the community in widening its definition, so that community becomes synonymous with the environment itself,[3] with the "nurture" that works upon the "nature" of the child.

Other studies and, it is to be hoped, to some extent this present one also, should offer a common meeting place within the communality of common seeking—a vantage point from which to appraise ourselves as we apprise ourselves of the conceptions of other groups. Among other things we can apply ourselves to is the study of these considerations: What is the basic attitude of each of the groups?—for not only teachers and mental hygienists have them. Once we learn that, each of us can more readily modify his to any necessary extent and join with the others, or present his viewpoint with the hope of modifying that of the other individuals or other groups to any degree that the situation appears to make desirable. This basic attitude divides itself into several facets:

Towards the child. One important advantage of filling out a questionnaire of this type is the undoubted fact that the child no longer appears as an undifferentiated entity, but as an omnitude which is composed of characteristics; and these rating sheets identify and bring out the separate traits of which the personality and character of children are composed. To analyze and integrate these characteristics and personality traits is the joint responsibility of teachers *and* parents *and* mental hygienists *and* the community at large. But to what extent shall the separate groups conjoin, where do their duties begin and their privileges end?—that is the basic conception underlying the formula of define and allot. And once we proceed to analyze the characteristics of the child, instead of thinking of him in monolithic terms, the function of each of the varying segments of the population will also outline itself more specifically, instead of merely revealing itself in general fashion.

Studying of the questionnaires may disclose to us that we have unconsciously and unwittingly, perhaps, imposed upon the school systems vague requirements for vaguely outlined treatment of children, but demanded precision in execution; whereas, the reverse of the process should be instituted: greater precision in our knowledge of what is really involved, and more understanding and leniency in how the schools are to fulfill these requirements. In other words, what do we really consider *the function of the school* to be? By dredging up and expressing our thoughts on the undesirable behavior manifestations of children, our question would be: Who, really, should remedy conditions such as nervousness in a child, unhappiness in a child—is that the function of the school or is teaching alone the function of a school? Concomitantly, *what is the function of the home?* Beyond the basic ones of affording food and shelter, to what extent should the home provide the moral training and satisfy the spiritual needs of the growing young individual?

In this manner, instead of relegating all responsibility to one sphere or another, accompanied by a general and vaguely amorphous notion of child training and education, the various phases of the development of children should become more clear in our minds; and, with that, the individual responsibility of each group for specific aspects of each phase, and their joint responsibility for overlapping phases, should become palpable.

This conjointness of interest and enterprise has the power to create strength out of weakness, and to fill in lacunae of knowledge with the insight gathered from the other groups. The parent who is inclined to let Nature take care of unfavorable traits manifested in his child's behavior, such as fearfulness or shyness, and wait for him to "outgrow" them, may find the standpoint of the mental hygienist of incalculable value in the direction of a more appropriate understanding of the meaning of such characteristics. Not that this is to imply that wherever such characteristics are evidenced, the parent is hastily to seek psychotherapeutic aid. To some extent and in most cases, the parent may be justified in expecting the situation to correct itself. Karen Horney has gone so far as to express the view that even in the case of established psychoneuroses, Life itself may act as a therapeutic agent. The present writer does not necessarily subscribe to, or against, this judgment, except to point out that indications which *may* be symptomatic of deeper, and stubborn, disturbances are not necessarily so whenever they appear. But, even with this more relaxed attitude, the meaning of the expressions can, obviously, be more readily understood when expert knowledge is invoked and diagnostically applied.

Then, on the other hand, the teachers who stress schoolroom problems, etc.—the less important ones from a mental hygiene viewpoint— may have their opinions bolstered by the parents; *who, according to our data, as groups of fathers or mothers or both, have for the somewhat greater part of items taken an intervenient stand between the mental hygienists and the teachers, with a leaning towards the viewpoint of the teachers in the majority of these instances.* That is, the parents, being in a strategic position to stress both mental hygiene items and schoolroom items, can fortify the standpoint of the teachers when the sentiments of these two groups coincide; and can likewise support the viewpoint of the mental hygienists to the extent, or beyond, that mental hygienists and parents are in accord. Thus, instead of these differences of attitudes acting as sterile divisive forces, here too there is the opportunity of productive coalition, of the pooling of assets.

But before pooling these resources, it may be wise to analyze further, even if superficially, to ascertain what these resources are. More specifically, to find out wherein we disagree, and wherein we agree.

Wherein Do We Disagree: How Ideal Is the Mental Hygiene Ideal?

It is with respect to characteristics that we have called schoolroom, overt and aggressive types of problems, as against those we have named mental hygiene items, that there seems to be the greatest disparity in outlook between the mental hygienist and the teacher, traits which we have alternatively suggested might be called objective as against subjective in nature. In some respects, however, there is an identity of meaning even between these two seemingly antagonistic sets of items which could be invoked to coördinate the efforts of mental hygienists and teachers, if this connaturality were only realized more fully and the principles derived from it were applied more freely. Unfortunately, however, separating the objective phase from the subjective phase may be as difficult of success as separating the outer coating of a cell into outer and inner layers: for the external side may be only the outward coating of the inner side—while the inner, in its turn, may be only the inverted manifestation of the environment as it confronts the inner reality of the personality. In the actual expression of this duality, the outer misconduct may be the extroverting of inner experiences of maladjustment. Restlessness, for instance, may be only the outward phase of a felt but inarticulate inner tension; selfishness, may be the outward reflection of an internally mirrored frustration which expresses itself in the aggressiveness of self-seeking. Analogously, there exist opposing counterparts to these manifestations.

Not only do these conditions of duality exist but, in the presence of psychic unease, a definite emotional set may arise: as a sore thumb draws attention to itself and is not easily ignored, so may a wounded or smarting ego become the focal point of an individual's concern, an absorption which is oftentimes glibly and too callously termed ego-centrism—a centripetal force creating a vortex into the orbit of which all manner of assorted behavior characteristics may repair.

By the very nature of their calling, by the very fact that the success or failure of their work is systematized and schematized into cold statistical facts—so many passed, so many failed, so many conformed to an outward code of assimilation of facts—teachers, in more ways than one, are bound only to view these assorted bits of behavior without having the time or opportunity to conceive of the vacuum in the child which attracts them.

Mental hygienists, on the other hand, do—at least, theoretically—stress the source of this centripetal force, this vacuum, the psychic status of the personality, and regard the unfavorable outer and outward behavior evincements as something the wind merely blew in, to continue our figure of speech. And also, in contradistinction to teachers, in clinical work results are sometimes measured over periods of months or years, perhaps even never, any improvement being accepted gratefully. There is no set schedule, no standards of achievement that have to be met at stipulated times. Consequently, the mental hygienists could, in any event, afford to take the long-range view which is what is so often called the theoretical one, the view that *may* come to practical fulfillment in the future, but is not necessarily measured by the touchstone of concrete results.

The position of the mental hygienists has been used as the point of reference throughout this investigation, in parallel to Wickman's study, as representing the most advanced view, rightly or wrongly. Or, at least, as a fixed point from which to make comparisons and contrasts (whether or not necessarily odious ones). For the patent tendency is towards approximation of the mental hygiene viewpoint, rather than any other course—that is, the mental hygienist's outlook is not apt to reconvert to the tenor of the teachers' ratings; even if slowly, that of parents, children, and teachers is going to follow his lead. So, from the standpoint of physical locus, if nothing else, we may label the mental hygienist's post the most advanced one.

But, although we consider this mental hygiene attitude as being the most *advanced,* we do not commit ourselves as to whether it is necessarily the *best* one. For one thing, we could hardly be so unscientific as to make moral judgments about moral judgments. For another, as John Dewey and other philosophers have repeatedly pointed out, morals and conduct are relative, depending largely upon time and place. Even the words *morals* and *ethics* carry the functional connotation: what is best for a given community from the practical consideration of *outcome* of certain behaviors.

From this pragmatic point of assessment, then, we may ask: (1) How ideal is the mental hygiene ideal? (2) Is it more feasible as a theoretical concept than as an actual rule of conduct for practical existence? (3) Is it the ideal for pedagogy, also?—To what extent is this universal, fixed standard—which, like the ethical ideal "is felt to be *ideal*—that is, *not actual*"[4]—to what extent is this applicable to the teaching profession with its measured and measurable objectives? Instead of pleading extenuating circumstances when teachers do not altogether reach this standard, the assertion may conceivably be made that this nonattainment does not necessarily connote that they are falling short of this goal, but rather, that they are keeping their distance from it.

In barely touching upon answers to these suggestive questions, we find, for example, that the mental hygienists rate stealing as being thirteenth in importance, compared with all the other groups rating it as being the most serious problem. In a sense, one may say that the clinicians' ranking shows a skew distribution of judgment. One must wonder how universal such an evaluation could be in practical application in a practical world; if we would want teachers and parents—even children—to consider stealing so comparatively low in undesirability, and as a yardstick of conduct.

Some of the grave considerations that arise in this connection are: What about the value judgments, as against clinical judgments, that the child will find confronting him in the outside, adult world? To what extent will he receive the intimate, special consideration which mental hygienists are professionally bound to give? The child will have to meet and measure up to objective standards; the appraisements of the world will not be endowed with the professional leniency that mental hygienists evidence.

Education is one type of preparation for this adult world. In a sense, his first contact with school marks the first time that the outer world impinges upon the life of the child and, to some extent, then, it is desirable that the teacher act towards him as the world will later. Rather graphically, in his "L'Éducation Morale," Durkheim expresses this thought by stating that "in the same way that the priest is the interpreter of God, he [the teacher] is the interpreter of the great moral ideas of his time and of his country."[5] It behooves us, then, to study her attitudes with the proper realization that the child must acquire this as well as other types of training and discipline, along with the expression of self.

Morally, ethically, behaviorally, the child is an unformed being full of potentialities, whose realization must involve the twofold process of reaction from within in response to stimuli from without and, correspondingly, reactions to the outside which are prompted by motivations from within. Thus, the development of these potentialities is dependent not only on what lies internally, but on what forces are applied externally. To be sure sometimes the former, especially in the case of boys, may be quite invisible, not to say occult. A simple example would be the boy sitting in a classroom who seemingly has no outward incitement to deliver himself of a spitball, yet whose inner-acting goad of boredom, or frustration, or the need to show off, may inspire this juvenile form of jet propulsion. This, in turn, evoking dynamic energy from the external world, crystallized here in the person of the teacher, will determine his future conduct so far as that particular type of internal stimulus is concerned.

More broadly, and eventually, these externally imposed standards form one of the bases for inner codes of conduct. For, and analogous to the manner in which we translate our inner beliefs into exteriorized behavior, criteria originating from without are introjected by the personality and become absorbed as its own.

Not only is it the teacher's task thus to render her share of assistance in training children to meet the requirements imposed by social standards and by society's standards, but, additionally and primarily, to educate children in the fullest and yet more narrow sense of the word. School examinations are not given to ascertain who is the most cheerful or best adjusted child in the classroom; nor are promotions of children (or teachers!) based on the felicity of the teacher's record in inducing such a happy state of affairs. In fact, there may often be a negative—although temporary—correlation between the cheerfulness of the child and the state of his marks. In this connection, the following would seem to be very pertinent: Expressing his opinion that in speaking of the authority of the schoolmaster, he by no means states that it is necessary to conduct a class like a regiment, Durkheim continues on, however, with the enunciation that, "all is not play in life; it is necessary that the child prepare himself for effort, pain, and, consequently, it would be disastrous to allow him to believe that all can be done as though it were a game."[6]

It is a simple matter to indulge in a policy of great liberality with children from a safely prognostic standpoint and distance—while the teacher has to struggle with what may be termed the facts of life. These facts she deals with and which deal so hard with her. Anyone wishing to pursue this point in more detail would be well rewarded by reading a doctoral thesis which has the rather revealing title of "A Psychological Study of the Annoyances or Irritations of Teachers"[7] (both of which terms are synonymous, according to the author). Despite the potential levity which might seem to lurk in the title, this study is a soberly factual account and interpretation of the problems that beset the teacher.

Using as her subjects teachers of all levels, and including irritations arising both in school and out of school,[8] the investigator, Kathleen E. O'Malley, elicited a total of 1334 useable annoyances from them; to which the author then added 68 more, derived from the literature (Ossa upon Pelion!), for a total of 1402![9] Of this total of 1402 items, 75.7 per cent were representative of school irritations.[10]

But the contributions of the *elementary* school teachers, comprising 50.3 per cent of the 1334 items submitted,[11] accounted for 41.8 per cent of the irritations listed among the 1334 as arising in the school situation.[12] In other words, simple arithmetical computation would show then that 83.1 per cent of the irritations or annoyances submitted by the elementary school teachers to this grouping was attributed to the school milieu.

Further, there were thirteen types of school irritations listed "which were submitted with the greatest frequency"; of which, annoyances such as "Clerical work," "Physical environment," "Rules, Regulations, and Requirements (School)," formed part of a diversified grouping.[13]

From this briefly schematized summary of one phase of a very interesting investigation, one is adequately prepared for the author's conclusion upon analysis that pupils (male or female) are not even included among "the types of irritations which are most irritating."[14]

Thus, from the aspect of administration alone, when one realizes that, in droves, technically illiterate young individuals enter the schools, young minds which have only recently learned to speak and to understand, and that these children are developed into educated young men and young women, ready for trades, skilled occupations, professional training, universities—one appreciates the magnitude of the tasks assigned to and carried out by the school systems of the land.

The summarized import of these adductions is then that for these two specialists, teacher and mental hygienist, there is bound to be a difference not so much of view, perhaps, but of viewpoint, of emphasis. The mental hygienist not only occupies himself more fully with the theoretical aspects of childhood development than the teacher does, but he is also concerned with problems that define the maladjusted personality of the child, and with the treatment of characteristics such as shyness, unsociability, etc., that interfere with proper reorientation. The teacher is concerned with matters that affect his primary orientation, with his educational development and the correction of impedimental traits that interfere with this learning, such as cheating, creating of classroom disturbances, and the like. Put more succinctly, one may say that education is the function of the teacher, whereas re-education is the function of the mental hygienist.

All the foregoing may be said to represent the functional view, the functional approach in interpreting the teachers' interpretations.

However, the next problem is: Having fulfilled her major and primary duties satisfactorily all these years, how much further should she go? Also, how much further should we expect her to go without additional assistance? Or, rather, do we expect the teacher, like an actor in a Chinese company, to play too many roles?

To be sure a desideratum would be the major one that even though the teacher is not a practicing mental hygienist, that she be practicing mental hygiene, basically. For, obviously, the teaching and mental hygiene professions can best work efficiently when they act in reciprocity. Reverting back to our earlier example of the reversible equation, we may note again the effect that one trait of the child may have upon the other. So that the child who does poorly in arithmetic, say, may as a consequence be unhappy; while the child who is unhappy, for emotional reasons of one sort or another, may do very poorly in arithmetic: with the possibility of a compounding mechanism thereby being set up and entering in as a further factor. Additionally, it would be most estimable for teachers to possess an understanding of mental hygiene principles competent enough to discern when a child is evidencing a degree of maladjustment sufficient to require specialized or specialist's treatment. The advantages of a teacher's having a working knowledge of child psychology and children (the distinction is not necessarily always fortuitous) are, by now, too widely known and too widely discussed in the literature to require any further dissemination here.

But, the problem should be set in these terms: *that of increased duties and responsibilities for the school system, rather than an unreflecting indictment that its members have been remiss in their duties or that they have failed to achieve standards set forth.* If we wish to integrate these extra benefits and tasks into the school system, they must be planned—by the community, through its constituents of taxpayers, Board of Education, officials, parents, etc.—and one of the important considerations must be the existing and future capacities of the school as an institution to cope with these expanding responsibilities. Again, we must define and allot. The teacher cannot do all and be all. Indeed, even if teachers had wanted to be all, it would have been an impossible task to choose her role of doing all, with any assurance of having made the proper choice. About her ears have been beating the storms of theoretical speculations: progressive education contra traditionalism, introvert contra extrovert, the three R's contra rest, recuperation, and rehabilitation. Who shall guide her?

Culminating in the last four months of the year 1944, the ebb and flow of these considerations had set up a tidal wave in the progressive education movement, not unmindful of the criticism that retrogression might well masquerade under the guise of progression; and by that time other very important developments had also taken place.

Child psychology had reached into the preschool stage for its contributions, in the form of Gesell's evidential tokens that the child of eighteen months, despite all his peregrinations while on outings, develops a sense of insecurity [more likely, a recrudescence of it] so that he finds it enjoyable to be back in his walking leash.[15] Further, that in his sequence of development, the child of three is glad to seek the protection of the parent, after brief forays into independence.[16]

Not only in respect of the younger children but also in pertinence to adolescents, recognition was not lacking by then that in the upgrade to independence, there were little footholds of recurrent (but welcome!) retreat to parental standards and firmness.[17] And the motivating concept of permissiveness was yielding: more and more there was talk of children wanting a "structured relationship"—pedagogical-psychological-euphemistical nomenclature for old-fashioned words such as discipline and training.

And yet, and this present writer must interject a counterweight into the battle also, there exists danger that a strongly authoritarian system of training may bring about an equating of security with restraint. The feeling of being taken care of, even when primarily by prohibition, may give rise to a spurious feeling of protection and security. The consequences may be akin to those potential in M. C. Jones's classic experiment of reconditioning. In order to condition the child *away* from a strong fear of rabbits, the procedure of keeping the rabbit at a safe distance while the child was given appetizing food was decided upon.[18] However, unless three premises were sustained—that is, that the child be hungry, that the food be appetizing, that the rabbit be kept at a goodly distance—a conditioning in reverse, so to speak, would theoretically ensue. That is, instead of the food operating to aid the child in losing his fear of the rabbit, the opposite tendency would prevail; the result of this dominance phenomenon being that the child would now be afraid of the food! In similar fashion, the feeling of restraint may become the usurping surrogate for the feeling of security, to the consequent impairment of the individual's developmental pattern.

Literature had also long since entered the fray. Mr. Weller, Sr., modestly attributes the sterling qualities of his son to his paternal enlightenment, in the following fashion: "Wery glad it hear it, sir," replied the old man; "I took a good deal o' pains with his eddication, sir; let him run in the streets when he was wery young, and shift for his-self. It's the only way to make a boy sharp, sir."[19]

And the prototype of all progressive schools is presented by Mr. Squeer's establishment, employing Nicholas Nickleby, in which institution weeding of the garden, cleaning of windows, and currying of horses are some of the diversified activities included as part of the curriculum and deemed to be functionally related to classroom instruction.[20]

However, Mr. Squeer's "permissiveness" may have had a certain autogenetic quality educationallywise. For, approximately one hundred years later, the well-loved son of a well-esteemed professor at one of our great universities had chosen to spend an afternoon of his class time tending the furnace of his well-known secondary school. Doubtless, other authenticated cases can be cited, and at length. (Although, in fairness to progressive education, it must be added that this youngster later on achieved distinction of another variety as salutatorian at the exercises graduating him from this same above-mentioned university, despite or because of his progressive education.)

But matters reached a climax when the two Titans—considering their alternating effects in raising and calming our metaphorical wave, perhaps better said, the two Tritons—of the educational world set forth their views:

On the one hand, after a premonitory flash of lightning in 1942,[21]

Dr. Nicholas Murray Butler hurled a thunderbolt in an address delivered on September 27, 1944, on the occasion of the exercises opening Columbia University's 191st academic year. In his discourse, which bore the interesting title of "Men or Machines?" and the challenging subtitle of "The Reactionary Influence of So-called Progressive Education," President Butler asserted that the heritage of centuries of education and culture and civilization belongs of right to the oncoming generations; and that progressive education, "in its extreme form," would divest them of these rights and would put on their young and inexperienced shoulders the burden of starting anew.[22]

In rebuttal, were the responses of Dr. John Dewey pointing out the imperatives (rather said, the permissivenesses) of progressive education.[23]

Not only did the principles as well as the principals cross swords, but their seconds and followers crossed letters in a voluminous and spirited correspondence which involved various communication channels, with here and there a more neutral voice being heard.[24]

Inspired by the consummated transformation of the Progressive Education Association into the American Education Fellowship, a final touch was lent by the requiem offered in the form of a "Funeral Oration for the Late Progressive Educator"[25] over the body of the progressive education movement. Although there, too, the report of dissolution appeared to be greatly exaggerated.

With this storm beating about her ears, perhaps it is not invidious but rather meritorious that the teacher has maintained a fidelity of affirmation that education, too, is a definite and important phase of development and that if she, the teacher, does not stress it, who will! Progressive education journals may come and go but the syllabus goes —or worse, perhaps, stays—on forever. It is not to be wondered at then, and very likely less adventitious than advantageous, that the teachers as a group, paraphrase and cherish the old injunction: *Teacher, stick to your text.*

Wherein Do We Agree?

However, all these occasional tornadoes notwithstanding, here too there exists the great inner area of calm to be found in the very heart of tornadoes—a deep area of agreement between parents and teachers. Chart IV which, with one exception, deals with school and home-school items, gives evidence that despite disruptive forces at large, in practical administration teachers and parents maintain a bulwark of responsible and impressive cooperation, for the most part.

CHART IV

REPRESENTATION OF THE BACKGROUND OF DIFFERENTIAL INFLUENCE ON THE VIEWS OF CHILDREN

I—Items Wherein Parents and Teachers Agree Closely as to Seriousness (*and may be presumed to reinforce each other's discipline— or show equal tolerance*)*

School items	Home-school items
Tardiness	Untruthfulness
Truancy	Imaginative lying
Destroying school materials	Stealing
Whispering	Smoking
Carelessness in work	Unreliableness
	Cruelty
	Quarrelsomeness
	Inquisitiveness

II—Items Wherein Teachers Show More Influence (*augmenting parents' milder judgments*)

School items	Home-school items
Interrupting	Profanity
Silliness	

III—Items Wherein Parents Show More Influence (*augmenting teachers' milder judgments*)

Mental hygiene items	Home-school items
Easily discouraged	Tattling
	Selfishness
	Overcritical
	Thoughtlessness
	(forgetting)
	Sullenness
	Slovenly

IV—Items Which Both Groups Regard Seriously (*with reinforcement of each other's opinions*)

	Home-school items
	Disobedience
	Impudence

* All references to teachers, in this chart, are based upon data obtained from Teachers 1a.

CHART IV—*Continued*

V—Items Wherein Parents' Ratings Do Not Back Up Teachers' More
      Serious Views
            (*thereby producing a negative type of influence*)

School items	Home-school items
Disorderliness	Laziness
Restlessness	Impertinence
Inattention	Stubbornness
Dreaminess	Temper tantrums

VI—Items Which Both Groups Regard Seriously
      (*parents more so, but without tending to augment teachers'
      discipline*)

School items
Cheating

Thus we find for the first category of traits listed, that teachers
and parents are in close accord as to their seriousness, the rated positions for each of these items being four steps, or closer, in approximation of evaluated judgment. This group includes some of the most
important school items as well as some of the most important characteristics which play their part in the life of the child away from school.
For problems, then, such as truancy, destroying school materials,
stealing, cruelty, and quarrelsomeness, among others, we feel justified
in making the assumption that the influence of teachers and of the
parents on children is about equal, and that these two groups of adults
would reinforce each other's authority in the training of the child.

The second category indicates that for traits such as interrupting,
silliness, and profanity the attitudes of the children are more strongly
influenced by the teachers; and that, even though the parents regard
them with comparative lenity, this lesser degree of strictness would,
nevertheless, be augmented in practical administration by the teachers,
in accordance with the more serious views expressed by them.

The third category demonstrates that parents appear to exercise
more direction over their children in the items of tattling, overcritical,
thoughtlessness, selfishness, sullenness, and slovenly than is true of
teachers. And that, as in the above classification, but conversely, the
teachers' less severe evaluations are augmented in actual home training; the premise here also being that the parents' stricter attitudes,
as expressed in their ratings, make for firmer corrective measures.

The fourth category—disobedience and impudence: both home-school items and both regarded with considerable concern by the parents and the teachers—also shows the effects of this reciprocity of training on the attitudes of the children.

It is only upon coming to the fifth category that we fail to find this complementary reinforcement of training; for these characteristics there is a divergence of opinion between the teachers and parents as to relative undesirability. That is, so far as disorderliness, restlessness, inattention, dreaminess, laziness, impertinence, stubbornness, and temper tantrums are concerned, the parents take a milder stand as to the degree of their seriousness. And the incomplete strengthening of the opinions of the teachers is educed from the finding that the children, also, attribute less importance to these traits than the teachers do.

As has already been noted in the preceding chapter, an additional explanation for the first five items, and one perhaps representing more closely the core of the matter, may be that disorderliness, restlessness, inattention, dreaminess, and laziness are not representative of home situations to any material extent, and therefore the lack of complementary supportive procedures on the part of the parents may be as attributable to their attention not being engaged by them as to their more tolerant appraisement of such behavior.

The other three items, impertinence, stubbornness, and temper tantrums, which would play a part in home difficulties as well as in school, are evidently explainable primarily on the single basis also noted earlier: They are not treated by parents along the lines augured by the teachers' judgments because parents do not regard these traits as seriously as teachers do, and therefore do not exercise as much deterring control over them as the rated opinions of teachers would prescribe.

The sixth category consists only of the one item, cheating. Cheating, already termed an anomaly, viewed with more concern by the parents than by the teachers, also shows this lack of reinforcement on the part of the parents: our criterion being the children's lesser view of its importance as evinced by their close conformity with the teachers' ratings. Here, too, it may be presumed that this lack of augmentation is due primarily to the fact that cheating is not a situation which would normally or formally arise in the home environment, and hence does not become the object of stressed parental guidance.

But, on the whole, and for the majority of these essential items, *our chart illustrates that the views of parents and teachers do coincide to a sizable extent; and that in practical administration judgments are reinforced by both groups of adults to a very effective degree.*

Coming now to those we have called mental hygiene items, and having reference only to the more typical ones (for, in one sense, unreliableness, selfishness, domineering, and many others, could also be titled mental hygiene traits), we find that there is less correspondence of opinion between the parents and Teachers 1a. Of these nine problems—shyness, unsocial, unhappy, nervousness, fearfulness, suspiciousness, easily discouraged, suggestible, and sensitiveness—eight are regarded with less seriousness by the teachers than by the parents.

TABLE XXVI

RELATIVE RATINGS GIVEN TO SALIENT MENTAL HYGIENE ITEMS BY THE FATHERS, MOTHERS, AND TEACHERS°

	Fathers	Mothers	Teachers Schedule 1a	Teachers Schedule 1b
Shyness	37	39	44	39
Unsocial	19	21	26	25
Unhappy	6	6	16	15
Nervousness	16	12	24	26
Fearfulness	14	13	32	30
Suspiciousness	32	28	37	28
Easily discouraged	9	15	28	22.5
Suggestible	15	23	15	10
Sensitiveness	41	38	43	35

Sensitiveness is rated lower by both Teachers 1a and the fathers than by the mothers; while suggestible is considered more undesirable by these groups than by the mothers. Interpretation for this last characteristic, suggestibility, may at first blush be dubious for, as has already been noted, it does have its classroom counterpart of inducement to mischievous activity. But the rating given by teachers for this same item in Schedule 1b, wherein it was elevated in importance by five places, tends to support the belief that teachers were in the first instance also regarding it from the standpoint of mental hygiene and were assuredly doing so in Schedule 1b.

However, their evaluations of characteristics such as unhappy, unsocial, nervousness, and easily discouraged, although comparatively lower than those made by the parents, still do indicate a definite amount of concern on the part of the teachers; for all four are deemed by them to be among the twenty-eight most serious traits.

───────────────

° This table is based on Table XIV, for consistency; and seven items therein will therefore show some slight discrepancies in comparison with their appearance in "Arrangement One" (Chapter VI), which is based on Table VI.

Additionally, in judging these nine items for *Schedule 1b,* where conditions were set forth to make for comparability with the circumstances under which mental hygienists were asked to express their attitudes, the views of the teachers (except for one trait) more closely approximated or went beyond those of the parents; and, by the same token, came closer to those of the mental hygienists. As Table XXVI shows, all problems (with the exception of nervousness, for some unaccountable reason) were *appreciated* in importance by the teachers; the greatest shifts being made for suspiciousness and sensitiveness, which were raised from 37th to 28th place, and from 43d to 35th place, respectively. And we have also seen in a previous chapter that some of the school items were *lowered* in rank by the teachers, in the framework of this new conception of their role.

SUMMARY

Parents and Teachers Reinforce Each Other's Views:

School items
- Tardiness
- Truancy
- Destroying school materials
- Whispering
- Carelessness in work
- Interrupting
- Silliness

Mental hygiene items
- Easily discouraged

Home-school items
- Untruthfulness
- Imaginative lying
- Stealing
- Smoking
- Unreliableness
- Cruelty
- Quarrelsomeness
- Inquisitiveness
- Profanity
- Tattling
- Overcritical
- Thoughtlessness (forgetting)
- Selfishness
- Disobedience
- Impudence

Parents Do Not Appear to Reinforce Teachers' Views:

School items
- Disorderliness
- Restlessness
- Inattention
- Dreaminess
- Cheating

Home-school items
- Laziness
- Impertinence
- Stubbornness
- Temper tantrums

Parents Do Not Appear to Augment Teachers' Views:

Mental hygiene items
- Shyness   Nervousness
- Unsocial   Fearfulness
- Unhappy   Suspiciousness

From these concrete pieces of evidence we may hypothesize that in our problem of defining and allotting, the teacher will offer no obstacle; that, contrary to interpretation put forth, there is no uniquely emotional actuation behind her ratings which would have to be dealt with in mediative and premeditative fashion. Further, these results offer no evidence of any deeply rooted schism; nor do our findings attest that the teachers have any feeling of vested interest being vested in their opinions.

Rather, we may fairly conclude that the teachers, as a group, are flexible in their views and capable of and willing to cope with new responsibility; not only from our understanding of the functional standpoint already discussed but from the basis of their rated judgments. That, basically, their attitudes are intellectually conditioned and can successfully thus be approached.

Shall Parents Abdicate a Primary Responsibility?

This study, and many other discussions of relative responsibility, may present the appearance of severe crisis upon crisis developing in the movements of child education and training, but in reality may be very favorable signs, as was pointed out in the bulletin to parents. Oftentimes, under more enlightened circumstances, it is not the problems that increase but, rather, our *awareness* of the existence of the problems. And, indeed, sometimes to the extent that new ones are created or, the old ones at least seemingly, transplanted to areas where they had hitherto not played a very important part.

The controversy which took place in the fall of 1945 regarding racial tolerance, erupting on October 17,[26] is a case in point. Some sources severely criticized the school system for the presence of racial prejudice, angrily charging that the schools were at fault. In the noise and fury, this note was seemingly lost sight of: that the children assimilate their standards from their parents, from the community at large, for the most part; that the children reflect our views, they do not create them nor imbue us with them. Rather than issuance of such strictures on school systems, as though the children were the pacemakers, aided and abetted—or instigated—by the teachers, the more logical view would have recognized that the site for changes lies within the purview of higher sources.

Here too, though, the situation was not essentially one of an increasing racial friction but, instead, of a greater consciousness of the problem. The manifestations of racial intolerance were not markedly rising, only our sensitization, our intolerance of such intolerance. (It may be added parenthetically, however, that *if carried to excess,* this desire to force others to conform to standards arbitrarily set for them may in itself develop the vice of the very intolerance it seeks to correct.)

Germane to this general problem is the specialized question of: When and where is the true genesis of maladjustment in the child? From sources as far apart as Shaffer,[27] Gesell,[28] and Freud,[29] come persuasive evidence that the inception is to be looked for in the pre-school home environment of the child; that just as the maturation pattern of organic and behavioral growth of the individual has been established,[30,31] so in early childhood will have been laid down the germinating factors which will determine the evolution of his emotional potentialities.

Not only persuasive but essentially conclusive are the studies made during the war which offer startling corroboration of Freud's discoveries on this subject. One that deserves special commendation is the book entitled "Men Under Stress," of which the chief author is Roy R. Grinker.[32] This work on military psychiatry displays not only deep psychological insight but also (and perhaps to some extent because of) a quality comparatively rare, a deep feeling of compassion for the young men of whom and with whom it deals.

To put it briefly, one may state that, although latent possibilities are enhanced or ameliorated by environmental circumstances, rarely can the *inception* of mental or emotional disturbance be found in the classroom or in the school. This belongs primarily to the home. One may, as it were, catch measles in school but not basic conflicts! Even to summarize the types and number of emotional problems that may develop at home and then manifest themselves in school misconduct, openly or in disguised fashion, would be entirely beyond the scope and projected size of this study.

The manifold mainsprings and undercurrents of children's behavior whereby their conduct, so to speak, *repels* because it is trying to *attract,* are overshadowed only by the manner in which their emotions are translated into seeming opposites behaviorally. Wickman has discussed at length and given a highly developed and valuable presentation of withdrawing tendencies and aggressive tendencies, their ramifications, evolvement, and the like. The present writer wishes to go even further and enunciate that aggressive traits and withdrawing traits may have not only the same psychological meaning, as Wickman suggests, *but even the same psychological identity;* that they can be different and differing forms and mutations of the same reaction, according to what circumstances bring forth and allow expression of; and that which alternate form of expression emerges in response to the underlying turmoil and unease depends on a multiplicity of factors surrounding and inherent in the child.

The structure and extent of such expression can be briefly exemplified. One may introject the aggressive desire and by the alchemy of mind it becomes a recessive, withdrawing trait. But this mechanism may show great deviousness and complexity. Aggression, undischarged, may not only cause withdrawing traits but actually become introverted so that it is *felt* as depression, unhappiness, shyness, or a combination of all three. Then, there may be such transformation into various types of recessive, retiring traits which are not *felt* as such, but more likely are only manifested in behavior. Uriah Heep would be a good example. To use an ultimate and more complicated instance: In some cases homicidal tendencies may thus be restrained and inverted into suicidal tendencies. The utmost in aggressiveness has turned inward on itself and has been converted into the utmost of withdrawment. This concatenation of unhappy events is paced by an emotional gamut which forms a descending order from pure external aggression to total self-immolation.

Conversely, and in milder illustration, if the child desires affection and recognition, and sarcasm is meted out instead, the reaction to this affront may very well be impertinence or the like. He has been hurt, and here the aggressive trait is really one of inner retreat, turned inside out.

One may generalize the foregoing into the formula that what is *aggressive* may express itself in *recessionary* fashion and what is *recessionary* may express itself in *aggressive* fashion. And further, aggressive traits may become introverted and assimilated by the individual's personality and *experienced* as withdrawing traits; while extroversion of withdrawing traits may cause them to be *experienced* as outgoing ones, in analogous manner. These phenomena, this present writer should like to term the *mutation of emotions* and, considering the infinite variety-potential, may be seen as existing within the scope of incalculable permutations.

However, to delve any deeper into these fields of depth psychology would lead us too far astray from the purpose of this investigation. These analyses of emotional possibilities have been offered primarily to furnish inklings of the complexities of the problem, of the need to know what we are doing when we attempt to regulate the well-springs of the child's personality, lest we quell them; and to put in a warning note against turning the schoolroom into a mental hygiene clinic for psychotherapeutic training, a result which would lie within the implications of remedial suggestions offered now and again.

This realization of the complexity and delicacy of the factors involved, and of the developmental phases, would seem to emphasize that the duty and the capacity are lodged primarily in the home; and that the school system could reasonably be expected to bear only an adjunct and supplementary responsibility to a process already instituted rather than a basic one for its inculcation.

That enlightened parenthood shares these views and expresses them with eloquence has been attested to during the years. Indeed, it underwrites them with the asseveration that not only has the home its specified responsibility for moral education but the further one of transforming its principles into sincere practice. To quote Mrs. A. H. Reeve (former president, National Congress of Parents and Teachers, Philadelphia), who is demonstrably representative of this forward-looking category: "For the morality which is preached and not practiced is as sounding brass in the sensitive ears of the child."[33]

* * * * *

And so this study has developed these phases of the general problem, like many of the others dealt with, to a minimum degree; its purposiveness truly confined to suggestiveness, in order to maintain the balance of its investigatory scope and conclusions, and to avoid expatiation of any phase which might be of magnitude sufficient to distract from its main intention: To determine, compare, and analyze attitudes on the part of the major protagonists—teachers, parents, and children; to determine experimentally and statistically whether they are protagonists or antagonists; to offer definitions without venturing to be definitive; to present these factual findings into the pooled resources of the community, with the hope that—even in small measure, perhaps—this analysis will help lead to synthesis.

REFERENCES

1. ZACHRY, CAROLINE B. *Emotion and Conduct in Adolescence.* New York: Appleton-Century-Crofts, Inc., 1940. Pp. 231-32, 238-40, 243-45.

2. *Ibid.,* pp. 415, 419-20.

3. BRADFORD, MRS. HUGH. "Interesting the Community in Character Building," the *National Education Association,* LXX (June 25-July 1, 1932), 396-97.

4. BALDWIN, JAMES MARK. *Genetic Theory of Reality.* New York: Knickerbocker Press, 1915. P. 103.

5. DURKHEIM, ÉMILE. *L'Éducation Morale.* Paris: Librairie Félix Alcan, 1925. P. 177.

6. *Ibid.,* p. 183.

7. O'MALLEY, KATHLEEN E. "A Psychological Study of the Annoyances or Irritations of Teachers." Unpublished Ph.D. dissertation, School of Education, New York University, 1935.

8. *Ibid.,* p. 2.

9. *Ibid.,* pp. 23-24.

10. *Ibid.,* p. 29.

11. *Ibid.,* p. 50.

12. *Ibid.,* p. 51.

13. *Ibid.,* pp. 31-33.

14. *Ibid.,* p. 134.

15. GESELL, ARNOLD, *et al. The First Five Years of Life.* 4th edition. New York: Harper, 1940. P. 258.

16. *Ibid.,* p. 46.

17. ZACHRY, *op. cit.,* pp. 308-10, 312, 345.

18. MURPHY, GARDNER, MURPHY, LOIS BARCLAY, and NEWCOMB, THEODORE M. *Experimental Social Psychology.* New York: Harper, 1937 (revised). P. 166.

19. DICKENS, CHARLES. *The Posthumous Papers of the Pickwick Club.* Vol. I. New York: Thomas Y. Crowell & Co., n.d. P. 300.

20. DICKENS, CHARLES. *The Life and Adventures of Nicholas Nickleby.* Vol. I. New York: Thomas Y. Crowell & Co., n.d. Pp. 100-101.

21. Columbia University Bulletin of Information. *Report of the President of Columbia University for 1942.* New York: Columbia University Press, 1943. Pp. 39-40.

22. BUTLER, NICHOLAS MURRAY. "Men or Machines?", *Vital Speeches of the Day,* X (October 1, 1944), 755-56.
    Also reported in:
    The New York Times, September 28, 1944, p. 21.

23. *Ibid.,* October 20, 1944, p. 32.

24. The participants were represented in the following publications, among others:
    WARREN, CONSTANCE to the *New York Times,* October 4, 1944, p. 18.
    McNELLIE, ESTELLE, *ibid.*
    "Sticks and Stones," *Progressive Education,* XXII (November, 1944), 3, 18, 20.

MEIKLEJOHN, ALEXANDER. "A Reply to John Dewey," *Fortune*, XXXI (January, 1945), 207-8, 210, 212, 214, 217, 219.

BAGLEY, WILLIAM C. Editorial, *School and Society*, LX (November 4, 1944), 292.

The New York Times, editorial, October 20, 1944, p. 18.

25. PRATT, KARL C. "Funeral Oration for the Late Progressive Educator," *School and Society*, LX (July 29, 1944), 76-77.

26. A running account of the controversy may be partially found in the following:

New York Herald Tribune, editorial, October 20, 1945.
Ibid., October 23, 1945.
New York Sun, October 27, 1945. (Letters to the Editor.)
New York Herald Tribune, November 9, 1945.
Ibid., November 17, 1945.
Ibid., November 18, 1945. (Two references.)

27. SHAFFER, LAURANCE FREDERIC. *The Psychology of Adjustment*. Edited by Leonard Carmichael. Boston: Houghton Mifflin Company, 1936. Pp. 206-7, 217-18, 246-48, 362-81.

28. GESELL, *op. cit.*, pp. 314-15.

29. FREUD, SIGMUND. *Gesammelte Schriften*. Erster Band. Leipzig: Internationaler Psychoanalytischer Verlag, 1925. Pp. 416-18, 458-59, 364-65, 367-70, are some of the references for this primary principle.

30. STONE, CALVIN P. "The Factor of Maturation." In *Handbook of General Experimental Psychology*. Worcester, Mass.: Clark University Press, 1934. Pp. 352-54, 361.

31. LASHLEY, K. S. "Nervous Mechanisms in Learning." *Ibid.*, pp. 457, 460-61.

32. GRINKER, ROY R., and SPIEGEL, JOHN P. *Men Under Stress*. Philadelphia: Blakiston, 1945. Pp. 42, 60-64, 129, 236-40, 247-48, 292-93, 303, 316-19, 366-67.

33. REEVE, MRS. A. H. "The Parent's Responsibility for Moral Education," the *National Education Association*, LXIII (June 28-July 3, 1925), 135-38.

Appendix A

List of Schedules

Schedule 1a. This schedule was distributed to 130 public school teachers, constituting the full faculties of five elementary schools in the City of New York, during the academic year of 1944-45. To make for strict comparability, this schedule and the instructions pertaining to it were identical with Schedule B-4 which, during the course of his investigation, had been devised by E. K. Wickman and administered to 511 teachers in the year 1927. (The slip appended to the instruction sheet in this present investigation was issued, among other reasons, to serve as a check upon the time actually spent by the teachers on their rating procedures; but none exceeded the maximum time period of twenty minutes which had been specified.)

Schedule 1b. One week after Schedule 1a had been filled out, this schedule was presented to the same teachers for their evaluatory consideration. To ensure proper testing of theoretical concepts this schedule was, designedly so, an exact reproduction of Wickman's Schedule B-5 which, as part of his study, had been utilized in 1926-27 to obtain the ratings from thirty mental hygienists. And the instructions accompanying Schedule 1b were also identical with those issued in the earlier investigation.

Schedule 2. This was utilized in eliciting the views of parents, and was submitted to 460 fathers and mothers in 1945. The behavior items and the captions were kept the same as those of Schedule B-5, but the instructions were devised by the present investigator to present a modified and different approach, in conformity with the requirements occasioned by this group of raters.

Schedule 3. This was administered in the academic year of 1944-45 to more than 406 boys and girls attending grades 5A, 7A, and 8B in a number of public schools in New York City. It had also been filled out by children in grade 4B, but their responses had to be discarded. This schedule, unlike the three for the adults, contained forty-six instead of fifty items, due to the necessity of four deletions. The instructions were simplified and in other ways prepared by the present investigator for appropriate guidance of children.

SCHEDULE 1a

1. In case you cannot finish in the expected twenty minutes, take as much extra time as you may require.

But please state the total number of minutes utilized, on the first page of the rating sheets, top left.

2. All data will be considered confidential; no individual's ratings will be reported upon as such. Please put all material back in accompanying envelope, and seal.

SCHEDULE 1a

Explanation. Behavior problems of children have recently become a subject for systematic and objective study. It is essential to secure reliable information on the causes and effects of behavior disorders of children. One of the first requirements in securing this body of knowledge is to ascertain the comparative seriousness of various behavior problems as they affect the welfare of children and society. Teachers, who are constantly meeting these problems, have a fund of information on the subject, much of which has never been accurately tabulated. In order to secure some of this information you are asked to cooperate in spending twenty minutes in filling out this questionnaire.

A list of behavior problems has been tabulated on the attached sheets. The list was obtained by a previous questionnaire to school teachers in which they were asked to report on the kinds of undesirable behavior they had encountered in their teaching experiences.

You are requested to rate each of these behavior items according to the degree of seriousness of the particular behavior for any child. In other words, how undesirable is it for any child to manifest the behavior described in this list of problems? To what extent does it make him a difficult child?

Your ratings will be made by marking on a "scale of seriousness" provided for this purpose. A line has been drawn to the right of each behavior item. Each line has four divisional points coinciding with captions at the top of the page to denote the degree of difficulty (or seriousness) caused by such behavior in any child.

Directions

1.   First read the list of behavior items on the two sheets.

2.   Then answer the questions of the degree of seriousness and undesirability of each behavior item when manifested by any child by making a vertical stroke, like this (/) at any point on the line according to the captions at the top of the page.

3.   You may make your rating at *any point on the line.* You do not need to make it directly on any divisional point. If you think your rating falls somewhere between two divisional points, make your mark at the appropriate point just where you think it ought to go. This will permit you to distinguish finely in your ratings between the different behavior problems. The following examples will illustrate this.

How serious (or undesirable) is this behavior in *any* child?

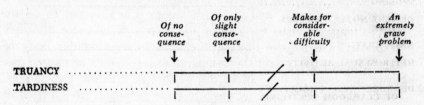

4.   *Avoid* rating how frequently the particular behavior occurs in children. Some of the items of behavior you may have observed to occur very seldom. Rate only *how undesirable it is for any child when it does occur.*

5.   Make your ratings as rapidly as possible.

6.   Please do not consult anyone in answering this questionnaire.

SCHEDULE 1a

How serious (or undesirable) is this behavior in *any* child?

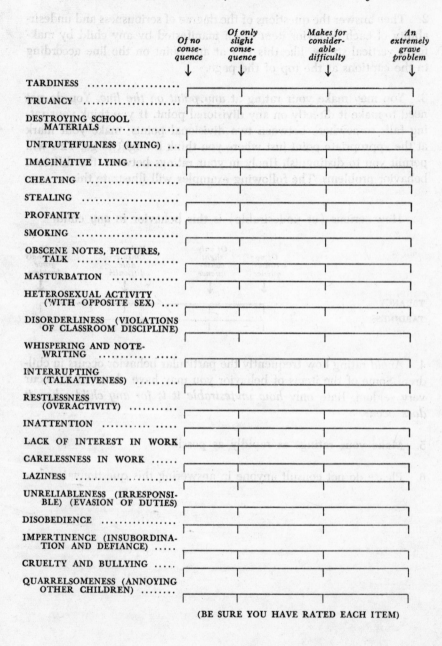

	Of no consequence ↓	Of only slight consequence ↓	Makes for considerable difficulty ↓	An extremely grave problem ↓
TARDINESS				
TRUANCY				
DESTROYING SCHOOL MATERIALS				
UNTRUTHFULNESS (LYING) ...				
IMAGINATIVE LYING				
CHEATING				
STEALING				
PROFANITY				
SMOKING				
OBSCENE NOTES, PICTURES, TALK				
MASTURBATION				
HETEROSEXUAL ACTIVITY (WITH OPPOSITE SEX)				
DISORDERLINESS (VIOLATIONS OF CLASSROOM DISCIPLINE)				
WHISPERING AND NOTE-WRITING				
INTERRUPTING (TALKATIVENESS)				
RESTLESSNESS (OVERACTIVITY)				
INATTENTION				
LACK OF INTEREST IN WORK				
CARELESSNESS IN WORK				
LAZINESS				
UNRELIABLENESS (IRRESPONSIBLE) (EVASION OF DUTIES)				
DISOBEDIENCE				
IMPERTINENCE (INSUBORDINATION AND DEFIANCE)				
CRUELTY AND BULLYING				
QUARRELSOMENESS (ANNOYING OTHER CHILDREN)				

(BE SURE YOU HAVE RATED EACH ITEM)

SCHEDULE 1a—Continued

	Of no consequence	Of only slight consequence	Makes for considerable difficulty	An extremely grave problem
	↓	↓	↓	↓
TATTLING				
STUBBORNNESS (CONTRARINESS)				
SULLENNESS (SULKINESS)				
TEMPER TANTRUMS				
IMPUDENCE, IMPOLITENESS, RUDENESS				
SELFISHNESS (AND UNSPORTS-MANSHIP)				
DOMINEERING, OVERBEARING, DICTATORIAL				
SHYNESS, BASHFULNESS				
SENSITIVENESS				
UNSOCIAL, WITHDRAWING				
OVERCRITICAL OF OTHERS ...				
THOUGHTLESSNESS (FORGETTING)				
INQUISITIVENESS, MEDDLESOMENESS				
SILLINESS, "SMARTNESS," ATTRACTING ATTENTION .				
UNHAPPY, DEPRESSED, DISSAT-ISFIED				
RESENTFUL				
NERVOUSNESS				
FEARFULNESS (EASILY FRIGHTENED)				
ENURESIS (WETTING SELF) ...				
DREAMINESS				
SLOVENLY IN PERSONAL AP-PEARANCE				
SUSPICIOUSNESS				
PHYSICAL COWARD				
EASILY DISCOURAGED				
SUGGESTIBLE (ACCEPTS SUG-GESTION OF ANYONE)				

(BE SURE YOU HAVE RATED EACH ITEM)

SCHEDULE 1*b*

Please note: This questionnaire is very much like the one filled out about a week ago, by you, but in this case the basis for evaluation of these behavior problems is somewhat different.

There Is No Time Limit for This Questionnaire
All data will be considered confidential. No individual's ratings will be reported upon as such. Please put all material back in accompanying envelope, and seal.

SCHEDULE 1*b* (Alternative One for Teachers)

Explanation. This questionnaire is designed to supplement a study that has been made in one elementary public school in Cleveland. The attached sheets contain a list of 50 behavior problems in children. This list was secured from two sources: (1) from a questionnaire to the teachers of this school in which they were asked to enumerate all behavior problems that they had encountered in their teaching experience; and (2) from the compiled list of problems as referred in the first 300 cases of the Cleveland Child Guidance Clinic Demonstration.

The immediate purpose of this questionnaire is to secure a professional evaluation of the seriousness or importance of these behavior traits as they may affect the future welfare of the child who shows such traits.

The graphic rating method has been employed for this investigation. To the right of each behavior item a line has been drawn. This line has four divisional points. These points correspond to captions at the top of the page. In order to rate the items according to the directions below, you will make a vertical stroke, like this /, at any point through the lines with reference to the captions at the top.

Directions — Read Carefully

1. First read all the 50 behavior items in order to distinguish carefully between them. Where more than one descriptive noun appears

for any item, it is designed thereby to qualify or explain more fully the particular behavior trait in question.

2.   Then rate each of these items according to this criterion: What is your professional opinion of the seriousness or importance of this behavior when occurring in any school child with regard to its future effect in limiting his or her happiness, success, and general welfare after leaving school and on entering adult social and industrial life. In other words, how much will the possession of this behavior trait by a child generally handicap him in his future adjustments as an adult.

3.   Observe these three limitations in your interpretations of the traits and your evaluations of them:

(a)   Any behavior trait when extended to the extreme may produce very serious difficulties in the child's future. Confine your ratings to the usual or general developments of these traits.

(b)   These traits may occur at one time or another in almost any child. In your ratings you will interpret the separate behavior trait as being manifested by the child just so frequently that it has become a *"problem."*

(c)   It is assumed that no modern psychiatric, psychological or visiting teacher efforts have been applied to these problems in the course of the child's development.

4.   Try to make this a professional opinion that is as free as possible from your own emotional reactions.

5.   You will make your ratings with reference to the answers established by the captions at the top of the page. However, you need *not* mark exactly *on* any divisional point corresponding to these captions; but you may rate at *any* point on the line whether on the divisional points or anywhere between them. This will permit you to distinguish very finely in your ratings between the different items.

6.   It is essential that you do not confer with *anyone* in answering this questionnaire.

SCHEDULE 1*b*

How serious (or undesirable) is this behavior in *any* child?

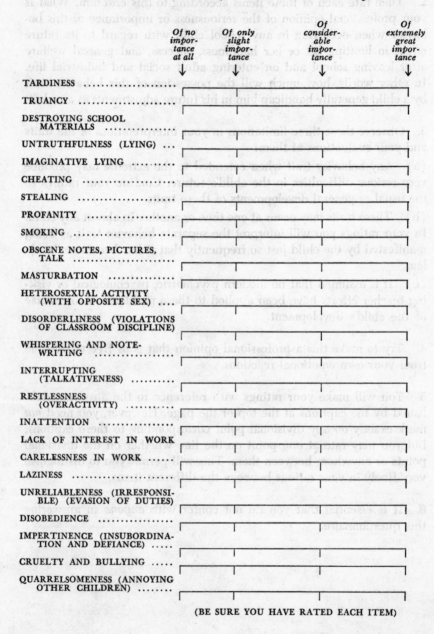

	Of no importance at all	Of only slight importance	Of considerable importance	Of extremely great importance
TARDINESS				
TRUANCY				
DESTROYING SCHOOL MATERIALS				
UNTRUTHFULNESS (LYING)				
IMAGINATIVE LYING				
CHEATING				
STEALING				
PROFANITY				
SMOKING				
OBSCENE NOTES, PICTURES, TALK				
MASTURBATION				
HETEROSEXUAL ACTIVITY (WITH OPPOSITE SEX)				
DISORDERLINESS (VIOLATIONS OF CLASSROOM DISCIPLINE)				
WHISPERING AND NOTE-WRITING				
INTERRUPTING (TALKATIVENESS)				
RESTLESSNESS (OVERACTIVITY)				
INATTENTION				
LACK OF INTEREST IN WORK				
CARELESSNESS IN WORK				
LAZINESS				
UNRELIABLENESS (IRRESPONSIBLE) (EVASION OF DUTIES)				
DISOBEDIENCE				
IMPERTINENCE (INSUBORDINATION AND DEFIANCE)				
CRUELTY AND BULLYING				
QUARRELSOMENESS (ANNOYING OTHER CHILDREN)				

(BE SURE YOU HAVE RATED EACH ITEM)

SCHEDULE 1*b*—*Continued*

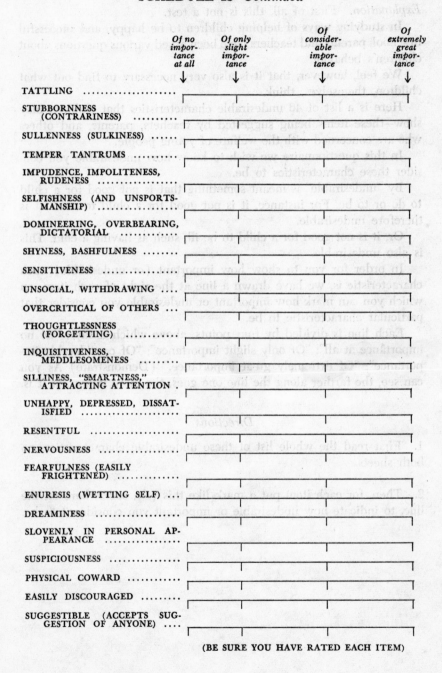

	Of no importance at all ↓	Of only slight importance ↓	Of considerable importance ↓	Of extremely great importance ↓
TATTLING				
STUBBORNNESS (CONTRARINESS)				
SULLENNESS (SULKINESS)				
TEMPER TANTRUMS				
IMPUDENCE, IMPOLITENESS, RUDENESS				
SELFISHNESS (AND UNSPORTS-MANSHIP)				
DOMINEERING, OVERBEARING, DICTATORIAL				
SHYNESS, BASHFULNESS				
SENSITIVENESS				
UNSOCIAL, WITHDRAWING				
OVERCRITICAL OF OTHERS ...				
THOUGHTLESSNESS (FORGETTING)				
INQUISITIVENESS, MEDDLESOMENESS				
SILLINESS, "SMARTNESS," ATTRACTING ATTENTION .				
UNHAPPY, DEPRESSED, DISSAT-ISFIED				
RESENTFUL				
NERVOUSNESS				
FEARFULNESS (EASILY FRIGHTENED)				
ENURESIS (WETTING SELF) ...				
DREAMINESS				
SLOVENLY IN PERSONAL AP-PEARANCE				
SUSPICIOUSNESS				
PHYSICAL COWARD				
EASILY DISCOURAGED				
SUGGESTIBLE (ACCEPTS SUG-GESTION OF ANYONE)				

(BE SURE YOU HAVE RATED EACH ITEM)

SCHEDULE 3 (For Children)

Explanation.   First of all, this is not a test.

In studying ways of helping children to be happy, and successful in school, parents and teachers have been asked various questions about children's behavior.

We feel, however, that it is also very necessary to find out what children, themselves, think.

Here is a list of 46 undesirable characteristics that children may show—these items being suggested by teachers, parents, and others who are concerned with the welfare of young people.

In this questionnaire we wish to know how undesirable you consider these characteristics to be.

By "undesirable" is meant something that is not good for a child to do or to be. For instance, it is not good for a child to steal. It is therefore undesirable.

Or, it is not good for a child to be ill, such as having a cold. This is also undesirable.

In order for you to show how important (or undesirable) each characteristic is, we have drawn a line at the right of each item, on which you can mark how important or undesirable you consider that particular characteristic to be.

Each line is divided by four points, above which it says: "Of no importance at all"; "Of only slight importance"; "Of considerable importance"; "Of extremely great importance." (Demonstrate) As you can see, the farther along the line one goes, the more important it is.

Directions

1. First read the whole list of these undesirable characteristics, on both sheets.

2. Then, for each item put a mark like this (/), somewhere on the line, to indicate how undesirable or important you consider it to be.

For instance, if you think that stealing is of great importance you put your mark here. (Demonstrate)

	Of no importance at all	Of only slight importance	Of considerable importance	Of extremely great importance
	↓	↓	↓	↓
STEALING				
HAVING A COLD				

3.   However, *you need not make your mark at any of these four points, you may make it anywhere along the line.*

For example, if you think that having a cold is a little more serious than "of only slight importance," but not as serious as "of considerable importance," you may put your mark anywhere along the line, as you choose. (Demonstrate) Just so long as it shows how important, or undesirable, *you* consider it to be.

4.   It does not matter whether you have or show these undesirable characteristics; whether you have ever been tardy, or not, for instance —just mark on the line how undesirable these characteristics are, when *any* child has or shows them.

5.   Please do not put down your marks according to what you think you *ought* to say, nor according to what you feel your teachers or parents think. We want *your own opinion.*

6.   *This is not a test* of any sort. Nobody will see your responses except the investigator. Your names will not be used in any fashion.

7.   If anything is not clear, please let me know.

SCHEDULE 3

How serious (or undesirable) is this behavior in *any* child?

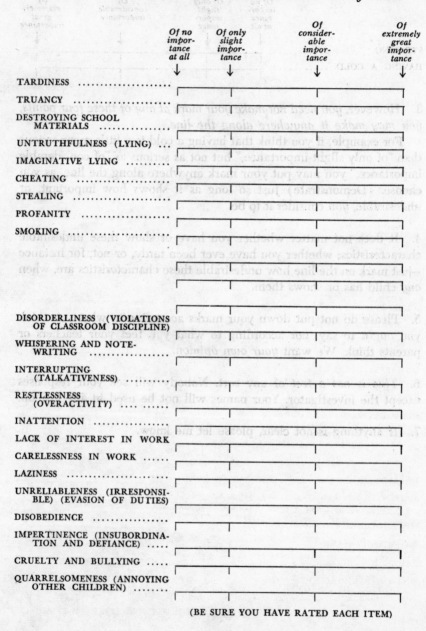

	Of no importance at all ↓	Of only slight importance ↓	Of considerable importance ↓	Of extremely great importance ↓
TARDINESS				
TRUANCY				
DESTROYING SCHOOL MATERIALS				
UNTRUTHFULNESS (LYING)				
IMAGINATIVE LYING				
CHEATING				
STEALING				
PROFANITY				
SMOKING				
DISORDERLINESS (VIOLATIONS OF CLASSROOM DISCIPLINE)				
WHISPERING AND NOTE-WRITING				
INTERRUPTING (TALKATIVENESS)				
RESTLESSNESS (OVERACTIVITY)				
INATTENTION				
LACK OF INTEREST IN WORK				
CARELESSNESS IN WORK				
LAZINESS				
UNRELIABLENESS (IRRESPONSIBLE) (EVASION OF DUTIES)				
DISOBEDIENCE				
IMPERTINENCE (INSUBORDINATION AND DEFIANCE)				
CRUELTY AND BULLYING				
QUARRELSOMENESS (ANNOYING OTHER CHILDREN)				

(BE SURE YOU HAVE RATED EACH ITEM)

SCHEDULE 3—*Continued*

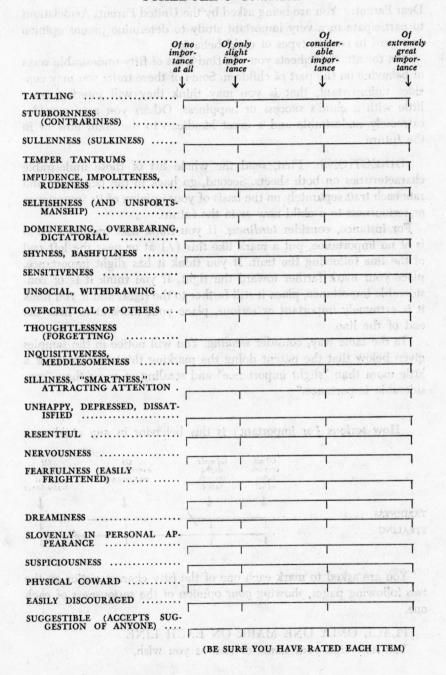

	Of no importance at all	Of only slight importance	Of considerable importance	Of extremely great importance
TATTLING				
STUBBORNNESS (CONTRARINESS)				
SULLENNESS (SULKINESS)				
TEMPER TANTRUMS				
IMPUDENCE, IMPOLITENESS, RUDENESS				
SELFISHNESS (AND UNSPORTS-MANSHIP)				
DOMINEERING, OVERBEARING, DICTATORIAL				
SHYNESS, BASHFULNESS				
SENSITIVENESS				
UNSOCIAL, WITHDRAWING				
OVERCRITICAL OF OTHERS ...				
THOUGHTLESSNESS (FORGETTING)				
INQUISITIVENESS, MEDDLESOMENESS				
SILLINESS, "SMARTNESS," ATTRACTING ATTENTION .				
UNHAPPY, DEPRESSED, DISSAT-ISFIED				
RESENTFUL				
NERVOUSNESS				
FEARFULNESS (EASILY FRIGHTENED)				
DREAMINESS				
SLOVENLY IN PERSONAL AP-PEARANCE				
SUSPICIOUSNESS				
PHYSICAL COWARD				
EASILY DISCOURAGED				
SUGGESTIBLE (ACCEPTS SUG-GESTION OF ANYONE)				

(BE SURE YOU HAVE RATED EACH ITEM)

PARENT OPINION

Dear Parent: You are being asked by the United Parents Associations to participate in a very important study to determine parent opinion in regard to certain types of child behavior.

On the attached sheets you will find a list of fifty undesirable ways of behaving on the part of children. Some of these traits you may consider unimportant, that is you may think they will interfere very little with a child's success or happiness. Others you may consider extremely undesirable and a great handicap to the child now or in the future.

DIRECTIONS: First, read the whole list of these undesirable characteristics on both sheets. Second, go back to the beginning and rate each trait separately on the basis of your opinion of its importance or seriousness to a child now or in the future.

For instance, consider *tardiness*. If you think that trait in a child is of no importance, put a mark like this (/) at or near the left end of the line following the trait. If you think it has slight importance, place your mark farther toward the right. If you think it is of considerable importance, place it still farther to the right; and if you think it is extremely important or serious, place your mark at or near the end of the line.

In the same way, consider *stealing*. You will notice in the samples given below that the parent doing the marking thinks tardiness of a little more than "slight importance" and stealing of more than "considerable importance."

How serious (or important) is this behavior in *any* child?

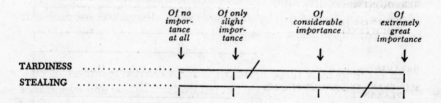

You are asked to mark each one of the fifty characteristics on the two following pages, showing *your* opinion of the seriousness of each one.

PLACE ONLY ONE MARK ON EACH LINE.
You may sign your name or not, as you wish.

Weighing and comparing the seriousness of these problems will be of value to you as a parent, as well as of value to those making this important study. Mark both pages of traits and mail them in the envelope attached, as soon as possible.

SCHEDULE 2 (For Parents)

Explanation. For a number of years, behavior and personality disorders of children have been the subject of intensive research and scientific study, a field of investigation which has developed in accelerative fashion as the amount of information has accumulated, with the separate and combined endeavors of the workers in the field.

But, along with the increase of knowledge, there has developed the growing realization of how much more needs to be known. The problem has, perhaps, not increased—but, rather, our increasing insight makes more evident to us the true magnitude of the problem.

For this effort, the cooperation of the parents of our school children, and the information that only they can furnish us, is a first essential.

* * *

On the attached sheet, there are listed fifty behavior problems of children. The sources of this tabulation are:

1. A questionnaire filled out by school teachers in which they enumerated items of undesirable behavior in children, as they had experienced it in their professional capacity.

2. A list compiled from the problems of the first three hundred cases which were referred to the Child Guidance Clinic Demonstration of Cleveland, these referrals being made by parents, social agencies, juvenile courts, and teachers. Many behavior and personality disorders not mentioned by teachers, were designated as problems by the parents in these cases.

* * *

In order to treat these personality and behavior disorders of children, it is necessary to ascertain the relative seriousness and importance of these traits, from the viewpoint of a parent.

For the purpose of this questionnaire, it is suggested that you think of your child not only as your son (or daughter) in terms of your affection and concern for him, but as a young person in his own right, who will be expected to acquire an education and take his proper place in the world; and the bearing which these unfavorable characteristics would have on his present development and future happiness—or on that of *any* child who may manifest them.

It may, perhaps, seem somewhat irksome to dwell only on the unfavorable characteristics of children, when they have so many delightful ones, but these are not meant to be personal evaluations. The purpose of these ratings is to assay the consequences and undesirableness of these personality and behavior characteristics, *as they may appear in any child, not necessarily in yours!*

A scale of seriousness and importance is provided, along with these behavior items. To the right of each item, a line has been drawn. On each of the lines, four points have been marked, above each of which is an explanatory phrase, denoting the degree of importance or seriousness of such behavior or personality characteristic, as it may appear in *any* child.

For example:

How serious (or important) is this behavior in *any* child?

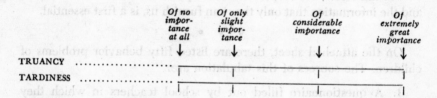

Directions.   1. Read all of the fifty behavior items on the two sheets.

2. Then indicate the importance of any item, when evidenced by a child, by making a vertical line, like this (/), at any point along the line. It is not necessary that you confine yourself to the four divisional points. To express any gradation of opinion, you may draw a line at any place between divisional points. Indeed, for finer discrimination, it may be necessary to do so very often.

3. The frequency of such behavior is of no importance in this rating. Nor is it necessary that your child should have exhibited any of the characteristics under immediate scrutiny. The only requirement is that you show, by your rating mark, what its degree of importance or undesirability is, *when it does occur.*

4. You may take as much time as you require for making *careful* ratings, bearing in mind the consequences of these undesirable characteristics in children from the standpoint of the child and the society in which he lives; his present happiness, educability, adjust-

ments; and his future adjustment—socially, vocationally, and emotionally—as an adult.

      5. These ratings apply only to children of elementary school age.

      6. All information will be considered confidential; no individual's returns will be reported upon as such.

SCHEDULE 2

How serious (or undesirable) is this behavior in *any* child?

Please Check Whether Father ☐ Mother ☐	Of no importance at all ↓	Of only slight importance ↓	Of considerable importance ↓	Of extremely great importance ↓
TARDINESS				
TRUANCY				
DESTROYING SCHOOL MATERIALS				
UNTRUTHFULNESS (LYING) ...				
IMAGINATIVE LYING				
CHEATING				
STEALING				
PROFANITY				
SMOKING				
OBSCENE NOTES, PICTURES, TALK				
MASTURBATION				
HETEROSEXUAL ACTIVITY (WITH OPPOSITE SEX)				
DISORDERLINESS (VIOLATIONS OF CLASSROOM DISCIPLINE)				
WHISPERING AND NOTE-WRITING				
INTERRUPTING (TALKATIVENESS)				
RESTLESSNESS (OVERACTIVITY)				
INATTENTION				
LACK OF INTEREST IN WORK				
CARELESSNESS IN WORK				
LAZINESS				
UNRELIABLENESS (IRRESPONSIBLE) (EVASION OF DUTIES)				
DISOBEDIENCE				
IMPERTINENCE (INSUBORDINATION AND DEFIANCE)				
CRUELTY AND BULLYING				
QUARRELSOMENESS (ANNOYING OTHER CHILDREN)				

(BE SURE YOU HAVE RATED EACH ITEM)

SCHEDULE 2—*Continued*

Please Check Whether — Father ☐ Mother ☐	Of no importance at all ↓	Of only slight importance ↓	Of considerable importance ↓	Of extremely great importance ↓
TATTLING				
STUBBORNNESS (CONTRARINESS)				
SULLENNESS (SULKINESS)				
TEMPER TANTRUMS				
IMPUDENCE, IMPOLITENESS, RUDENESS				
SELFISHNESS (AND UNSPORTS-MANSHIP)				
DOMINEERING, OVERBEARING, DICTATORIAL				
SHYNESS, BASHFULNESS				
SENSITIVENESS				
UNSOCIAL, WITHDRAWING				
OVERCRITICAL OF OTHERS ...				
THOUGHTLESSNESS (FORGETTING)				
INQUISITIVENESS, MEDDLESOMENESS				
SILLINESS, "SMARTNESS," ATTRACTING ATTENTION .				
UNHAPPY, DEPRESSED, DISSAT-ISFIED				
RESENTFUL				
NERVOUSNESS				
FEARFULNESS (EASILY FRIGHTENED)				
ENURESIS (WETTING SELF) ...				
DREAMINESS				
SLOVENLY IN PERSONAL AP-PEARANCE				
SUSPICIOUSNESS				
PHYSICAL COWARD				
EASILY DISCOURAGED				
SUGGESTIBLE (ACCEPTS SUG-GESTION OF ANYONE)				

(BE SURE YOU HAVE RATED EACH ITEM)

Appendix B

FIGURES

Figures 1-46 are based on the data obtained in this present investigation; while the percentages yielded in McGrath's study supplied the source for the present investigator's preparation of Figures 47-49.

Figures 6 and 49, 7 and 48, 11 and 47, may be matched as pairs of comparable items which appear in both studies.

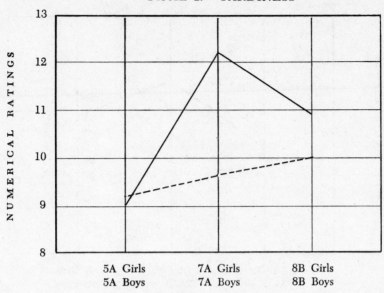

FIGURE 1. – TARDINESS

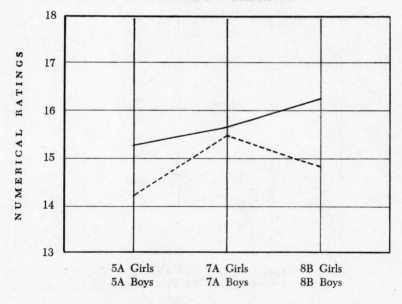

FIGURE 2. – TRUANCY

───── Represents judgments made by the three groups of girls.
- - - - - Represents judgments made by the three groups of boys.

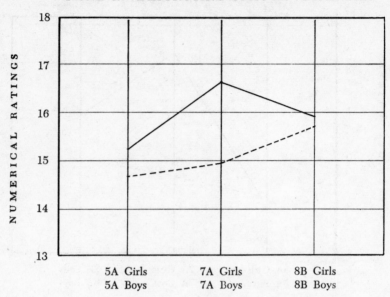

FIGURE 3. — DESTROYING SCHOOL MATERIALS

| | 5A Girls | 7A Girls | 8B Girls |
| | 5A Boys | 7A Boys | 8B Boys |

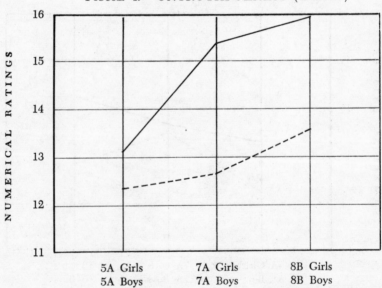

FIGURE 4. — UNTRUTHFULNESS (LYING)

| | 5A Girls | 7A Girls | 8B Girls |
| | 5A Boys | 7A Boys | 8B Boys |

——— Represents judgments made by the three groups of girls.

- - - - - Represents judgments made by the three groups of boys.

FIGURE 5. – IMAGINATIVE LYING

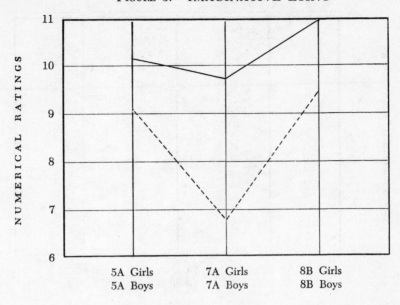

5A Girls   7A Girls   8B Girls
5A Boys   7A Boys   8B Boys

FIGURE 6. – CHEATING

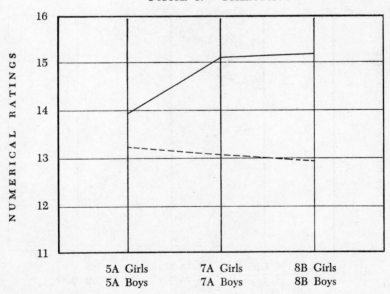

5A Girls   7A Girls   8B Girls
5A Boys   7A Boys   8B Boys

————— Represents judgments made by the three groups of girls.
----- Represents judgments made by the three groups of boys.

199

FIGURE 7. – STEALING

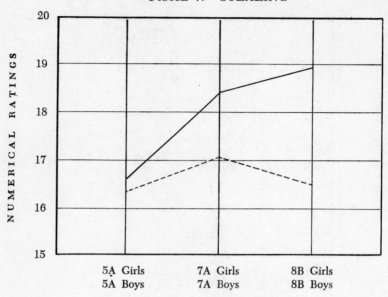

5A Girls   7A Girls   8B Girls
5A Boys   7A Boys   8B Boys

FIGURE 8. – PROFANITY

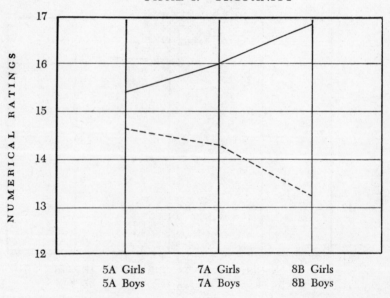

5A Girls   7A Girls   8B Girls
5A Boys   7A Boys   8B Boys

——— Represents judgments made by the three groups of girls.
------ Represents judgments made by the three groups of boys.

Figure 9. — SMOKING

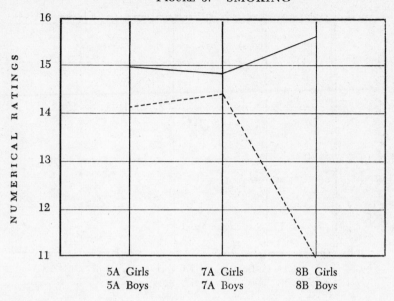

Figure 10. — DISORDERLINESS

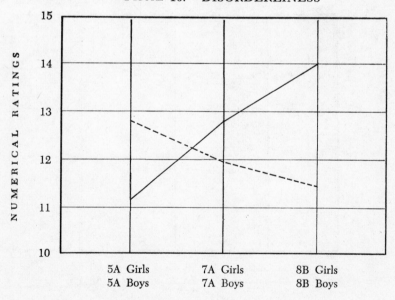

——— Represents judgments made by the three groups of girls.
------ Represents judgments made by the three groups of boys.

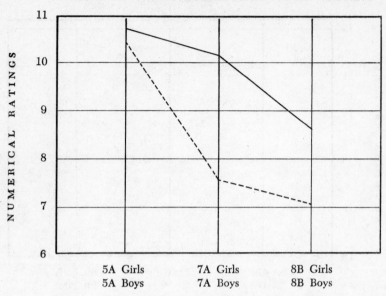

FIGURE 11. — WHISPERING AND NOTE-WRITING

NUMERICAL RATINGS

5A Girls   7A Girls   8B Girls
5A Boys   7A Boys   8B Boys

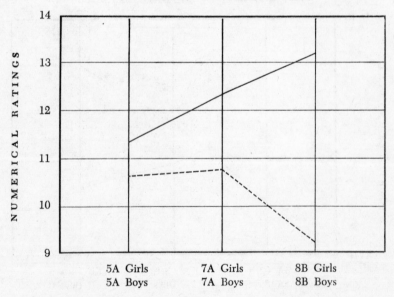

FIGURE 12. — INTERRUPTING

NUMERICAL RATINGS

5A Girls   7A Girls   8B Girls
5A Boys   7A Boys   8B Boys

———— Represents judgments made by the three groups of girls.
------ Represents judgments made by the three groups of boys.

Figure 13. – RESTLESSNESS

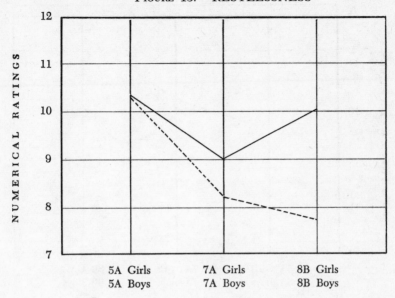

Figure 14. – INATTENTION

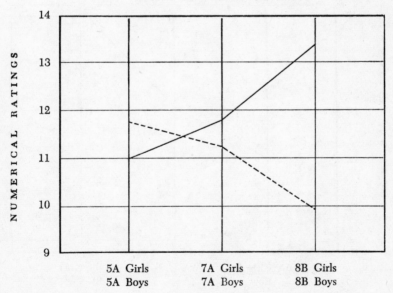

——— Represents judgments made by the three groups of girls.

- - - - - Represents judgments made by the three groups of boys.

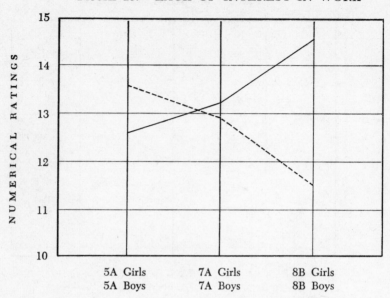

FIGURE 15. — LACK OF INTEREST IN WORK

5A Girls   7A Girls   8B Girls
5A Boys   7A Boys   8B Boys

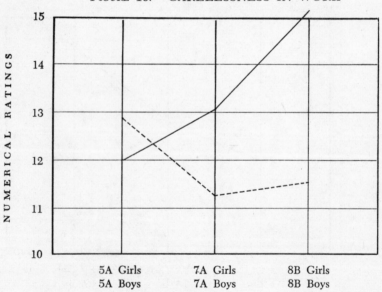

FIGURE 16. — CARELESSNESS IN WORK

5A Girls   7A Girls   8B Girls
5A Boys   7A Boys   8B Boys

———— Represents judgments made by the three groups of girls.

------ Represents judgments made by the three groups of boys.

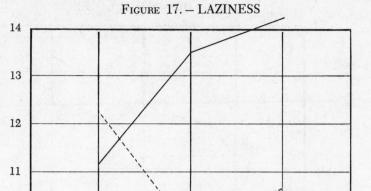

FIGURE 17. — LAZINESS

| 5A Girls | 7A Girls | 8B Girls |
| 5A Boys | 7A Boys | 8B Boys |

FIGURE 18. — UNRELIABLENESS

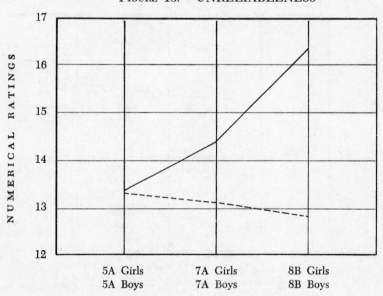

| 5A Girls | 7A Girls | 8B Girls |
| 5A Boys | 7A Boys | 8B Boys |

———— Represents judgments made by the three groups of girls.

------ Represents judgments made by the three groups of boys.

Figure 19. – DISOBEDIENCE

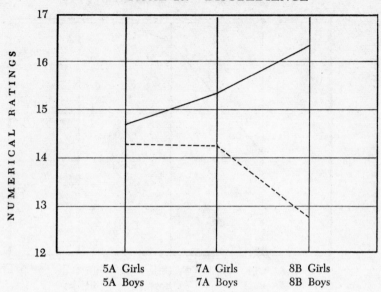

Figure 20. – IMPERTINENCE

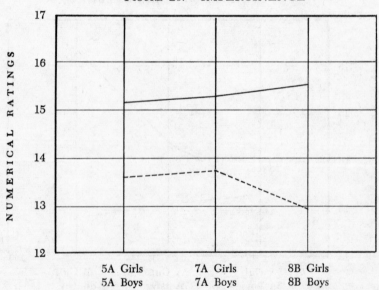

——— Represents judgments made by the three groups of girls.
- - - - - Represents judgments made by the three groups of boys.

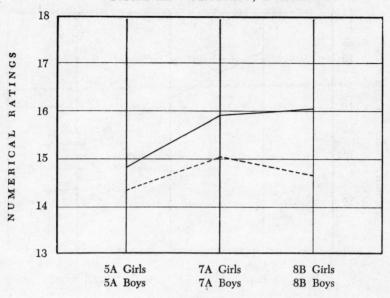

FIGURE 21. – CRUELTY, BULLYING

NUMERICAL RATINGS

18
17
16
15
14
13

5A Girls   7A Girls   8B Girls
5A Boys   7A Boys   8B Boys

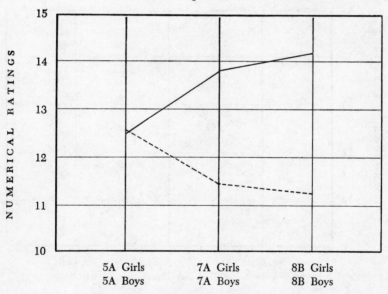

FIGURE 22. – QUARRELSOMENESS

NUMERICAL RATINGS

15
14
13
12
11
10

5A Girls   7A Girls   8B Girls
5A Boys   7A Boys   8B Boys

——— Represents judgments made by the three groups of girls.
----- Represents judgments made by the three groups of boys.

Figure 23. – TATTLING

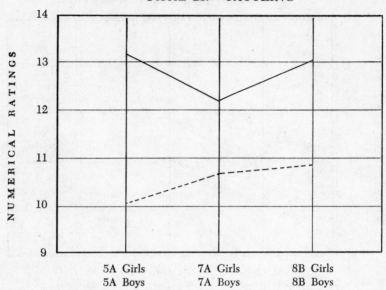

Figure 24. – STUBBORNNESS, CONTRARINESS

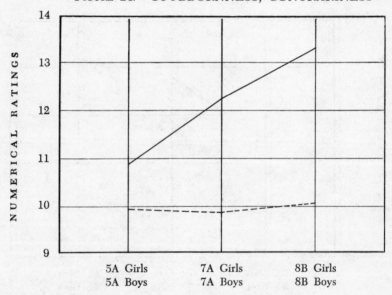

——— Represents judgments made by the three groups of girls.
----- Represents judgments made by the three groups of boys.

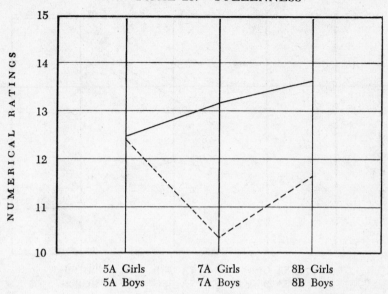

FIGURE 25. — SULLENNESS

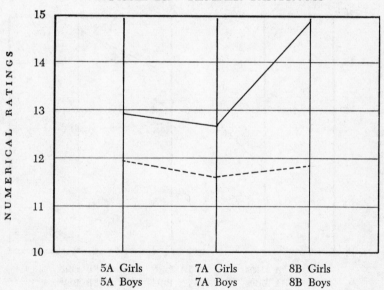

FIGURE 26. — TEMPER TANTRUMS

———— Represents judgments made by the three groups of girls.
------ Represents judgments made by the three groups of boys.

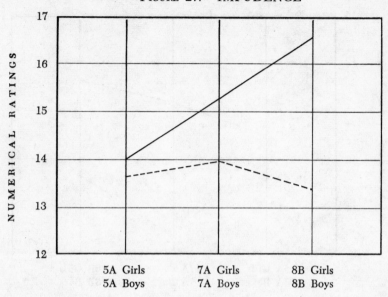

FIGURE 27. – IMPUDENCE

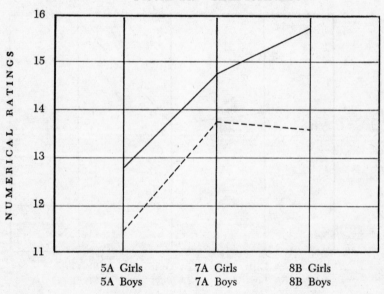

FIGURE 28. – SELFISHNESS

—— Represents judgments made by the three groups of girls.
----- Represents judgments made by the three groups of boys.

210

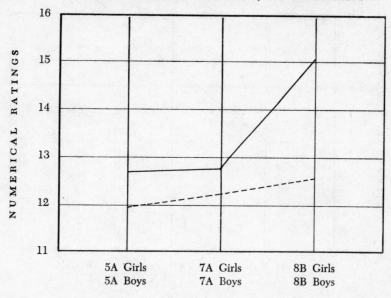

FIGURE 29. – DOMINEERING, OVERBEARING

NUMERICAL RATINGS

| | 5A Girls | 7A Girls | 8B Girls |
| | 5A Boys | 7A Boys | 8B Boys |

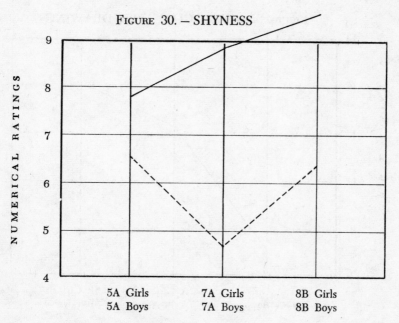

FIGURE 30. – SHYNESS

NUMERICAL RATINGS

| | 5A Girls | 7A Girls | 8B Girls |
| | 5A Boys | 7A Boys | 8B Boys |

——— Represents judgments made by the three groups of girls.
------ Represents judgments made by the three groups of boys.

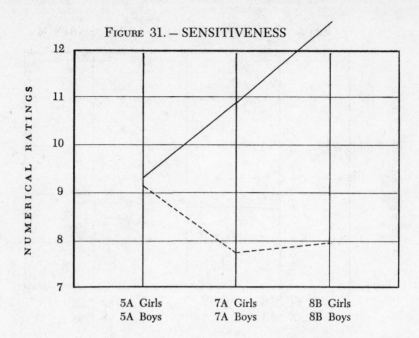

FIGURE 31. – SENSITIVENESS

NUMERICAL RATINGS

| | 5A Girls | 7A Girls | 8B Girls |
| | 5A Boys | 7A Boys | 8B Boys |

FIGURE 32. – UNSOCIAL, WITHDRAWING

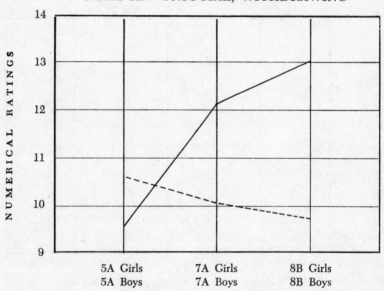

NUMERICAL RATINGS

| | 5A Girls | 7A Girls | 8B Girls |
| | 5A Boys | 7A Boys | 8B Boys |

——— Represents judgments made by the three groups of girls.
------ Represents judgments made by the three groups of boys.

212

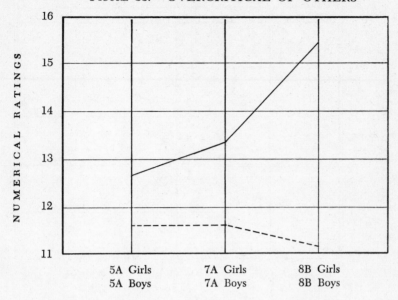

FIGURE 33. – OVERCRITICAL OF OTHERS

NUMERICAL RATINGS

5A Girls   7A Girls   8B Girls
5A Boys   7A Boys   8B Boys

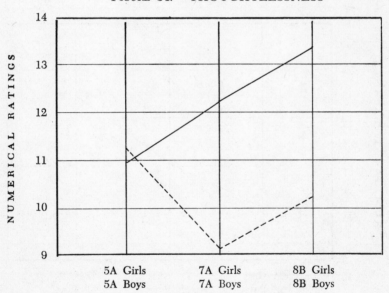

FIGURE 34. – THOUGHTLESSNESS

NUMERICAL RATINGS

5A Girls   7A Girls   8B Girls
5A Boys   7A Boys   8B Boys

———— Represents judgments made by the three groups of girls.
- - - - - Represents judgments made by the three groups of boys.

213

FIGURE 35. – INQUISITIVENESS

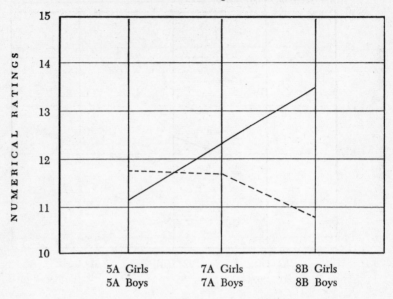

FIGURE 36. – SILLINESS

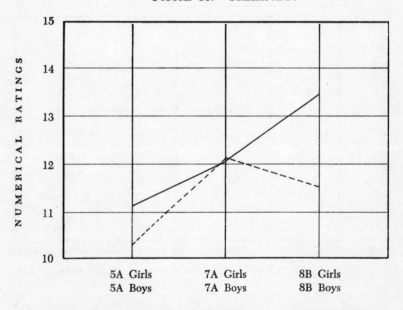

——— Represents judgments made by the three groups of girls.
- - - - - Represents judgments made by the three groups of boys.

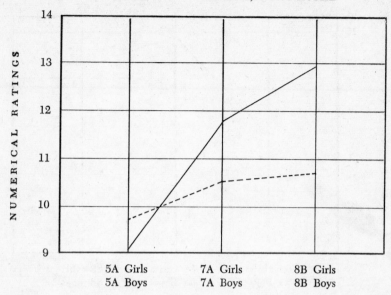

FIGURE 37. — UNHAPPY, DEPRESSED

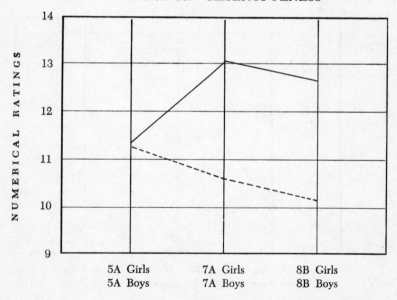

FIGURE 38. — RESENTFULNESS

—————— Represents judgments made by the three groups of girls.
- - - - - - Represents judgments made by the three groups of boys.

215

FIGURE 39. — NERVOUSNESS

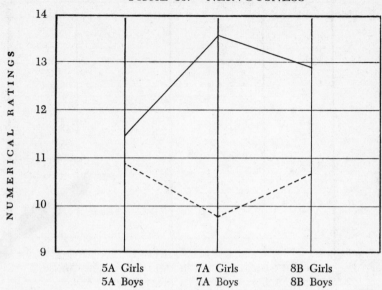

FIGURE 40. — FEARFULNESS

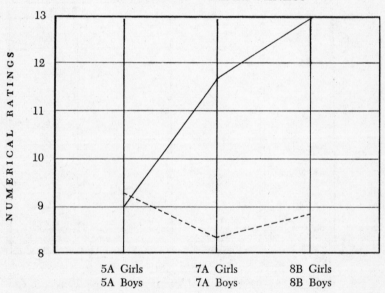

——— Represents judgments made by the three groups of girls.

- - - - - Represents judgments made by the three groups of boys.

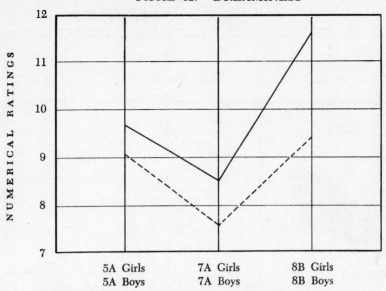

FIGURE 41. — DREAMINESS

5A Girls   7A Girls   8B Girls
5A Boys   7A Boys   8B Boys

FIGURE 42. — SLOVENLY IN PERSONAL
APPEARANCE

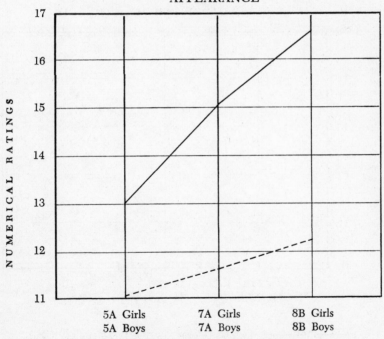

5A Girls   7A Girls   8B Girls
5A Boys   7A Boys   8B Boys

——— Represents judgments made by the three groups of girls.
------ Represents judgments made by the three groups of boys.

FIGURE 43. – SUSPICIOUSNESS

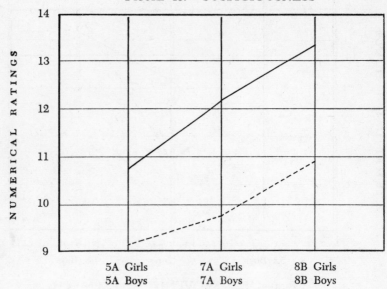

FIGURE 44. – PHYSICAL COWARD

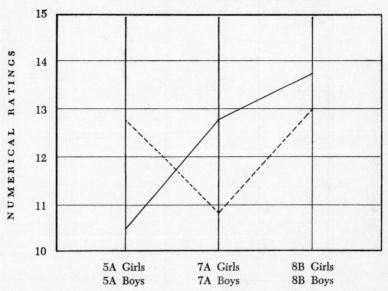

——— Represents judgments made by the three groups of girls.
------ Represents judgments made by the three groups of boys.

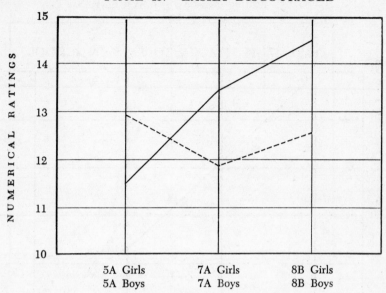

FIGURE 45. — EASILY DISCOURAGED

NUMERICAL RATINGS

15
14
13
12
11
10

5A Girls   7A Girls   8B Girls
5A Boys   7A Boys   8B Boys

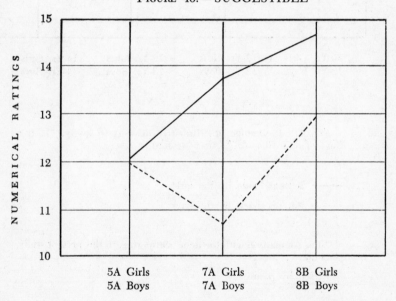

FIGURE 46. — SUGGESTIBLE

NUMERICAL RATINGS

15
14
13
12
11
10

5A Girls   7A Girls   8B Girls
5A Boys   7A Boys   8B Boys

———— Represents judgments made by the three groups of girls.
- - - - - Represents judgments made by the three groups of boys.

219

FIGURE 47.—IS IT A SIN TO TALK IN SCHOOL?

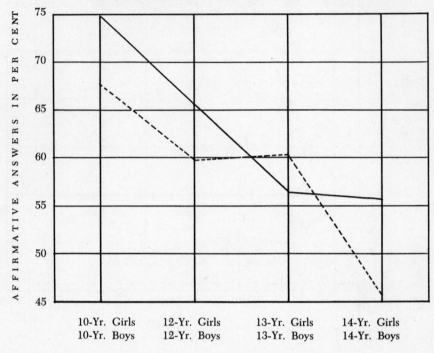

Fig. 47. Percentage of affirmative answers to query: "Is It a Sin to Talk in School?"° (After McGrath.)†

———— Ratings made by the girls.

------ Ratings made by the boys.

° For comparison with the item, whispering, in this present study, see Figure 11.

† Used by permission.

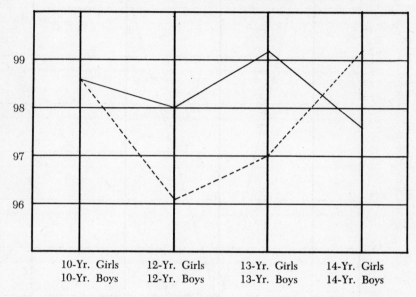

FIGURE 48.—WOULD IT BE WRONG TO TAKE A
NICKEL OUT OF YOUR MOTHER'S POCKET-
BOOK WITHOUT ASKING HER?

Fig. 48. Percentage of affirmative answers to query: "Would It
Be Wrong to Take a Nickel out of Your Mother's Pocketbook without Asking Her?"* (After McGrath.)†

——— Ratings made by the girls.

------ Ratings made by the boys.

* For comparison with the item, stealing, in this present study,
see Figure 7.

† Used by permission.

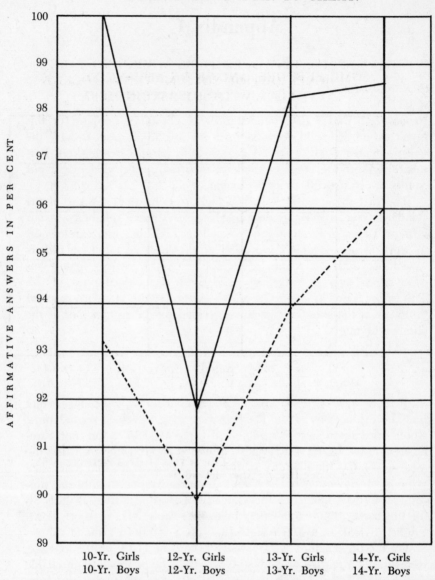

FIGURE 49.—IS IT A SIN TO CHEAT?

Fig. 49. Percentage of affirmative answers to query: "It It a Sin to Cheat?"° (After McGrath.)†

——— Ratings made by the girls.

------ Ratings made by the boys.

° For comparison with the item, cheating, in this present study, see Figure 6.

† Used by permission.

222

Appendix C

SOME FURTHER, AND MORE ADVANCED, STATISTICAL CONSIDERATIONS

Reliability. Under the circumstances of obtaining samples for this investigation, it would not have been feasible in all cases to have the questionnaires rated a second time by the parents or children. Fortunately, there are other methods of ascertaining to what extent our results are statistically reliable, or not.

The first depends on statistical logic, and involves the use of the standard error of measurement as a measure of the reliability of our ratings. To make it more concrete, let us take the item carelessness in work as an example. Inspection of this trait as rated by fathers (twenty-seventh down the list in Table XXIII), reveals that it has received an average rating of 11.18; with a standard error of .75. This latter figure is derived from the formula: the standard error of the mean is the standard deviation divided by the square root of the number of raters,

$$\sigma_m = \frac{\sigma}{\sqrt{N}}$$

If there were no deviation and no standard error, we could predict that the evaluations of the fathers, were they to rate a second time, would once again ascribe a numerical value of 11.18 to the trait, carelessness in work. But the actuality of the standard error furnishes the measure of the unreliability of this arithmetic mean, due to chance error; such deviation being a normal accompaniment of rating procedures in experiments of this type. Similarly, the ratings of girls 8B for this same item, carelessness in work (Table XII, sixteenth down the list), yield an average of 15.12, with a standard error of .57.

On the other hand, if the fathers' ratings of 11.18, on the average, were purely a matter of chance, they would be completely unreliable statistically. And, again, if the average rating of 15.12 obtained from girls 8B was solely due to chance, it would also be completely unreliable statistically. Further, if these conditions existed in the present instance, that is, if the means of the two groups differed from each other only by chance, we could not obtain a statistically significant difference between the averages of the ratings for this item.

But reference to our Table XXIV shows that the critical ratio between fathers and girls 8B for this item, carelessness in work, is 4.19. In other words, the means obtained from these two groups of raters are found to differ from each other to an extent which may be termed statistically significant. As a corollary, the presumption must be made that these original ratings were not, for the most part, fortuitous, but do have reliability and do have some real basis of existence.

This type of reasoning is applicable to all of our intergroup combinations, where comparable conditions obtain. That is, for each of our groups of raters there is at least one instance (for most, more) where comparison with another group produces a critical ratio of 3 or more.

The conclusion may therefore be drawn that this item, carelessness in work, does have adequate reliability for purposes of this study. (The contrary does not necessarily follow, however: absence of critical ratios, significantly high, would not mean that the ratings were not reliable.) And, since we have found this item to be reliable, and since the rating of each of all the various traits is a highly similar task, it is very probable that the remaining items are also reliable.

However, there is another way of establishing reliability in the absence of actual repetition of the experiment, and that is offered by analysis of the meaning of our correlation coefficients. Reliability is the correlation of a measure with itself; administration of two equivalent forms of a test is one common way of obtaining the reliability figure. A correlation coefficient is limited by the reliability of the measures being correlated. Since reliability is the correlation of a measure with itself, ordinarily we would not expect any measure to correlate more highly with another measure than it does with itself. Thus, if we obtain a correlation of .9 between two measures, say, it is highly probable that each of these has a minimum reliability of .9. Further, squaring of our correlation figure permits us to obtain enhanced confidence in our reliability figure. So that, in this case, by squaring the correlation figure of .9, just given as an example, we obtain the figure of .81, at least, *and the chances are 1000 to 1 that such is actually true.* In other words, we thus see that squaring decreases the coefficient of reliability but increases the certainty.

Both sets of reliability figures for each of our ten groups have been set forth in the arrangement following, entitled, "Reliability of the Ratings."

Reference to our table of correlations (Table V) and to this table of reliability, will furnish the actual figures for the ratings made in this investigation. We find, for instance, that the correlation coefficient between the ratings of fathers and that of mothers is .945. Hence, the reliability of the ratings of the fathers and of the mothers is probably at least .945 for *each* of these two groups. Similarly, the correlation between 5A boys and 7A boys is .866. So, the reliability for each of these two groups must be at least .866. But going farther down the table, we find that the correlation between 7A boys versus 8B girls is .895. Now we can state that the ratings of our group of 7A boys have at least a reliability of .895. And so on for each of our ten groups.

Then, as has just been pointed out, if we wish to be almost entirely certain of the correctness of our reliability coefficients, to a proportionate extent of one thousand chances to one, we square each of our reliability coefficients. In this manner, our reliability coefficient for fathers has now become .893 (.945 squared), and the same is naturally true for the ratings of the mothers; and so on.

Inspection of the reliability table as a whole sanctions the determination that even the attenuated figures on the right-hand side of the table constitute high reliability coefficients for an investigation of this type.

RELIABILITY OF THE RATINGS

	Highest correlation coefficient	Square of highest correlation coefficient
FATHERS	.945	.893
MOTHERS	.945	.893
5A BOYS	.866	.750
5A GIRLS	.893	.797
7A BOYS	.895	.801
7A GIRLS	.893	.797
8B BOYS	.883	.780
8B GIRLS	.895	.801
TEACHERS 1a	.922	.850
TEACHERS 1b	.921	.848

Intragroup critical ratios. Another statistical question that came up dealt with the problem of obtaining critical ratios for the items within a group of raters (intragroup critical ratios) in correspondence with our having obtained intergroup critical ratios. That is, the first would deal with all of the items rated by one group, Teachers 1a, say, so that we would obtain the critical ratios when we compared the means of any two items of the list of fifty items, proceeding consecutively or in any other manner down the list of items, thereby making a vertical

comparison in each case. (In the case of each of the respective groups
of children, forty-six items would thus be compared.)

The intergroup critical ratio deals with the means of any single
given item compared horizontally group as against group. So that, as
Table XXIV shows, for example, we have the critical ratios for tardiness as rated by fathers in comparison with tardiness as rated by any
and all of our nine other groups; truancy as rated by fathers in comparison with truancy as rated by any and all of our nine other groups;
and in like fashion, crosswise comparisons are shown for each of the
fifty items (with the exception of the four items deleted in the case
of the children's groups). Tables VII, XV-XXI, XXIV, and XXV offer,
in sequence, a complete presentation of the critical ratios for each item
as between each of our ten groups of raters involved, with Wickman's
group of mental hygienists forming the eleventh.

However, when the attempt is made to compute critical ratios for
intragroup items, one cannot use the formula that is used for intergroup ratios, which is

$$\sigma_d = \sqrt{\sigma^2_{m_1} + \sigma^2_{m_2}}$$

Perhaps the word "cannot" is incorrectly employed for they sometimes are computed by that formula, although not correctly so, in an
investigation of this general type. In a listing such as ours one is bound
statistically to take cognizance of the correlation, if any, between the
two items in question whose means are being compared. Therefore
the more involved formula must be used:

$$\sigma_d = \sqrt{\sigma^2_{m_1} + \sigma^2_{m_2} - 2r_{12}\,\sigma_{m_1}\,\sigma_{m_2}}$$

Under certain circumstances, the numerical value of the correlation
could more or less be dispensed with. If one knew that the correlation
was zero, for instance, the whole term beginning with 2r would, of
course, become zero and of no further importance. Also, in studies
dealing with achievement score tests—to offer another example—where
there is always some positive correlation, one may simply ignore this
whole term $(2r_{12}\sigma_{m_1}\,\sigma_{m_2})$ and compute the critical ratios without it,
knowing then that the critical ratios thus obtained were minimal. How-
ever, one cannot make comparable blanket assumptions in this present
type of study, the rating of traits, for there is nothing in the literature
to justify any assumption that our correlation coefficients would be
positive in all cases; and despite the theoretical expectation of its in-

frequence, a negative correlation, whenever it did exist, would increase the denominator and consequently lower the numerical value of our critical ratio.

These considerations led to the regretful decision that the simpler formula would not be generally applicable. However, utilization of the more extensive computation would involve the calculation of 1225 correlation coefficients for each of the complete lists of items, some- what less for the lists given to the children's groups, thus making a total of almost 12,250 correlation figures; these alone representing an equivalence in hours of statistical work, without taking account of the other statistical operations required. Under these circumstances, the results thus obtainable would not seem to warrant the involvement of so much labor, since the presentation as constituted does still retain its descriptive value and more. Even without the correlation figures, much statistical data has already been supplied, such as the means, standard deviations, and the like. And it is suggested that small sections, or items which arouse special interest, will lend themselves to develop- ment along certain lines productive of a great deal of information, statistically as well as descriptively.

Let us take as an example stealing and whispering as evaluated by Teachers 1a, Table I. Judging from the averages (means) given to these two items by all the adult groups and the children, we are permitted to make the assumption that these two characteristics would offer one of the greatest contrasts in rated seriousness. But extending this contrast to the utmost and assuming that *every* teacher would rate stealing *first* and whispering *last* in importance, a complete re- versal which would, of course, not actually be the case; and assuming further that the correlation was therefore completely negative for these two items, giving the correlation coefficient (r) of minus 1.00; we could calculate the minimum critical ratio for the difference of the means between the two items, using the formula after all:

Standard error of the mean for stealing:

$$\sigma_{m_1} = \frac{6.71}{\sqrt{110}} = .64$$

Standard error of the mean for whispering:

$$\sigma_{m_2} = \frac{4.11}{\sqrt{110}} = .392$$

The actual difference in means (D) between stealing and whispering is 7.67

Hence, according to our formula:

$$CR = \frac{D}{\sigma_d} = \sqrt{\sigma^2_{m_1} + \sigma^2_{m_2} - (2\text{-}r_{12}\sigma_{m_1}\sigma_{m_2})} \quad \frac{M_1 - M_2}{}$$

$$\frac{D}{\sigma_d} = \frac{7.67}{1.032} = 7.43$$

So, this critical ratio of 7.43 even where the negative correlation is assumed to be as large as 1.00, is still more than twice as large as it needs to be for statistical significance. Which means that we have this extremely large margin of certainty in concluding that the difference between the rated seriousness of stealing and whispering is a true one. Or, put somewhat differently, if the difference between the averages for stealing and whispering were only 3.096 we would still have statistical warranty that the true difference between these items was more than zero, and that further rating procedures by these teachers would have produced the same relative positions in rated seriousness of these two items. Along with this, the preponderance of likelihood would be that in actuality the difference of 3.096 could be even lower and still represent a statistically reliable difference.

We may go even further and generalize for all items in this distribution of Teachers 1a, by computing the maximum numerical value for our denominator, in this fashion: Except for obscene notes and masturbation, which could not even hypothetically be assumed to have inverse relationship with heterosexual activity, smoking bears the highest sigma, next to that of heterosexual activity (6.78 and 7.04, respectively). Let us use these sigmas in our formulae, and let us again assume that the correlation is negative and as high as −1.00, the maximum of inverse relationship, between these two items of smoking and heterosexual activity.

Thus,

$$\sigma_{m_1} = \frac{6.78}{10.488} = .646 \quad \text{and} \quad \sigma_{m_2} = \frac{7.04}{10.488} = .671$$

$$\sigma_d = \sqrt{(.646)^2 + (.671)^2 - (2 \times -1 \times .646 \times .671)} = 1.317$$

$$\frac{D}{\sigma_d} = \frac{6.05}{1.317} = \text{CR of } 4.593$$

This then yields a critical ratio of 4.593 and hence, considerably more than the guarantee required. For, as we have already noted, D/σ_d need only yield 3; so that in this list, whenever the difference between any two items is 3.951 the difference is a significant one. And this is a *minimum* guarantee for, as between any two means where the reversal is less complete (and complete reversal is rarely conceivable), the difference of 3.951 can be proportionately less to make it a significantly reliable one. A comparable and proportionate diminution of the required difference between the means would also arise in all cases where one or both of the standard deviations were less than 7.04 and/or 6.78.

In cases where the correlation is *zero*, the term beginning with the minus sign $(2r_{12\sigma_{m_1}\sigma_{m_2}})$ would drop out, thereby lowering the numerical value of our denominator; so that our figure of 3.951 could now be commensurately lower and still yield a significant critical ratio. For example, still using our high sigmas but now assuming that r is 0.

$$\sigma_d = \sqrt{(.646)^2 + (.671)^2 - (2 \times 0 \times .646 \times .671)} = \sqrt{.417316 + .450241 - 0}$$

$$CR = \frac{2.793}{.931} = 3.0$$

Hence, the figure of 2.793 would now generally ensure that the difference between any two items in question, so far as the ratings of Teachers 1a were concerned, was a statistically significant one.

And in those instances where the correlation is a *positive* one, keeping all our other terms constant, we could go further and state that our raw difference between means could now be 2.793 or lower for significance; that the greater the degree of positive correlation (and therefore the larger our minus term in the denominator), the smaller need our difference be to produce a significant critical ratio.

The summary of these statistical manipulations, using the ratings of Teachers 1a as illustrative material, would be:

1. Even if the correlation were completely negative for a given two items (that is, there was a complete reversal in the ratings), and these two items had standard deviations of 6.71 and 4.11, respectively,

we could consider it as reliable when the actual difference between the averages of these two items was 3.096; with the likelihood being that in most cases the difference could be less and still produce the significant critical ratio of 3. With one or both sigmas lower, the figure 3.096 could be proportionately less to produce a significant quotient.

2. Again assuming a negative correlation of 1.00, a generalization may now be made, broad enough to cover all of the items in the distribution of Teachers 1a: Since the sigmas of 7.04 and 6.78 are the highest in this listing which have even a remote possibility of a completely negative correlation being involved, we know that in all other comparisons for this distribution the difference between the means can be lower than 3.951 to produce a statistically significant difference. Furthermore, to the extent that the correlation coefficient recedes from the numerical value of minus 1.00, to that extent can the difference between means be decreased to produce a statistically reliable difference.

3. Where the correlation is zero, with these same high sigmas of 7.04 and 6.78, the critical ratio of 3 would be obtained if the difference between the means were 2.793; this required figure decreasing proportionately with the decrease in one or both of the sigmas.

4. When the correlation is positive, this raw difference of 2.793 between means can be even lower; the *higher* the positive correlation, the *lower* will our figure of 2.793 need to be to produce statistical significance.

As thus instanced, one may make general rule of thumb assumptions concerning broad correlation relationships; and to a considerable extent, distinctions finer than are afforded by our wider generalizations may be made for concrete items under consideration:

So that, for instance, if we compare disobedience and destroying school materials, as rated by Teachers 1a, we may assume that there would be a positive correlation; probably more but at least to the extent of .3. Using our formula, we find then that

$$\sigma_{m_1} \text{ (disobedience)} = .546$$

$$\sigma_{m_2} \text{ (destroying school materials)} = .533$$

Thus our critical ratio is 1.426

This would mean that we do not have the quotient of 3, which is required for statistical significance, but that the chances are approximately 92.6 in 100 that this obtained difference between the means of disobedience and destroying school materials is a real one. In other words, that teachers would rate these two items in the same relative positions of seriousness if subsequent ratings were made.

In like fashion, we may now compare disobedience with disorderliness, as a further example. Here,

$$\sigma_{m_1} \text{ (disobedience) is again .546}$$

$$\sigma_{m_2} \text{ (disorderliness) is .439}$$

Hence our critical ratio is 3.82

This critical ratio of 3.82 is greater than the required figure of 3.0, and therefore is more than large enough to offer virtual certainty that the average of ratings for disobedience on the part of teachers would always be higher than their average of ratings for disorderliness.

These series of statistical exercises have been performed to illustrate, then, that a great deal of information is available for various computations of varying nature; and it naturally follows that any type of calculation carried out in reference to these ratings made by Teachers 1a may also properly be applied to items rated by fathers, mothers, and any and all of the other groups concerned in this present study.

Animosity, *see* Resentfulness

Anxiety, *see* Fearfulness

Appearance, *see* Slovenly in Appearance

Attracting Attention, *see* Silliness

Bashfulness, *see* Shyness

Boys: analysis of ratings, 104-6, 109-10; correlation with boys, 112-14; correlation with girls, 112

Boys (Grade 5A): analysis of ratings, 104-6; critical ratios vs. 5A girls, 7A boys, 7A girls, 8B boys, 8B girls, and teachers, 87, 92-93 (Table XVI); ratings on behavior problems, 72-73 (Table IX)

Boys (Grade 7A): critical ratios vs. 7A girls, 8B boys, 8B girls, and teachers, 87, 96-97 (Table XVIII); ratings on behavior problems, 76-77 (Table XI)

Boys (Grade 8B): critical ratios vs. 8B girls and teachers, 87, 100-101 (Table XX); ratings on behavior problems, 80-81 (Table XIII)

Bradford, Mrs. Hugh, 152, 171

Bullying, *see* Cruelty

Butler, Nicholas Murray, on progressive education, 162, 172

Careless in Work (ratings): boys, 5A, 72; 7A, 77; 8B, 81; boys and girls, 204 (Fig. 16); fathers, 125; girls, 5A, 71; 7A, 75; 8B, 78; mental hygienists (Wickman), 43; mothers, 123; rank-order, 6 groups, 58, 11 groups, 88; teachers, 39, 53; teachers (Wickman), 41

Cheating, 140, 165; relation to McGrath study, 111-12, 222 (Fig. 49)

Cheating (ratings): boys, 5A, 72; 7A, 76; 8B, 80; boys and girls, 199 (Fig. 6); fathers, 124; girls, 5A, 70; 7A, 74; 8B, 78; mental hygienists (Wickman), 43; mothers, 122; rank-order, 6 groups, 58, 11 groups, 88; teachers, 38, 52; teachers (Wickman), 40

Children: analysis of ratings, 106-7; application of findings to, 151-73; correlation grade by grade, age by age, sex by sex, 112-14; general trends shown by ratings, 85-86; influence of adults on judgments, 84-85; influences on, 136-50; rating comparisons: fathers, teachers, and mothers, 148-50, 148 (Group IV), 149 (Group V), 149 (Group VI), 150 (Group VII), mental hygienists, 69, 82, 83, parents, 144-45, teachers, 69, 82, 85, teachers and parents, 146-48, 146-47 (Chart III); ratings on behavior problems, 64-115; teachers' attitudes towards, 44-45; *see also* Boys; Girls

Children in Study: administration of questionnaire, 66-68; distribution by age, grade, and school, 68-69; instructions to, 66; schedules, 33, 34, 65-67, 175, 184-87 (App. A)

Clinicians, *see* Mental Hygienists

Commonwealth Fund, 12

Community, influence on child through parents, 152

Consistency, *see under* Statistics

Contrariness, *see* Stubborness

Correlation, *see under* Statistics

Correlation of Data: all groups, 51, 54 (Table V); boys with boys, 112-14; children, grade by grade, age by age, sex by sex, 112-14; children with fathers, 136; children with mental hygienists, 83; children with mothers, 136; children with teachers, 82, 136; girls with boys, 112; girls with girls, 112-14; teachers with mental hygienists, 51, 54; teachers with teachers, 37, 51

Cowardice, *see* Physical Coward

Critical Ratios of Ratings: between 5A boys vs. 5A girls, 7A boys, 7A girls, 8B boys, 8B girls, and teachers, 87, 92-93 (Table XVI); between 7A boys vs. 7A girls, 8B boys, 8B girls, and teachers, 87, 96-97 (Table XVIII); between 8B boys vs. 8B girls and teachers, 87, 100-101 (Table

XX); between fathers and 9 groups, 126-27 (Table XXIV); between 5A girls vs. 7A boys, 7A girls, 8B boys, 8B girls, and teachers, 87, 90-91 (Table XV); between 7A girls vs. 8B boys, 8B girls, and teachers, 87, 94-95 (Table XVII); between 8B girls and teachers, 87, 98-99 (Table XIX); between mental hygienists and all 10 groups, 87, 102-3 (Table XXI); between mothers vs. 5A boys, 5A girls, 7A boys, 7A girls, 8B boys, 8B girls, and teachers, 128-29 (Table XXV); between Teachers 1a and 1b, 60-61 (Table VII), 62-63; see also under Statistics
Criticism, see Overcriticism of Others
Cruelty and Bullying (ratings): boys, 5A, 72; 7A, 76; 8B, 80; boys and girls, 207 (Fig. 21); fathers, 124; girls, 5A, 70; 7A, 74; 8B, 78; mental hygienists (Wickman), 42; mothers, 122; rank-order, 6 groups, 58, 11 groups, 89; teachers, 38, 52; teachers (Wickman), 40
Curiosity, see Inquisitiveness

Daydreaming, see Dreaminess; Inattention
Defiance, see Impertinence
Depressed, see Unhappy
Destroying School Materials (ratings): boys, 5A, 72; 7A, 76; 8B, 80; boys and girls, 198 (Fig. 3); fathers, 124; girls, 5A, 70; 7A, 74; 8B, 78; mental hygienists (Wickman), 43; mothers, 122; rank-order, 6 groups, 58, 11 groups, 88; teachers, 38, 52; teachers (Wickman), 40
Deviation, Standard, see under Statistics
Dewey, John, on progressive education, 162; on relation of morals and conduct, 156
Dickens, Charles, on out-of-school activities of children, 161, 172
Dictatorial, see Domineering
Discipline, Classroom, see Disorderliness
Discouragement, see Easily Discouraged
Disobedience (ratings): boys, 5A, 72; 7A, 76; 8B, 80; boys and girls, 206 (Fig. 19); fathers, 125; girls, 5A, 70; 7A, 74; 8B, 78; mental hygienists (Wickman), 43; mothers, 123; rank-order, 6 groups, 58, 11 groups, 88;

teachers, 38, 52; teachers (Wickman), 40
Disorderliness (Violations of Classroom Discipline), ratings: boys, 5A, 72; 7A, 76; 8B, 81; boys and girls, 201 (Fig. 10); fathers, 125; girls, 5A, 71; 7A, 75; 8B, 79; mental hygienists (Wickman), 43; mothers, 123; rank-order, 6 groups, 58, 11 groups, 88; teachers, 38, 52; teachers (Wickman), 41
Dissatisfied, see Unhappy
Domineering, Overbearing, Dictatorial (ratings): boys, 5A, 73; 7A, 76; 8B, 80; boys and girls, 211 (Fig. 29); fathers, 125; girls, 5A, 70; 7A, 75; 8B, 78; mental hygienists (Wickman), 42; mothers, 122; rank-order, 6 groups, 59, 11 groups, 89; teachers, 39, 52; teachers (Wickman), 41
Dreaminess (ratings): boys, 5A, 73; 7A, 77; 8B, 81; boys and girls, 217 (Fig. 41); fathers, 125; girls, 5A, 71; 7A, 75; 8B, 79; mental hygienists (Wickman), 42; mothers, 123; rank-order, 6 groups, 59, 11 groups, 89; teachers, 39, 53; teachers (Wickman), 41
Durkheim, Émile, L'Éducation Morale, 64, 114; on teacher as interpreter of moral ideas, 157, 158, 172

Easily Discouraged (ratings): boys, 5A, 72; 7A, 76; 8B, 80; boys and girls, 219 (Fig. 45); fathers, 124; girls, 5A, 71; 7A, 75; 8B, 79; mental hygienists (Wickman), 42; mothers, 122; rank-order, 6 groups, 59, 11 groups, 89; teachers, 39, 53; teachers (Wickman), 41
Emotions, mutation of, 170
Enuresis (Wetting Self), ratings: fathers, 125; mental hygienists, 43; mothers, 123; rank-order, 6 groups, 59; teachers, 39, 53; teachers (Wickman), 40

Falsehoods, see Lying
Fathers: critical ratios vs. 9 groups, 126-27 (Table XXIV); ratings compared with those of teachers, 130-32 (Chart I), 132-33 (Chart II); ratings on behavior problems, 124-25 (Table XXIII); see also Parents

Fathers in Study, schedules, 34
Fearfulness (Easily Frightened), ratings: boys, 5A, 73; 7A, 77; 8B, 81; boys and girls, 216 (Fig. 40); fathers, 124; girls, 5A, 71; 7A, 75; 8B, 79; mental hygienists (Wickman), 42; mothers, 122; rank-order, 6 groups, 59, 11 groups, 89; teachers, 39, 53; teachers (Wickman), 41
Figures, 195-222 (App. B)
Foolishness, see Silliness
Forgetting, see Thoughtlessness
Freud, Sigmund, corroborating studies, 169; Gesammelte Schriften, 173

Gesell, Arnold, on dependence of the child, 160, 172; 169, 173
Girls: analysis of ratings, 109; correlation with boys, 112; correlation with girls, 112-14
Girls (Grade 5A): critical ratios vs. 7A boys, 7A girls, 8B boys, 8B girls, and teachers, 87, 90-91 (Table XV); ratings on behavior problems, 70-71 (Table VIII)
Girls (Grade 7A): critical ratios vs. 8B boys, 8B girls, and teachers, 87, 94-95 (Table XVII); ratings on behavior problems, 74-75 (Table X)
Girls (Grade 8B): critical ratios vs. teachers, 87, 98-99 (Table XIX); ratings on behavior problems, 78-79 (Table XII)
Grinker, Roy R., Men Under Stress, 169, 173

Heterosexual Activity (With Opposite Sex), ratings: fathers, 124; mental hygienists (Wickman), 43; mothers, 122; rank-order, 6 groups, 58; teachers, 38, 52; teachers (Wickman), 40
Home, application of ratings to functions of, 153; see also Parents
Home-school Items: agreement of children, parents, and teachers, 139-41, 139 (Group II), 141-43, 142 (Group III); agreement of children, fathers, mothers, and teachers, 148-50, 148 (Group IV), 149 (Group V), 150 (Group VII); agreement of fathers, mothers, and teachers, 137-38, 138 (Group I); agreement of parents and teachers, 162-65, 167-68, 163-64 (Chart IV); positions, mothers, fathers, teachers, 131-32 (Chart I), 132 (Chart II)
Horney, Karen, 153
Hurlock, Dr. Elizabeth B., 7-9, 136-37, 150

Imaginative Lying (ratings): boys, 5A, 73; 7A, 77; 8B, 81; boys and girls, 199 (Fig. 5); fathers, 125; girls, 5A, 71; 7A, 75; 8B, 79; mental hygienists (Wickman), 43; mothers, 123; rank-order, 6 groups, 58, 11 groups, 88; teachers, 39, 53; teachers (Wickman), 41
Impertinence, 143
Impertinence (Insubordination and Defiance), ratings: boys, 5A, 72; 7A, 76; 8B, 80; boys and girls, 206 (Fig. 20); fathers, 124; girls, 5A, 70; 7A, 74; 8B, 78; mental hygienists (Wickman), 43; mothers, 122; rank-order, 6 groups, 58, 11 groups, 88; teachers, 38, 52; teachers (Wickman), 40
Impudence, Impoliteness, Rudeness (ratings): boys, 5A, 72; 7A, 76; 8B, 80; boys and girls, 210 (Fig. 27); fathers, 124; girls, 5A, 70; 7A, 74; 8B, 78; mental hygienists (Wickman), 43; mothers, 123; rank-order, 6 groups, 59, 11 groups, 89; teachers, 38, 52; teachers (Wickman), 40
Inattention (ratings): boys, 5A, 73; 7A, 77; 8B, 81; boys and girls, 203 (Fig. 14); fathers, 125; girls, 5A, 71; 7A, 75; 8B, 79; mental hygienists (Wickman), 43; mothers, 123; rank-order, 6 groups, 58, 11 groups, 88; teachers, 39, 53; teachers (Wickman), 41
Indolence, see Laziness
Influence: of adults on children, 136-50, on children's judgments, 84-85; of grade on boys' ratings, 109-10, on girls' ratings, 109; of parents on children, 168-71; of school accomplishment on ratings of teachers, parents, and mental hygienists, 120-21; of teachers' functions on their ratings, 44-45, 47-49, 157-59
Inquisitiveness, Meddlesomeness (ratings): boys, 5A, 73; 7A, 77; 8B, 81; boys and girls, 214 (Fig. 35); fathers, 125; girls, 5A, 71; 7A, 75; 8B, 79; mental hygienists (Wickman), 43; mothers, 123; rank-order, 6

groups, 59, 11 groups, 89; teachers, 39, 53; teachers (Wickman), 41

Insubordination, *see* Impertinence

Interest in Work, Lack of, *see* Lack of Interest in Work

Interrupting (Talkativeness), ratings: boys, 5A, 73; 7A, 77; 8B, 81; boys and girls, 202 (Fig. 12); fathers, 125; girls, 5A, 71; 7A, 75; 8B, 79; mental hygienists (Wickman), 43; mothers, 123; rank-order, 6 groups, 58, 11 groups, 88; teachers, 39, 53; teachers (Wickman), 41

Irresponsible, *see* Unreliableness

Jones, M. C., experiment on conditioning children, 161, 172

Lack of Interest in Work (ratings): boys, 5A, 72; 7A, 76; 8B, 81; boys and girls, 204 (Fig. 15); fathers, 125; girls, 5A, 71; 7A, 75; 8B, 79; mental hygienists (Wickman), 43; mothers, 122; rank-order, 6 groups, 58, 11 groups, 88; teachers, 38, 52; teachers (Wickman), 40

Lane, Mrs. Bess B., 11, 116

Lateness, *see* Tardiness

Lazar, Dr. May, 11

Laziness, 143

Laziness (ratings): boys, 5A, 73; 7A, 77; 8B, 81; boys and girls, 205 (Fig. 17); fathers, 125; girls, 5A, 71; 7A, 74; 8B, 79; mental hygienists (Wickman), 43; mothers, 123; rank-order, 6 groups, 58, 11 groups, 88; teachers, 38, 53; teachers (Wickman), 40

Lying, *see* Imaginative Lying; Untruthfulness

Maladjustment, appropriate understanding of, 153-54; expression of, 170; genesis of, 169

McGrath, M. C., *A Study of the Moral Development of Children,* 110-12, 114, 220 (Fig. 47), 221 (Fig. 48), 222 (Fig. 49)

Masturbation (ratings): fathers, 124; mental hygienists (Wickman), 43; mothers, 122; rank-order, 6 groups, 58; teachers, 38, 52; teachers (Wickman), 40

Meddlesomeness, *see* Inquisitiveness

Mental Hygiene Items: agreement of children, parents, and teachers, 139-41, 139 (Group II), 142 (Group III); agreement of children, fathers, mothers, and teachers, 148-49, 149 (Group V), 149 (Group VI); agreement of parents and teachers, 166-67, 163 (Chart IV); agreement of teachers and mental hygienists, 154-59; positions, mothers, fathers, and teachers, 131 (Chart I), 132 (Chart II); ratings of fathers, mothers, and teachers, 166 (Table XXVI)

Mental Hygienists: contrast with viewpoint of teachers, 154-59; critical ratios vs. all 10 groups, 87, 102-3 (Table XXI); ratings compared with those of children, 69, 82, 83; ratings compared with those of teachers, 37, 44, 47-48, 51-63; ratings in Wickman study, 42-43 (Table III)

Mothers: critical ratios vs. 5A boys, 5A girls, 7A boys, 7A girls, 8B boys, 8B girls, and teachers, 128-29 (Table XXV); ratings compared with those of teachers, 130-32 (Chart I), 132-33 (Chart II); ratings on behavior problems, 122-23 (Table XXII); *see also* Fathers; Parents

Mothers in Study, schedules, 34

Nervousness, 45

Nervousness (ratings): boys, 5A, 73; 7A, 77; 8B, 81; boys and girls, 216 (Fig. 39); fathers, 124; girls, 5A, 71; 7A, 74; 8B, 79; mental hygienists (Wickman), 42; mothers, 122; rank-order, 6 groups, 59, 11 groups, 89; teachers, 39, 53; teachers (Wickman), 40

Nifenecker, Dr. Eugene A., 11

Objectivity in ratings of teachers, 45-46, 48-50

Obscene Notes, Pictures, Talk (ratings): fathers, 124; mental hygienists (Wickman), 43; mothers, 122; rank-order, 6 groups, 58; teachers, 38, 52; teachers (Wickman), 40

O'Malley, Kathleen E., *Annoyances or Irritations of Teachers,* 158, 172

Overactivity, *see* Restlessness

Overbearing, *see* Domineering

Overcritical of Others (ratings): boys, 5A, 73; 7A, 77; 8B, 81; boys and girls, 213 (Fig. 33); fathers, 125; girls, 5A, 70; 7A, 75; 8B, 78; mental hygienists (Wickman), 42; mothers, 123; rank-order, 6 groups, 59, 11 groups, 89; teachers, 39, 53; teachers (Wickman), 41

Parents: agreement with ratings of teachers, 162-68, 163-64 (Chart IV); rating comparisons: children, 144-45, children and teachers, 146-48, 146-47 (Chart III), 148-50, 148 (Group IV), 149 (Group V), 149 (Group VI), 150 (Group VII), teachers, 120-21, 130-32 (Chart I), 132-33 (Chart II); ratings on behavior problems, 116-35, 122-23 (Table XXII), 124-25 (Table XXIII); responsibility of, 168-71; see also Fathers; Home; Mothers

Parents in Study: administration of questionnaire, 116-18; instructions to, 116-18; number in study, 33, 34, 175; schedules, 116-17, 188-93 (App. A)

Personal Appearance, see Slovenly

Physical Coward (ratings): boys, 5A, 72; 7A, 77; 8B, 80; boys and girls, 218 (Fig. 44); fathers, 124; girls, 5A, 71; 7A, 75; 8B, 79; mental hygienists (Wickman), 42; mothers, 123; rank-order, 6 groups, 59, 11 groups, 89; teachers, 39, 53; teachers (Wickman), 41

Piaget, Jean, Moral Judgment of the Child, 64, 65, 83, 108, 113, 114, 115, 139, 150

Pictures, see Obscene Notes, Pictures, etc.

Profanity (ratings): boys, 5A, 72; 7A, 76; 8B, 80; boys and girls, 200 (Fig. 8); fathers, 125; girls, 5A, 70; 7A, 74; 8B, 78; mental hygienists (Wickman), 43; mothers, 123; rank-order, 6 groups, 58, 11 groups, 88; teachers, 39, 53; teachers (Wickman), 40

Progressive education, controversy concerning, 160-62; references on, 172-73

Progressive Education Association, 162, 173

Purpose of Study, 32-34

Quarrelsomeness (Annoying Other Children), ratings: boys, 5A, 72; 7A, 77; 8B, 81; boys and girls, 207 (Fig. 22); fathers, 124; girls, 5A, 71; 7A, 74; 8B, 79; mental hygienists (Wickman), 43; mothers, 122; rank-order, 6 groups, 59, 11 groups, 89; teachers, 38, 53; teachers (Wickman), 41

Rank-order of Ratings on All Items: eleven groups, including grades, 86-87, 88-89 (Table XIV); six groups, 86-87, 58-59 (Table VI)

Ratio, Critical, see under Statistics

Reeve, Mrs. A. H., on parent's responsibility for moral education, 171, 173

Relationship, see under Correlation of Data; Statistics

Reliability, see under Statistics

Reliability of Data, teachers, 57, 62

Resentfulness (ratings): boys, 5A, 73; 7A, 77; 8B, 81; boys and girls, 215 (Fig. 38); fathers, 125; girls, 5A, 71; 7A, 75; 8B, 79; mental hygienists (Wickman), 42; mothers, 122; rank-order, 6 groups, 59, 11 groups, 89; teachers, 39, 53; teachers (Wickman), 41

Restlessness (Overactivity), ratings: boys, 5A, 73; 7A, 77; 8B, 81; boys and girls, 203 (Fig. 13); fathers, 125; girls, 5A, 71; 7A, 75; 8B, 79; mental hygienists (Wickman), 43; mothers, 123; rank-order, 6 groups, 58, 11 groups, 88; teachers, 39, 53; teachers (Wickman), 41

Rudeness, see Impudence

Schedules in Study, 175-93 (Appendix A): children, 33, 34, 65-67, 175, 184-87 (App. A); fathers, 34; mothers, 34; number used, 34, 175; parents, 33, 34, 116-17, 188-93 (App. A); teachers, 33, 34, 36-37, 175, 176-79 (App. A), 180-83 (App. A)

School, application of ratings to functions of, 153, 158-62

School Children, see Children

School Items: agreement of children, fathers, mothers, and teachers, 148-49, 148 (Group IV), 149 (Group V), 149 (Group VI), of children, parents, and teachers, 139-40, 139 (Group II), 141-43, 142 (Group III), of fathers, mothers, and teachers, 137-38, 138 (Group I), of parents and teachers, 162-68, 163-64 (Chart IV); positions, mothers, fathers, and teachers, 130, 130 (Chart I), 133 (Chart II)

School Materials, Destroying, *see* Destroying School Materials

Selfishness (and Unsportsmanship), ratings: boys, 5A, 73; 7A, 76; 8B, 80; boys and girls, 210 (Fig. 28); fathers, 124; girls, 5A, 70; 7A, 74; 8B, 78; mental hygienists (Wickman), 42; mothers, 122; rank-order, 6 groups, 59, 11 groups, 89; teachers, 39, 52; teachers (Wickman), 41

Sensitiveness, 166

Sensitiveness (ratings): boys, 5A, 73; 7A, 77; 8B, 81; boys and girls, 212 (Fig. 31); fathers, 125; girls, 5A, 71; 7A, 75; 8B, 79; mental hygienists (Wickman), 42; mothers, 123; rank-order, 6 groups, 59, 11 groups, 89; teachers, 39, 53; teachers (Wickman), 41

Shaffer, Laurance Frederic, 169, 173

Sherif, Muzafer, *Psychology of Social Norms*, 44, 46

Shyness, Bashfulness (ratings): boys, 5A, 73; 7A, 77; 8B, 81; boys and girls, 211 (Fig. 30); fathers, 125; girls, 5A, 71; 7A, 75; 8B, 79; mental hygienists (Wickman), 42; mothers, 123; rank-order, 6 groups, 59, 11 groups, 89; teachers, 39, 53; teachers (Wickman), 41

Silliness, "Smartness," Attracting Attention (ratings): boys, 5A, 73; 7A, 76; 8B, 81; boys and girls, 214 (Fig. 36); fathers, 125; girls, 5A, 71; 7A, 75; 8B, 79; mental hygienists (Wickman), 43; mothers, 123; rank-order, 6 groups, 59, 11 groups, 89; teachers, 39, 53; teachers (Wickman), 41

Slovenly in Personal Appearance, 146

Slovenly in Personal Appearance (ratings): boys, 5A, 73; 7A, 77; 8B, 80; boys and girls, 217 (Fig. 42); fathers, 125; girls, 5A, 70; 7A, 74; 8B, 78; mental hygienists (Wickman), 43; mothers, 123; rank-order, 6 groups, 59, 11 groups, 89; teachers, 39, 53; teachers (Wickman), 41

"Smartness," *see* Silliness

Smoking (ratings): boys, 5A, 72; 7A, 76; 8B, 81; boys and girls, 201 (Fig. 9); fathers, 125; girls, 5A, 70; 7A, 74; 8B, 78; mental hygienists (Wickman), 43; mothers, 123; rank-order, 6 groups, 58, 11 groups, 88; teachers, 39, 53; teachers (Wickman), 40

Standard Deviation, *see under* Statistics

Standard Error of the Mean, *see under* Statistics

Statistics, 22-28, 223-31: anthropomorphism of, 151-73; consistency, 27-28; correlation, 22-24; critical ratio, 26-27; relationship, 22-24; reliability, 25-28; standard deviation, 24-25; standard error of the mean, 24-25

Stealing, relation to McGrath study, 110-11, 221 (Fig. 48)

Stealing (ratings): boys, 5A, 72; 7A, 76; 8B, 80; boys and girls, 200 (Fig. 7); fathers, 124; girls, 5A, 70; 7A, 74; 8B, 78; mental hygienists (Wickman), 42; mothers, 122; rank-order, 6 groups, 58, 11 groups, 88; teachers, 38, 52; teachers (Wickman), 40

Stubbornness, 143

Stubbornness (Contrariness), ratings: boys, 5A, 73; 7A, 77; 8B, 81; boys and girls, 208 (Fig. 24); fathers, 125; girls, 5A, 71; 7A, 75; 8B, 79; mental hygienists (Wickman), 42; mothers, 123; rank-order, 6 groups, 59, 11 groups, 89; teachers, 39, 53; teachers (Wickman), 41

Subjectivity in ratings of teachers, 45-46, 48-50

Suggestible (Accepts Suggestion of Anyone), ratings: boys, 5A, 73; 7A, 77; 8B, 80; boys and girls, 219 (Fig. 46); fathers, 124; girls, 5A, 71; 7A, 74; 8B, 79; mental hygienists (Wickman), 42; mothers, 123; rank-order, 6 groups, 59, 11 groups, 89; teachers, 38, 52; teachers (Wickman), 41

Sullenness (Sulkiness), ratings: boys, 5A, 73; 7A, 77; 8B, 81; boys and girls, 209 (Fig. 25); fathers, 125; girls, 5A, 71; 7A, 75; 8B, 79; mental hygienists (Wickman), 42; mothers, 123; rank-order, 6 groups, 59, 11 groups, 89; teachers, 39, 53; teachers (Wickman), 41

Suspiciousness (ratings): boys, 5A, 73; 7A, 77; 8B, 81; boys and girls, 218 (Fig. 43); fathers, 125; girls, 5A,

71; 7A, 75; 8B, 79; mental hygienists (Wickman), 42; mothers, 123; rank-order, 6 groups, 59, 11 groups, 89; teachers, 39, 53; teachers (Wickman), 41

Swearing, *see* Profanity

Talkativeness, *see* Interrupting

Tardiness (ratings): boys, 5A, 73; 7A, 77; 8B, 81; boys and girls, 197 (Fig. 1); fathers, 125; girls, 5A, 71; 7A, 75; 8B, 79; mental hygienists (Wickman), 43; mothers, 123; rank-order, 6 groups, 58, 11 groups, 88; teachers, 39, 53; teachers (Wickman), 41

Tattling (ratings): boys, 5A, 73; 7A, 77; 8B, 81; boys and girls, 208 (Fig. 23); fathers, 125; girls, 5A, 70; 7A, 75; 8B, 79; mental hygienists (Wickman), 43; mothers, 123; rank-order, 6 groups, 59, 11 groups, 89; teachers, 39, 53; teachers (Wickman), 41

Teachers: agreement with views of parents, 162-68, 163-64 (Chart IV); application of ratings to function of, 159; attitude towards children, 44-45, 47-50; contrast with viewpoint of mental hygienists, 154-59; rating comparisons: children, 69, 82, 83, 85, children and parents, 146-48, 146-47 (Chart III), 148-50, 148 (Group IV), 149 (Group V), 149 (Group VI), 150 (Group VII), mental hygienists, 37, 44, 47-48, 51-63, parents, 120-21, 130-32 (Chart I), 132-33 (Chart II); ratings on children's behavior, 36-46, 38-39 (Table I), 52-53 (Table IV); shifts in ratings: upward, 55 (Arrangement One), downward, 56 (Arrangement Two), changed, 57 (Arrangement Three); subjective vs. objective responses in ratings, 45-46, 48-50

Teachers (Wickman), ratings on children's behavior, 40-41 (Table II)

Teachers in Study, schedules, 33, 34, 36-37, 175, 176-79 (App. A), 180-83 (App. A)

Temper Tantrums, 143

Temper Tantrums (ratings): boys, 5A, 73; 7A, 77; 8B, 80; boys and girls, 209 (Fig. 26); fathers, 125; girls, 5A, 70; 7A, 75; 8B, 78; mental hygienists (Wickman), 42; mothers,

123; rank-order, 6 groups, 59, 11 groups, 89; teachers, 38, 52; teachers (Wickman), 40

Theft, *see* Stealing

Thoughtlessness (Forgetting), ratings: boys, 5A, 73; 7A, 77; 8B, 81; boys and girls, 213 (Fig. 34); fathers, 125; girls, 5A, 71; 7A, 75; 8B, 79; mental hygienists (Wickman), 43; mothers, 123; rank-order, 6 groups, 59, 11 groups, 89; teachers, 39, 53; teachers (Wickman), 41

Timidity, *see* Shyness

Truancy, 45

Truancy (ratings): boys, 5A, 72; 7A, 76; 8B, 80; boys and girls, 197 (Fig. 2); fathers, 124; girls, 5A, 70; 7A, 74; 8B, 78; mental hygienists (Wickman), 43; mothers, 122; rank-order, 6 groups, 58, 11 groups, 88; teachers, 38, 52; teachers (Wickman), 40

Unhappy, Depressed, Dissatisfied (ratings): boys, 5A, 73; 7A, 77; 8B, 81; boys and girls, 215 (Fig. 37); fathers, 124; girls, 5A, 71; 7A, 75; 8B, 79; mental hygienists (Wickman), 42; mothers, 122; rank-order, 6 groups, 59, 11 groups, 89; teachers, 38, 52; teachers (Wickman), 41

Unreliableness (Irresponsible, Evasion of Duties), ratings: boys, 5A, 72; 7A, 76; 8B, 80; boys and girls, 205 (Fig. 18); fathers, 124; girls, 5A, 70; 7A, 74; 8B, 78; mental hygienists (Wickman), 42; mothers, 122; rank-order, 6 groups, 58, 11 groups, 88; teachers, 38, 52; teachers (Wickman), 40

Unsocial, Withdrawing (ratings): boys, 5A, 73; 7A, 77; 8B, 81; boys and girls, 212 (Fig. 32); fathers, 125; girls, 5A, 71; 7A, 75; 8B, 79; mental hygienists (Wickman), 42; mothers, 123; rank-order, 6 groups, 59, 11 groups, 89; teachers, 39, 53; teachers (Wickman), 41

Unsportsmanship, *see* Selfishness

Untidiness, *see* Disorderliness

Untruthfulness (Lying), ratings: boys, 5A, 73; 7A, 76; 8B, 80; boys and girls, 198 (Fig. 4); fathers, 124; girls, 5A, 70; 7A, 74; 8B, 78; mental hygienists (Wickman), 43; mothers, 122; rank-order, 6 groups, 58, 11 groups, 88; teachers, 38, 52; teachers (Wickman), 40

Wetting Self, *see* Enuresis

Whispering, relation to McGrath study, 110, 220 (Fig. 47)

Whispering and Note-writing (ratings): boys, 5A, 73; 7A, 77; 8B, 81; boys and girls, 202 (Fig. 11); fathers, 125; girls, 5A, 71; 7A, 75; 8B, 79; mental hygienists (Wickman), 43; mothers, 123; rank-order, 6 groups, 58, 11 groups, 88; teachers, 39, 53; teachers (Wickman), 41

Wickman, E. K., *Children's Behavior and Teachers' Attitudes*, 29-32, 35, 36-37, 46, 47, 49, 50, 51, 120, 135; ratings of mental hygienists (clinicians), 42-43 (Table III); ratings of teachers, 40-41 (Table II); relationship to present study, 32-34; résumé of a major phase of, 29-32; schedules in study, 175 (App. A)

Withdrawing, *see* Unsocial

Work, Carelessness in, *see* Carelessness in Work

Zachry, C. B., *Emotion and Conduct in Adolescence*, 152, 160, 171, 172